WHITE LAWYER
BLACK POWER

Don Jelinek with Stokely Carmichael, November 20, 1966
(Donald A. Jelinek papers [M2225]. Department of Special Collections and
University Archives, Stanford University Libraries, Stanford, California).

WHITE LAWYER BLACK POWER

A Memoir of Civil Rights Activism in the Deep South

Donald A. Jelinek

Foreword by John Dittmer

THE UNIVERSITY OF
SOUTH CAROLINA PRESS

© 2020 Estate of Donald A. Jelinek

Published by the University of South Carolina Press
Columbia, South Carolina 29208

www.uscpress.com

Manufactured in the United States of America

29 28 27 26 25 24 23 22 21 20
10 9 8 7 6 5 4 3 2 1

Library of Congress Cataloging-in-Publication Data
can be found at http://catalog.loc.gov/.

ISBN 978-1-64336-117-8 (hardback)
ISBN 978-1-64336-118-5 (paperback)
ISBN 978-1-64336-119-2 (ebook)

DEDICATED

to those who died in the Civil Rights struggle,
to those who fought and forever lost their innocence, and
to those who, still innocent, believe the years in the South
were as simple as "Love Your Enemies" and "Black and
White Together, We Shall Overcome."

"Those who profess to favor freedom, and yet depreciate agitation, are men who want crops without plowing up the ground. They want rain without thunder and lightning. They want the ocean without the awful roar of its many waters . . . Power concedes nothing without demand. It never did and it never will."

Fredrick Douglas,
Letter to an abolitionist associate (1857)

"First, I must confess that over the past few years I have been gravely disappointed with the white moderate. I have almost reached the regrettable conclusion that the Negro's great stumbling block in his stride toward freedom is not the White Citizen's Counciler or the Ku Klux Klanner, but the white moderate, who is more devoted to 'order' than to justice. . . ."

Rev. Martin Luther King Jr.,
Letter from a Birmingham Jail (1963)

"To equip ourselves to challenge the enemy we first have to distance ourselves from the friend who inhibits us. The liberal is no enemy, he's a friend—but for the moment he holds us back, offering a formula too gentle, too inadequate for our struggle."

Stephen Biko, a black South African arrested for his antiapartheid activities and slain in prison, quoted in BIKO by Donald Woods (1987)

CONTENTS

List of Illustrations *xi*

Foreword *xiii*
John Dittmer

Preface *xix*

Acknowledgments *xxiii*

List of Abbreviations *xxvi*

A Note on the Text *xxvii*

ONE
"Black and White Together, We Shall Overcome"

1. Going South *3*

2. Lawyers for the Movement *12*

3. On the Road *23*

4. Mississippi's Newest Civil Rights Worker *37*

5. Novice County Leader *49*

6. Time to Leave . . . and Return *63*

7. Full-Time Civil Rights Lawyer *75*

8. The "Rape" of the Plantation Owner's Wife *87*

TWO
Black Power Selma

9. A Crack in the Movement *99*

10. White Lawyer in Black Power Selma *114*

11. The Cotton Wars *132*

12. Black versus Black in the 1966 Elections *150*

13. The Dark Side of Two Federal Judges *166*

14. No Blacks on Southern Juries   *186*

15. Fired and Banished   *196*

16. Unsung Heroes of Selma: The Fathers of St. Edmund   *209*

17. The Unimaginable Poor   *217*

18. The Fight for Food   *224*

19. Goodbye to SNCC . . . and the South   *237*

Notes   *251*

Bibliography   *259*

Index   *265*

ILLUSTRATIONS

Don Jelinek with Stokely Carmichael   *ii*

Henry Schwarzschild   *120*

"Jean" with children   *129*

Dorothy Cotton   *140*

Shirley Mesher and Don Jelinek at Selma office   *153*

Selma police cruiser and SNCC sound truck   *157*

Police officer with shotgun approaching SNCC sound truck   *157*

Thomas Taylor being arrested   *158*

Stu House imploring gathered crowd to vote   *159*

Stu House speaking to assembled crowd   *159*

Stu House being led away by police   *160*

Stokely Carmichael protesting for voting rights   *161*

Stokely Carmichael speaking with Selma's chief of police   *162*

Stokely Carmichael being placed under arrest   *163*

Crowd watching police after Stokely Carmichael's arrest   *164*

Dick Reavis with Don Jelinek   *176*

Don Jelinek plowing on "Bokulich" land   *190*

Don Jelinek with Stokely Carmichael and
Thomas Lorenzo Taylor   *210*

SRRP logo   *219*

Don Jelinek at food distribution center in Alabama   *235*

FOREWORD

The black freedom struggle of the 1950s and 1960s was a seminal moment in the American experience. Then, local people—sharecroppers, maids, small business owners and a handful of black professionals—joined with young volunteers from the outside to create a movement that literally changed the course of history. Several of these volunteer activists have written about their experiences in the Deep South. Add to this list the most recent memoir by a white civil rights lawyer named Donald Jelinek, who had worked in Mississippi and Alabama in the mid-1960s.

I had never heard of Jelinek, and as author of a book on the civil rights movement in Mississippi I was skeptical, to say the least. Once I started reading the manuscript, however, I put aside all my reservations. This is, quite simply, a compelling book. Jelinek was an acute observer of race relations during a critical time when the black freedom struggle was undergoing profound changes. The role he played, as attorney and activist, is unique in the history of the movement.

Don Jelinek was born in the Bronx in 1934. After graduating from New York University Law School he took a job in a Wall Street law firm. In the summer of 1965 he decided to spend three weeks in Mississippi, working in the Jackson office of the American Civil Liberties Union, headed by the veteran attorney Al Bronstein. Jelinek was not the typical summer volunteer. To begin with, he was headstrong, as he readily admits, and when he was assigned to litigate a case in the small, tough north Mississippi town of Okolona he took chances and, while securing a verdict in favor of his client, he angered both local whites and Al Bronstein. But Jelinek had experienced the "'Mississippi High': the intoxication felt by white middle class civil rights workers who suddenly found themselves thrust into the idealism of the civil rights cause" (30), and at the end of his three weeks working for the ACLU he returned to Okolona, mentored by movement veteran Aviva Futorian, as both an independent attorney and as a civil rights worker.

It doesn't take the reader long to realize that Jelinek is a marvelous storyteller. He writes beautifully, and with humor. (He spent his college and law school summers as a waiter and a standup comic "on the Borscht Circuit in upstate New York.") (30) He integrates relevant historical material seamlessly and uses his own experiences as a volunteer in the movement to illustrate larger themes.

His three-week stint as an ACLU attorney in northern Mississippi required him to spend much of his time in a Holly Springs courtroom, dealing with "the same judge, lawyers, and courtroom personnel," establishing personal relationships with them that helped him in the court. But "Unlike other civil rights lawyers, I could not cross-examine too vigorously, embarrass or humiliate witnesses *or* engage in dramatic outside civil rights matters." (55) Still, Jelinek was a white lawyer in hostile territory. He recounts in dramatic detail a harrowing car chase on a deserted rural road, where two men in a pickup armed with rifles shot up his car and wounded him before he managed to lose them.

What is clear throughout the book is that Jelinek felt at home with local people, especially the sharecroppers who took him in and fed and housed him. While gathering signatures for a petition demonstrating that local blacks were denied the right to vote, he spent a day in the fields picking cotton and hours at night just talking to people. It took him nearly two weeks to get twenty signatures!

At the end of his volunteer assignment, Jelinek returned to New York, only to come back to Mississippi when Bronstein needed a replacement so he could take his Christmas vacation. While at the ACLU office in Jackson getting ready for a Christmas Eve party, Jelinek got a frantic call from nearby Canton. Blacks there had initiated a "Black Christmas" boycott of local merchants, and authorities had responded with mass arrests. Canton was a tough town, and there were legitimate concerns about the treatment of the prisoners. Jelinek's call to the county's deputy sheriff elicited a hostile response. The FBI said it had no jurisdiction. Fearing for the safety of the inmates, Jelinek called the Canton police chief and told him that he was Walter Cronkite of CBS News. What follows is Jelinek at his creative and literary best, and is worth quoting in detail:

> Attempting valiantly to impersonate the TV commentator's neutral accent and sonorous baritone delivery, I inquired about the Christmas Eve arrests which "the whole country is aroused about." I was immediately told that everybody was safe, received a complete list of those arrested and learned the general nature of the charges and bail. The chief of police confided that he watched my show as often as he could but complained that its coverage of the

South did not tell the whole story. I (Cronkite) should visit there myself to see what is really happening. I assured him I would. (65)

The Canton prisoners were eventually freed, and soon Jelinek returned to New York, only to be recalled once again by the ACLU, this time to head up a new office in Alabama. The second half of the book begins with a discussion of black-white tensions within the movement as civil rights competed with black power. Jelinek offers a fresh perspective here. He arrived in the South just as veteran black activists, discouraged by the failure of the federal government to take decisive action against Jim Crow, became increasingly nationalistic, telling white volunteers they were no longer wanted or needed. Because Jelinek did not come South until the summer of 1965, he had not been subjected to the kind of mistrust and acrimony that many white volunteers had experienced in the months after Freedom Summer. While he was not immune to criticism because of his race, as a white attorney with a reputation for courage both inside and outside the courtroom, he had a certain cache with influential black nationalists.

ACLU leaders told Jelinek they chose him to head up their Alabama office "because you have the best chance of being accepted by Stokely Carmichael." (103) Jelinek's friendship with Stokely—and that is not too strong a characterization—began inauspiciously. In June of 1966 Jelinek was moving into his second-floor office in Selma when a black colleague told him that members of the Student Nonviolent Coordinating Committee (SNCC) had just posted a sign at the entrance, "No whites allowed upstairs without prior approval." Furious, the white attorney let it be known that he would not work for SNCC under such humiliating circumstances. Several days passed, and when one of his associates told him that the SNCC firebrand Rap Brown was in jail and needed a lawyer, Jelinek flatly refused. A few hours later he got a call from Stokely, fresh from his "black power" speech on the Meredith March. Carmichael told "Don" that he had "heard many fine things about you," and "I hope you will continue to be our friend and represent us." Adding, "There will be no more signs—and no more SNCC problems for you." (114) And there weren't. Their relationship was both professional and casual. After Jelinek's mother wrote asking what black power really meant, Stokely laughingly replied, "Tell your mama when I find out, I'll let her know." (SNCC expelled its white members in a famous meeting in upstate New York in December of 1966. Jelinek continued to represent SNCC workers in court until the middle of 1968.)

Don Jelinek did productive work for the ACLU in Alabama. He won a critical lawsuit gaining representation for black farmers on previously all-white local boards that distributed federal funds to white and black farmers. In pursuing this suit, he won the support of both Martin Luther King and Carmichael, who were at odds on the issue of tactics. Encouraged by this success, Jelinek continued his work on behalf of Alabama farmers. As director of the Southern Rural Research Project, he led a protest in Washington, DC, against the US Department of Agriculture, resulting in the federal agency providing the free distribution of food stamps and surplus food to the rural poor. He considered this victory "one of the proudest moments of my life." (200)

Jelinek was also involved in elections in Selma and Dallas County, and here he discusses the implications of black-against-black tensions in the 1966 elections. Until recently, scholars have characterized the civil rights movement as a struggle between black activists and white racists. With passage of the Voting Rights Act of 1965 fissures developed in some black communities, with activists dividing along ideological and class lines. The SNCC faction in Selma, which Jelinek supported, favored an independent, all-black ticket, while a more moderate and middle-class group, affiliated with King and the SCLC, worked within the Democratic Party to elect Wilson Baker, the white former public safety director, to replace the racist sheriff Jim Clark. The moderate group was successful, Baker was elected, and here Jelinek's identification with SNCC destroyed his relationship with Amelia Boynton, the local hero of the Selma Movement, and a leader of the moderates.

Alabama Judge Frank Johnson has always been one of my heroes. As Jelinek notes, he was "The most famous and revered federal judge in the South . . . [and] the most prominent desegregationist judge in the nation." (147) But I was surprised—and dismayed—to see another side of the famed jurist. Johnson was "a tough law and order man with sentences longer than the national average . . . [who] despised the concept of 'Black Power' as much as he did the beliefs and tactics of the Ku Klux Klan." (148) This judgment appears harsh, but he had plenty of reason to be fearful of the judge, who saw Jelinek as a SNCC lawyer constantly pushing the boundaries of acceptable legal practice. One transgression led to another, and ultimately Judge Johnson ruled against Jelinek on every major issue, driving the attorney to distraction.

Jelinek increasingly displayed what was often characterized as "movement burnout." Martin Luther King's assassination had a further devastating impact on the white lawyer's psychological fatigue. He called

Carmichael to tell him that his time in the South was nearing an end. Stokely replied that he was moving to Africa. The book ends as Jelinek leaves the South, for an uncertain future in California.

Eager to know more, I Googled Jelinek and was amazed to learn about his life after his sojourn in Mississippi and Alabama. In California he joined the Bay Area Veterans of the Civil Rights Movement. Continuing to practice law, he represented the group of Native Americans who seized Alcatraz Island in the 1969 occupation of that infamous prison. Beginning in 1971, he coordinated the defense of the inmates charged after the Attica prison riot in New York. Entering mainstream politics, he was elected to three terms on the Berkeley City Council. He ran for mayor of Berkeley in 1994 and 1998, but lost both races. Reading further, I saw his obituary. Donald Jelinek died in June of 2016 at age 82. He asked that his epitaph read "he was part of SNCC." Somehow the news of his death stunned me. I felt as though I had lost a friend.

White Lawyer, Black Power adds much to our knowledge of the black freedom struggle, especially in the years following passage of the Civil Rights Act of 1964. It belongs on that short shelf of movement memoirs by SNCC activists Cleveland Sellers, James Forman, Stokely Carmichael, and Bob Zellner. The University of South Carolina Press deserves our gratitude for making Jelinek's memoir available to a new generation of civil rights scholars and students, and to readers everywhere who believe in the possibilities of democracy.

John Dittmer
Professor Emeritus of History
DePauw University

PREFACE

I arrived in the Deep South in 1965 at a time of simmering unrest between black civil rights workers and their white counterparts. This turbulence eventually led to the ouster of most whites, although I had been allowed to remain at my post while "Black Power" spread throughout the Civil Rights Movement.

Prior to the Civil Rights Movement the post–Civil War Fourteenth and Fifteenth Amendments (equal protection and the right to vote) had been all but taken away by violence and segregationist laws in the South.

Well into the 1960s black residents of the "Jim Crow" South were excluded from "white" schools, restaurants, theaters, boardinghouses, public parks, hospitals, libraries, swimming pools and restrooms. They were confined to the rear of buses and to separate railroad cars. Separate bibles were kept in courtrooms for colored witnesses to kiss. Their blood was segregated by the American Red Cross. And they were denied the right to vote.

The years that preceded the passage of the landmark civil rights legislation were particularly vicious and bloody. During the summer of 1964 in the state of Mississippi alone three civil rights workers were murdered, more than one thousand protesters were arrested, and many others were beaten or shot at. Black churches were burned and homes were bombed.[1]

The overwhelming majority of civil rights workers did not fight back. Their most prominent leader, Rev. Martin Luther King Jr., had promoted a model of passive resistance and nonviolence in which all were urged to turn the other cheek.[2] But as the brutal backlash against the Movement intensified it increasingly took a toll on civil rights workers, especially those in their twenties who overwhelmingly comprised the most militant organization of that time: the Student Nonviolent Coordinating Committee (SNCC, pronounced "snick"). As they settled into small rural communities fighting for voting and other civil rights, these SNCC workers became the "shock troops" of the Movement, absorbing much of the physical abuse.

The enactment of the Civil Rights Act of 1964 and Voting Rights Act of 1965 did not, in itself, mark much immediate improvement in the lives of Southern blacks. Nor did civil rights bills, as noted by a SNCC worker at the time, address basic problems:

> They had no effect on the South's rigid system of caste and class oppression, and [the laws] were not addressed to the economic oppression of poor blacks. . . . Blacks [were] not being lynched and dumped into muddy rivers across the South because they [weren't] 'integrated.' Black babies [were] not dying of malnutrition because their parents [did] not own homes in white communities. Black men and women [were] not being forced to pick cotton for $3 a day because of segregation. 'Integration' [had] little or no effect on such problems.[3]

Having endured too much brutality and not enough progress, SNCC leaders increasingly adopted a more defiant approach that put them in conflict with Dr. King and most other civil rights organizations.

The tensions came to a head in June 1966 on a blistering hot day in Mississippi. Twenty-five-year-old Stokely Carmichael, the new leader of SNCC, was arrested without cause. Upon his release and seething with anger, he made his way back to address his supporters. His aggrieved words that day shocked a nation that, for the most part, had considered the battle for racial equality already won.

> "This is the twenty-seventh time I've been arrested—and I ain't goin' to jail no more. The only way we gonna stop them white men from whuppin' us is to take over. We been saying 'Freedom' for six years and we ain't got nothing. What we gonna start sayin' now is Black Power!"[4]
>
> "BLACK POWER!" the crowd roared in unison.
>
> "*What* do you want?"
>
> "BLACK POWER!"
>
> "WHAT *do* you want?"
>
> "BLACK POWER!"
>
> "*WHAT DO YOU WANT?*"
>
> "BLACK POWER!! BLACK POWER!!! BLACK POWER!!!!"[5]

For SNCC everything that followed was an echo of that moment. The national press latched on to the slogan "Black Power" and "embellished it with warnings of an imminent racial cataclysm."[6] Carmichael, the most charismatic new civil rights personality since Dr. King, personified and promoted the ideals of Black Power: "It is our position that black organizations should be black-led and essentially black-staffed, with policy being made by black people."[7]

In a sweeping move Carmichael reached beyond the South and roamed about the country—a "Johnny Appleseed" planting black pride as he spoke with sharecroppers, college audiences, and urban ghetto dwellers. The television cameras captured his good looks and devilish smile as, in the tradition of Malcolm X, he urged defiance of "the Man" and the US government. When he yelled, "Black Power!" his message was, "Respect yourself . . . and your mama."

I watched him when he gave a speech to students at Tuskegee Institute in Alabama. It was unlike anything I had ever heard from a major civil rights leader:

> Why do you girls insist on dressing like Jackie Kennedy? I know who you are. And you guys that slicked back hair ain't goin' to fool the Man. He know you a Nigger. . . . Okra and hominy grits are beautiful, black girls are beautiful, your daddy is beautiful, African clothes are beautiful, African hair is beautiful, YOU ARE BEAUTIFUL!!!

The roar of the students was deafening as they stood cheering and pounding on their chairs. BLACKNESS! This was to be Carmichael's greatest achievement. He urged black people to accept themselves, to stop trying to be white, to be proud of their skin and culture, and to demand equal access to the economic benefits of white America.

On June 16, 1966—the very day that Stokely Carmichael was delivering his "Black Power" speech—I was driving to Selma, Alabama, from Jackson, Mississippi, to open an Alabama civil rights legal office located on the floor below Carmichael's headquarters. I would remain in Alabama for two additional years.

In this book I will tell the story of the journey I traveled along with my civil rights colleagues through the once-harmonious Civil Rights Movement into the increasing influence of the militant Black Power movement and eventually to the end of the Movement as we had known it.

ACKNOWLEDGMENTS

My primary source for this book was the thousands of hours I spent with sharecroppers and civil rights workers in Mississippi and Alabama.

Brave, selfless black sharecroppers took me into their homes, fed me, and allowed me to join their community, which endangered them and potentially jeopardized the little they had. They also shared the stories of their lives with me.

The civil rights workers were breathtaking in their courage and dedication. I imagined a scenario where a civil rights worker had been invited to "Go South" but was told that the other side had the guns, police, judges, money, and centuries of oppression against anyone who attempted to alter Southern lives. The civil rights worker would answer: "Where do I sign up?"

It was my great fortune to work with Dr. Martin Luther King Jr. and Stokely Carmichael. Our discussions and work together are written about in this book—but the written details cannot match the experience of learning from these two world changers. They both are now dead and much missed.

This book benefitted greatly from me becoming a member of the Bay Area Veterans of the Civil Rights Movement (the Vets), who have met since 1999. In monthly meetings we compare notes and tape discussions of past experiences and current viewpoints. Afterward the conversations are edited and made available at crmvet.org.

Bruce Hartford, webmaster of this unique site, was on the field staff of Dr. King's SCLC from 1965 until 1967 and participated in the March to Montgomery. He has created an online encyclopedia of documents, history, and personal experiences of those who were there. Bruce read a draft of this book and applied his expertise to offer chapter-by-chapter critiques and corrections laced with arguments and perceptions of what occurred.

Chude Pam Parker Allen was twenty-one years old when she took part in the 1964 Mississippi Freedom Summer, a time when three of her fellow civil rights workers were murdered. She read an early draft of this book, applying her sensitive and poetic nature to search out both details and nuances of life in the South.

The Vets include Chude Allen, Ron Bridgeforth, Cathy Cade, Hardy Frye, Miriam (Cohn) Glickman, Bruce Hartford, Phil Hutchings, Marion Kwan, Elizabeth ("Betita") S. Martinez, Wazir Peacock, Jim Rogers, Gene Turitz and Jean Wiley. The experiences of the Vets and the taped accounts of many others have enriched this book.

Buttressing my personal experiences were matchless other books: Stokely Carmichael's and Charles V. Hamilton's *Black Power,* Stokely Carmichael's with Ekwueme Michael Thelwell's *Ready for Revolution: The Life and Struggles of Stokely Carmichael,* Clayborne Carson's *In Struggle: SNCC and the Black Awakening of the 1960s,* Charles E. Fager's *Selma, 1965,* James Forman's *The Making of Black Revolutionaries,* Hasan Kwame Jeffries' *Bloody Lowndes: Civil Rights and Black Power in Alabama's Black Belt,* Gunnar Myrdal's *An American Dilemma,* Arthur M. Schlesinger Jr.'s *The Age of Roosevelt: the Coming of the New Deal,* and many other exemplary books included in the bibliography.

I am grateful to additional volunteer readers who read the initial draft of this book, including my wife Jane Scherr, who read and commented on many drafts of this book while accepting living with my past, which encompassed an ex-wife and three ex-girlfriends; my brother Roger Jelinek, who helped with the text as well as the editing; Dr. Edith Folb, a former professor of speech and communication studies at San Francisco State University, who applied her many skills to advise me and correct the draft; Malcolm Bell, the whistleblower-prosecutor discussed in my earlier book, *Attica Justice,* who read the draft with his perceptive editing and guidance; Kathy Veit, who was part of the story as assistant director for SRRP and who read and corrected the draft of her own experiences and those of other civil rights workers; my literary agent, Amaryah Orenstein, who went above and beyond by providing perceptive editing and analysis; and my then-thirteen-year-old grandson Pascal Scherr, who read the entire text while attending middle school in Berkeley and shared with me his own views about the concept of Black Power.

My brilliant editor, John Raeside, overcame most of the problems of a writer who is a character in the storyline. He cast out many of my favorite passages but kept me on an even keel with a narrative and an arc that I often could not see.

I especially note Erika Andraca, who, as with my Attica book, was supposed to be assisting my legal work but in addition became an almost full-time, in-house editor and then some—whose final okay was necessary before I would painfully yield each part as completed. A master of the computer, she searched out information, indexed, and prepared the book for publication. She also read, corrected, and added her reader comments to every word from cover to cover.

Despite this great support, I am solely responsible for all errors.

ABBREVIATIONS

ACLU	American Civil Liberties Union
ASCS	Agriculture Stabilization and Conservation Service
COFO	Council of Federated Organizations
CORE	Congress of Racial Equality
CP	American Communist Party
FBI	Federal Bureau of Investigation
KKK	Ku Klux Klan
LCDC	Lawyers Constitutional Defense Committee
LCFO	Lowndes County Freedom Organization
MFDP	Mississippi Freedom Democratic Party
NAACP	National Association for the Advancement of Colored People
NAACP LDF	National Association for the Advancement of Colored People Legal Defense and Educational Fund, Inc.
NLG	National Lawyers Guild
NSF	National Sharecroppers Fund
SCLC	Southern Christian Leadership Conference
SNCC	Student Nonviolent Coordinating Committee
SRRP	Southern Rural Research Project
SWAFCA	Southwest Alabama Farmers Cooperative Association
USDA	US Department of Agriculture

A NOTE ON THE TEXT

The names of most sharecroppers have been changed throughout this book, not to protect them from exposure since they have already undergone the dangers of such exposure, but to avoid further invading their privacy. The names of some civil rights workers have been changed as well, also for reasons of privacy. Those whose names are changed are shown by quotation marks the first time the name is used.

ONE

"Black and White Together, We Shall Overcome"

1

Going South

On August 15, 1965, I flew to Jackson, Mississippi, for a three-week stint as a civil rights lawyer. I was unsure of what would greet me but I had some idea. It would not be my first encounter with the fearsome realities of the "Jim Crow" South.

While serving in the US Army in 1958 I was stationed at Fort Jackson in South Carolina—the first state to secede from the Union and where the first shots of the Civil War were fired. Ten years before my arrival at Fort Jackson President Harry Truman had integrated the US military, creating the only zone of equal rights in the South. As a result the military also became a major source of black employment in the former Confederate States.

At Fort Jackson my basic training was accompanied by the shouts of three black drill sergeants, which was not taken well by white trainees from the region. A few weeks after my arrival I was befriended by Morris, one of the black sergeants, who enjoyed talking with a Yankee lawyer. One day I suggested we go into town for a movie on my next weekend pass.

"Are you crazy?" Morris almost shouted. "I could be killed, and maybe you too!"

"Just for going to the movies?"

"Don't you know anything about where you are?" he asked angrily.

When I didn't reply he called over the other two black sergeants and repeated what I had proposed. Acting as if I wasn't present, one of the other sergeants snorted and said, "He obviously doesn't understand anything about the South. Does he even know about Emmett Till?"

"Do you know about Emmett Till?" Morris asked. "The 14-year-old boy from Chicago who was beaten and murdered because he spoke to a white woman."

They all looked at me but didn't wait for me to answer.

"Come with us," I was directed; and I followed the sergeants into their barracks. When we entered Morris looked around guiltily as if he were about to commit a serious crime.

"Look and see what they did to the boy." He opened his footlocker and pulled out a hidden copy of *Jet* magazine.[1] "Look at the photos!"

Under pressure and feeling I had done something seriously wrong, I looked at the photos. I didn't know what I was looking at.

"What is this?" I asked.

"It's the boy!" they responded, almost in chorus.

"Oh my God," I whispered, feeling woozy. I did not say what I was thinking: *Is this a human body?*

We would talk about many things in my remaining time at Fort Jackson, but never again about Emmett Till.

Much later I read his mother's account of what had happened. Emmett Till had traveled from Chicago to Mississippi to visit his uncle and cousins. Mamie Till had warned her son about danger in the South.

> Don't start up any conversation with white people in Mississippi. Only talk if you are spoken to. And you respond, 'Yes, sir.' 'Yes, Ma'am.' 'No, sir.' 'No, Ma'am.' . . . If you're walking down the street and a white woman is walking toward you, stay off the sidewalk, lower your head. Don't look her in the eye. Wait until she passes by, then get back on the sidewalk, keep going, don't look back. If you have to humble yourself, then just do it. Get on your knees if you have to.[2]

On August 28, 1955, a few days after arriving in Mississippi, Emmett Till entered a county store to purchase candy. As if he were still in Chicago the young man spoke to the white wife of the storekeeper. Later Till was accused of "chatting her up," and maybe "looking her over." Likely his only "crime" was speaking to her as an equal, showing a lack of deference to a white woman. Her husband told his brother after he learned of the encounter.

That night the two men seized the "boy from Chicago" and removed him from the home of his uncle. They dumped him in a truck and drove to a barn where they savagely tortured him. Till was pistol-whipped, had an eye gauged out, and was shot through the head before they dropped him into the Tallahatchie River, his body weighted down with a cotton gin fan tied around his neck with barbed wire. Three days later his swollen, disfigured, and nude body was found by two boys fishing in the river.[3]

A Mississippi relative telephoned Mamie Till to tell her of her son's death. Although near faint from shock and grief she demanded that his body not be buried in the South, and that it must be sent back to Chicago. When the corpse arrived she insisted there be no pre-burial cosmetic work and called for an open-casket memorial and funeral, saying, "There was just no way I could describe what was in that box. No way. And I just wanted the world to see."[4]

During the killers' murder trial their counsel claimed the body might not even be that of a human. The defense also argued that the body couldn't be identified as Emmett Till because the face of the corpse was unrecognizable due to the beatings and having been submerged in water for three days.

An all-white jury acquitted the two killers. One juror stated afterward that the panel believed the two men were guilty but that life imprisonment or the death penalty did not seem proper punishment for whites who had merely killed a disrespectful black person. After the verdict was rendered the murderers confessed their guilt in *Look* magazine in 1956. They were paid $4,000 for their story.[5]

The torture and murder of Emmett Till, with photographs of his mutilated body and press accounts of thousands who had lined up around the block to view his open casket, horrified most Americans and propelled some of them into action.[6]

The outrage eventually coalesced into marches, sit-ins, freedom rides, and the national convulsion that came to be known as the Civil Rights Movement. If the US Supreme Court's *Brown v. Board of Education* decision in 1954 had broken "the legal back of segregation," as the Rev. Jesse Jackson said, the murder of Emmett Till "broke the emotional back of segregation."[7]

Less than ninety days after Till's funeral, forty-two-year-old Rosa Parks was riding a bus in Montgomery, Alabama, returning home from her job as a seamstress sewing and pressing clothes at a local department store. Under bus segregation laws, whites sat in the front rows with black passengers in the back rows. If one white person boarded a full bus, everyone in the black row nearest the front was required to get up and stand so that a new whites-only row could become available.

When the bus driver noticed a white man standing he ordered Parks and three other black passengers in her row to get up and "make it light on ourselves." She refused, was arrested, and sparked a black boycott of the Montgomery city bus system. For over a year 42,000 blacks walked as far as twelve miles a day as part of the Montgomery Bus Boycott no matter the weather, even in heavy rain. Bus segregation eventually ended with a US Supreme Court decision.[8]

GREENWICH VILLAGE

As these events were unfolding in the South I was starting my legal studies at New York University.

I had grown up in a comfortable middle-class neighborhood in the Bronx where my friends were almost all white, Jewish, and, like me, first-generation Americans of Eastern European parents. In 1955 at the age of twenty-one I moved into a tenement, a fifteen-minute walk from the law school and Greenwich Village. To pay my rent I took a job as a janitor in the building, which had twenty-four units of mostly Ukrainian families and black men.

The Village was the bohemian mecca of New York at that time. My friends were literary and artsy, but only a few paid attention to events like those that were beginning to roil the nation. Although I took it upon myself to tell my friends what I had read about lurid tales of lynchings, shootings, and beatings in the Deep South, I remained on the sidelines. I might have stayed there if my friend and former law boss Phil Feiring had not quietly signed up to go to the South during the Mississippi Summer of 1964.

THE MISSISSIPPI FREEDOM SUMMER

The Council of Federated Organizations (COFO)—a coalition of primarily SNCC, Rev. Martin Luther King's Southern Christian Leadership Conference (SCLC), and the Congress of Racial Equality (CORE)— recruited more than a thousand volunteers to attempt to register as many potential black voters in Mississippi as possible. They also were to help set up Freedom Schools and community centers to aid the local black population. Volunteers were mostly students, 85 percent of them white, and an average age of 21. They joined medical, legal, and religious organizations and spread out across Mississippi.

Like most volunteers, Phil used his summer vacation to join the coalition, but this was not to be a day at the beach. Even the recruiting civil rights organizations warned potential volunteers that this could be a deadly experience and required each prospective recruit to sign a release of liability in the event of death or bodily injury.

The organizers' concerns were not exaggerated. Even before the first Freedom Summer volunteers arrived Mississippi's Klan mounted a pre-emptive strike. On a single night crosses were burned in sixty-four of the state's eighty-two counties and black churches were firebombed. In some instances fire insurance policies were suddenly cancelled by white insurance agents, shortly before the churches were burned.[9]

Meanwhile the Mississippi state legislature passed laws outlawing civil rights activities, officials were allowed to declare dawn-to-dusk curfews, and it became a crime to even pass out leaflets advocating boycotts. The number of state troopers were doubled, and towns hastily formed posses of armed white men—many of them Klansmen—to repel the "beatnik horde."

CORE, the old-timer in COFO having been founded in 1942, played a major role in the 1961 Freedom Rides and helped organize the 1963 March on Washington. Included in the first wave of Mississippi Summer workers were two CORE activists: twenty-four-year-old white CORE field secretary Mickey Schwerner and twenty-one-year-old black CORE leader James Chaney, a resident of Mississippi. On Saturday, June 21, 1964, these two CORE men along with twenty-year-old summer volunteer Andy Goodman were assigned to drive to Philadelphia, Mississippi, to investigate the burning of a church where the pastor had agreed to host a civil rights Freedom School. The trio were arrested on the road and then "released" into a Klan ambush. Chaney was tortured and all three men were shot to death. A New York pathologist later examined the body of Chaney and reported:

> I could barely believe the destruction to these frail young bones. In my 25 years as a pathologist and medical examiner, I have never seen bones so severely shattered, except in tremendously high speed accidents or airplane crashes. . . .This boy had been beaten to a pulp.[10]

Despite three deaths on the first days of the Freedom Summer, volunteers continued their efforts pushing for voter registration and operating Freedom Schools intended to begin to undo the effect of the state's segregated school system. They also opened community centers that offered cultural and educational programs such as adult literacy courses, health education classes, and vocational training centers.

The summer was marked by widespread violence against volunteers and local blacks. Thirty-five COFO workers were shot at with four people critically wounded, at least eighty were beaten, and more than 1,000 were arrested, including local blacks, COFO staff, and summer volunteers. At least thirty-seven black churches were bombed, and more than thirty black homes and businesses were burned.

When Phil returned to New York he told me what he and the others had gone through balanced by his delight at meeting up with Mississippi sharecroppers. As I heard him relate his experiences a great shame came over me. I had been vaguely aware that volunteers were heading for Mississippi, but I thought that this program was only for students and young people. I didn't believe there was any role for a lawyer in his thirties, but Phil having been there made all the difference. Like me he was a lawyer, not a student, and he encouraged me to apply.

Within weeks I was scheduled to spend my next year's summer vacation in Jackson, Mississippi.

WAITING FOR THE FLIGHT TO MISSISSIPPI

My parents accompanied me to the airport in August 1965. My mother was frightened for me and weepy. My father was glum and disapproving because he believed I was jeopardizing my career. My father's silence was deafening, so I made conversation with my mother about what I anticipated in the South, relaying what I had learned from Phil and his new civil rights allies.

Black residents in Mississippi, I told my mother, were still experiencing widespread discrimination and forced to suffer impoverished living conditions. Families with as many as fourteen children lived in dirt-floored wooden shacks with walls that had gaping holes were covered by newspapers and tapestries of their "Holy Trinity": Jesus Christ, President John F. Kennedy, and Rev. Martin Luther King Jr. Freezing winters were relieved, if at all, by a potbelly stove—the only source of heat as well as the sole implement for cooking. There was no relief from the sweltering summers.

Medical care, I added, was virtually nonexistent from birth to death although desperately needed for nutritionally starved adults and lethargic, malnourished children. Their diet was one of greens, cornbread, Kool-Aid, coffee, and occasional pork parts drowned in thick gravy. From dawn to dusk the sharecroppers farmed, but at the end of the year they were still in debt with even less money for decent living quarters, adequate food, and minimal medical care for the next year.

Despite their circumstances and vulnerability most blacks welcomed civil rights workers. Organizing was done in the open: sometimes in the plantation owner's cotton fields, other times at church meetings, and often on public roads. The sharecropper who listened and offered a bed or food to a civil rights worker was subject to retribution from the landowner, the merchant, the police chief, and the Klan.

My mother worried about the community where I would live. I reassured her, relaying Phil's description of the sharecroppers as kind, caring people who usually looked after large extended families, including elderly relatives and often the babies of their children working in the North. Serious crime and adultery within the black community were almost unheard of, and children were respectful of their parents and other adults. Few farmers even cursed and marriages didn't seem to break up. Even when they were down to their last meal, a sharecropper's family would share it with a black visitor or a civil rights worker.

When my mother asked me about the "dirty, long-haired youth" she had seen on TV—referring to the civil rights workers—I related Phil's depiction of them as a separate society with their own culture. Emulating the sharecroppers with whom they worked, the civil rights workers dressed in overalls, work shirts and boots, and spoke a bastardized Negro dialect saying things like, "The Peoples have a right to reddish to vote!" The Southern tradition of humiliating a black male by calling him "boy" or by his first name led civil rights workers to reverse the tradition. Every black adult was referred to by the honorific "Mr." or "Mrs." while civil rights workers, no matter what age, were called by their first names. And there was always the dilemma of how to refer to the former slaves. For Southern whites the term was "nigger" or "nigra." For the subjects themselves it was "colored." And to civil rights workers it was "negro"— "black" was yet to come.

I also told my mother of the social rituals I had heard so much about. If a civil rights worker drove up to a sharecropper's home and introduced himself he had to be prepared for a long visit. The farmer would typically tell someone to run inside and "get this man some Kool-Aid." Then, as all the children swarmed around, their elders would ask, "Where are you from? Do you have a family? What do you think of Mississippi? Hot 'nuf for you? Have you seen so-and-so? Is this one out of jail? Has that one recovered from his beating? Isn't it horrible that another one was shot?" Then their neighbors would arrive and ask the same questions. The civil rights worker would be invited for dinner, would play with the children, and probably stay overnight.

Civil rights workers joked that if Paul Revere had tried to warn black Mississippi, he would have ridden up, shouted "the British are coming!", and would still be at the first house eating and talking when the King's men arrived.

I related the warnings I had heard of conversation barriers volunteers had experienced with the sharecroppers and vice versa. Communication was often nearly impossible because the black farmers spoke very slowly, forcing the visitor to grit his teeth to avoid interrupting and finishing the sentence. On the other hand the abbreviated speech patterns of the newly arriving Northerner might roar ahead, seemingly out of control with the rhythm of a railroad train, overwhelming the rural listener.

Adding to the confusion were regional accents, drawls, colloquialisms, and style—the latter a very serious matter since the white Northerner spoke with ironic humor, exaggeration, and sarcasm while the black Southerner, holding a very straightforward view of life, considered hyperbole a falsehood. And there was the tendency of some black farmers, dating back to days of enslavement, to tell the white man what it was thought he or she wanted to hear. To achieve even the semblance of communication I was told that veteran civil rights workers were pressed into temporary service as interpreters.

Even time and directions had their own language. Since few black sharecroppers used clocks or calendars time was told by the sun (sunrise, sunset) or events (the day the candy man arrived, cotton choppin' week, the Sunday the preacher came to town). Directions depended upon nature (turn left at the big oak, then down a piece to the three cows—and there would be three cows!).

Although intrigued by my retelling of experiences I had heard from Phil, my parents still worried about my safety. When my father asked, "Isn't it dangerous?" I responded, "Not for a lawyer wearing a suit. The ones at risk are the civil rights workers." I did not mention the no-nonsense rules for survival.

Suit or no suit I was very aware that the struggle for civil rights in the South could provoke open warfare. Certain rules were intended to avoid the kind of provocations that would amplify the bloodlust of racist whites. A breach of those rules could mean death for the rule-breaker and those nearby. To remain alive in communities where the mere presence of a civil rights worker could be a provocation, one had to carefully follow the rules of survival:

If cursed, do not curse back.

If pushed, do not push back.

If struck, do not strike back.

Avoid bizarre or controversial behavior.

No facial hair; be neat.

Do not travel alone if possible.

Know all roads.

Keep doors, gas tanks, and hoods locked.

Do not sleep near open windows.

Do not stand in a doorway with light to your back.

Be sure all prescribed medicines are clearly marked [to avoid drug arrests].

Never tell the police or FBI who you live with.

Call in regularly.

Never drive with less than half a tank of gas.

Only fill up at franchise [minimum four pumps] gas stations. [The theory was that franchise dealers would be vulnerable to Northern economic pressure and therefore less likely to initiate or tolerate violence.]

When on the road eat only at Holiday Inn–type franchises [for the same reason as using gas station franchises].

Keep enough food in the car to last half a day [to avoid the necessity of dangerous stops].

Keep an empty bottle handy [to avoid bathroom stops].

Remove all inside car lights [to avoid being a target when the car door is opened].

As my flight was called my mother gave me a tearful bear hug. My father mustered himself to shake my hand and wish me good luck.

2

Lawyers for the Movement

I settled into my seat on the Jackson-bound Delta Airlines jet and tried to visualize my anticipated righteous struggle against Jim Crow laws and racial injustice.

But as we neared Jackson and the overhead panels lit up with "fasten seat belt," all my daydreams about the warm glow of future accomplishment were suddenly overwhelmed by a wave of anxiety at what would await me in the coming long, hot summer weeks. As the plane circled the small four-hangar airport I braced myself both for the landing and the need to prove myself.

"Please remain in your seats until the aircraft has come to a complete stop. Welcome to Jackson, Mississippi."

The sound of "Mississippi" spoken with a Southern accent sent yet another spasm of anxiety through my body. *Wasn't Mississippi basically Nazi Germany with a Southern accent? Was I, a Jew, completely out of my mind voluntarily flying to the crematorium?*

ARRIVING IN JACKSON

As the plane came to a halt and I walked down the aircraft steps onto firm Mississippi soil, the only violence I encountered was being jostled by joyous passengers rushing past me to greet family and friends. Discreetly placing myself in the midst of such a group I headed for the terminal hoping I did not appear as conspicuous as I felt. It was then that I heard someone calling out my name.

"Are you Donald Jelinek?" a stranger asked.

"Who y'all?" I ventured gamely.

A hearty laugh erupted from a man who turned out to be Mike, the lawyer assigned to drive me to the office of the American Civil Liberties Union (ACLU) where I was to work for the next three weeks. Mike assumed I had been joking.

Riding out of the airport I took my first look at Mississippi farmland.

"That's cotton," Mike said pointing at a field filled with the crop that had been the catalyst for American slavery.

I had expected to see vast acres of farmland and remnants of old plantations—which, I was to discover, was a fair description of much of the state but not of the capital city of Jackson. Having almost tripled its population to 150,000 over 20 years, the city was newly built-up and immaculately clean. Instead of a country store with a cracker barrel and spittoons I saw the same plastic restaurants, dime stores, and movie theaters as would be found in any Northern shopping center.

Surprised to see both races walking on the same streets and apparently shopping in the same stores, I questioned Mike. He explained that the famous "Southern hospitality" was available to blacks *if* they were not perceived as "uppity." They could even shop in most stores if they politely refrained from touching clothes they were not ready to purchase —and didn't sit down. Despite surface appearances, Jim Crow, he assured me, was alive and well in Jackson.

Now came the real tour. It began when we walked into the state capitol building, a dignified gray stone edifice featuring an impressive rotunda and a prominent bronze statue of Theodore Bilbo, a former Mississippi governor and US senator who had campaigned to send blacks "back to Africa" and was reelected on a platform of "Do not let a single Nigger vote!" Mike hustled me past a collection of memorabilia celebrating the state's major triumphs: life-size portraits of two winners of the Miss America pageant. He had more important stops to make.

"That," Mike pointed out, "is the bus terminal where the Freedom Riders rode into Mississippi." The Riders were integrated groups of young students who boarded Greyhound and Trailways buses to challenge segregated bus terminals in the Deep South. On May 15, 1961, over 100 Klansmen ambushed one of the buses in Anniston, Alabama, and set it on fire. Other riders were set upon by violent mobs in Birmingham and Montgomery, Alabama, before finally arriving in Jackson where they were arrested and then sent to the infamous Parchman prison.

Next we drove to the fairgrounds where only two months earlier Mike had seen hundreds of demonstrators arrested for challenging the legitimacy of white Mississippi legislators elected while black citizens were denied the vote. Protesters had been forced to run a gauntlet behind barbed wire as they were beaten and gassed. They were kept awake day and night and were issued no blankets and only one narrow mattress for every three prisoners. Women who asked for medical attention were subjected to physical examination in full view of staring policemen.[1]

"Now keep your eyes open!" Mike exclaimed as we turned the corner. That's when I saw it: Thompson's Tank—the infamous six-and-a-half ton battlewagon that had been readied by Mayor Allen Thompson for use in the event of a civil rights–instigated riot during the 1964 Freedom Summer. It contained steel walls, bullet-proof windows, teargas guns, a submachine gun, and numerous shotguns. "They won't have a chance!" the mayor had blared.[2]

Leaving the white downtown area, we made a sharp turn and drove two blocks into the black downtown.

Amazed at the close proximity of the two races, I wondered why so much blood was shed to keep them apart. "It's you Yankees who keep the races apart," segregationist Governor George Wallace of neighboring Alabama had proclaimed. "In the South, colored and white live right next to one 'nother." He was right. In Jackson a ten-minute walk from almost anywhere would take you across racial boundaries. A black sharecropper who had left the South for work in Detroit would later tell me how much he missed the contact, the trading of friendly "Hiya's" with the whites; he felt much more isolated in the "integrated" North.

"Southerners love blacks as individuals and hate them as a race," Mike said in an oft-repeated piece of racial folklore, "while Northerners love them as a race and avoid them as individuals." Southern whites debased, intimidated, and even lynched former slaves but also knew their names and frequently seemed genuinely solicitous of their health and family problems. Most Northerners I knew were cheerleaders for civil rights but had never in their entire lives truly socialized with a black person.

Still in the South there was steel behind that honeyed courtesy. Mike angrily pointed to the street where thousands of mourners had followed the coffin of Medgar Evers. The young NAACP civil rights leader and WWII veteran had been assassinated by racist whites in June 1963; he died minutes after President Kennedy delivered a landmark national address proclaiming a future Civil Rights Act. Evers was shot down in the driveway of his home in front of his wife and children.

Pausing only briefly in front of the place where Evers' funeral had been held, Mike perked up and said, "I forgot to mention, you're now on North Farish Street, the civil rights capital of the United States. We're home."

Unlike the sedate white downtown, here the sidewalks and streets were alive with smiling black faces, some capped with straight "conked" hair. The walkways and streets were filled with pedestrians, their blackness offset by bright clothing, often orange and chartreuse. Driving through this mass of black humanity, we rarely had to honk the horn. A strange harmony was apparent on North Farish Street. As we neared our next local landmark, Steven's Kitchen, the blast of jukeboxes increased the decibel level markedly. This was "Movement territory," where visiting civil rights dignitaries ate with the rank and file and planned for upcoming struggles.

As our car edged its way through the pedestrian traffic Mike rolled the windows down to reply to cheery greetings from the crowd. I heard my first chorus of the song of the black South: the infectious roar of raucous laughter, mock combat, and an almost indistinguishable mélange of accents emerging from behind decaying teeth in mouths that never seemed to open wide enough. Almost drowned out in the din was the twang issuing from the white faces dotting this black oasis: a confused dialect that sounded like John Wayne imitating Rhett Butler. These were the young civil rights workers, only faintly disguised behind their sharecropper jeans and work shirts, but their acceptance on the street was obvious.

LAWYERS ROW

Mike seemed oblivious to my awestruck reaction to this spectacle. "That's our destination up ahead!" he boomed. "Lawyers Row!" He pointed to a small sector of North Farish Street.

"See that ramshackle building?" he asked. "That's ACLU."

After thanking Mike for the ride and tour I bounded up a rickety flight of stairs and stepped into the top floor offices of the civil liberties group. Two glances were sufficient to take in the entire operation. The first glance revealed four small rooms, assorted desks, chairs, file cabinets, typewriters, a photocopy machine, and five telephones. The second revealed my boss for the next three weeks, Al Bronstein.

A short, stocky man, his career in the South paralleled the growth of the legal effort for basic civil rights in the region from its touch-and-go beginnings. Bronstein had been a practicing lawyer in New York City when he was first stirred by news of the sit-ins and Freedom Rides. As early as 1961 he had become a part-time fly-in-fly-out civil rights lawyer.

Eventually aspiring to practice in the South full time, he discovered that there was no organization devoted solely to civil rights lawyering based in Mississippi. Not even the venerable NAACP, the granddaddy of civil rights lawyering, with its sixty years of experience and victories including the historic school desegregation case of *Brown v. Board of Education.*[3]

The NAACP had no civil rights law office in the South. Nor did the so-called "President's Committee," a prestigious establishment group of lawyers allegedly solicited in 1963 by President Kennedy to grapple with the embarrassing specter of Southern racism. Neither did the ACLU, which had been battling for free speech and civil liberties for forty-five years and had been expanding its work in the racial justice arena.[4] However, after almost a thousand volunteer civil rights workers were arrested during the Freedom Summer of 1964, the necessity for on-the-spot legal response was clear.

The National Lawyers Guild (NLG), a left-oriented bar association with a history of involvement in racial causes, leaped in to support the Movement. Although impoverished and weakened by the House Un-American Activities Committee, which had falsely branded it as "an arm of the international Communist Conspiracy," the Guild recruited and financed black female lawyer Claudia Shropshire to open an office on North Farish Street, thereby creating a string of firsts: the first fulltime civil rights law office in Mississippi, the first law office in the Deep South headed by a black lawyer, and the first law office anywhere headed by a woman. Serving as a command post for lawyer volunteers from Guild chapters across the country, the Guild office provided critical support for the rapidly growing and increasingly needy Civil Rights Movement.

Bronstein of the ACLU and his counterparts in both the President's Committee and the NAACP Legal Defense Fund were chagrined. Embarrassed by the Guild's successes and concerned by its radical influence—*Freedom Now! Without Compromise!*), the "Reluctant Three," as they were contemptuously dubbed by the Guild, mobilized separately and raced southward in 1965, each opening an office on North Farish Street.

Pleased at having lured the others down, the underfinanced Guild gratefully closed its doors and thereafter operated on a case-by-case basis, representing the more militant elements of the movement. Guild lawyers maliciously liked to recall a cartoon that depicted a conversation between two prosperous white liberal lawyers: "The civil rights movement was great fun 'til the colored started joining." It was suggested that the well-heeled, well-educated lawyers, despite their commitment to the cause of civil rights, were uncomfortable in the presence of destitute, barely literate black sharecroppers and outright contemptuous of by-choice, beggared civil rights workers.

After the departure of the NLG the three remaining groups—which were often rather disdainful of one another—divided the turf according to their own ideological inclinations and comfort levels. The President's Committee preferred to represent ministers and community leaders, while the ACLU defended rank-and-file civil rights workers. Thus if a minister was arrested with a handful of civil rights workers, two sets of lawyers might travel many hours in separate cars and file separate sets of papers. The NAACP Legal Defense Fund mostly stayed out of the fray, concentrating on school desegregation and other long-range projects.

Soon each had the other labeled. The President's Committee protected only "big shots," the ACLU "shot from the hip," while the Legal Defense Fund cared only for constitutional issues and not people. Periodically each would cross into the other's terrain but coexistence was never established. Instead they sparred with one another even as they fought for racial harmony.

When the ACLU opened its Jackson office in March 1965—a mere five months before my arrival—Bronstein, then thirty-seven, set out to coordinate the efforts of three or at times four full-time staff lawyers supplemented by volunteer lawyers like me (sarcastically referred to by resident civil rights workers as "Summer Soldiers") who had given up their vacations to render assistance in the South.[5] Absorbing the varied skills of his many volunteers, Bronstein crafted their work into an effective whole.

After meeting Bronstein I advanced timidly into the office receiving a weak handshake from a visiting member of the Boston Brahmin Saltonstall family, a warm greeting from a celebrated Harvard law professor, and a glance from a renowned criminal law specialist from Pennsylvania. "Hi," I muttered, humbled. I had been imagining myself volunteering to enter into dangerous and uncharted territory, but it was as if I had arrived at the Harvard Faculty Club.

With pleasantries out of the way Bronstein assigned me to a small desk on top of which rested a case file. This case was apparently too small for the criminal law specialist, had no constitutional issues for the Harvard professor, was not worthy of the efforts of a Saltonstall, had no ministers involved for the President's Committee, and lacked enough national significance for the NAACP Legal Defense Fund. It was just insignificant enough for Bronstein's newest and most insignificant lawyer.

THE PIGGLY WIGGLY CASE

The case involved a group of young black and white civil rights activists who had been heckled and threatened by a band of young white toughs while picketing outside a Piggly Wiggly supermarket. They were demanding an end to discriminatory hiring. One white tough cuffed a protester on the ear. In shock she whirled around and *may have* brushed her sign against him. She was arrested, jailed for assault and battery, and then released after posting $200 cash bail.

After reading through the file I invited the twenty or so picketers to come to the ACLU office to reenact the "crime." *Who was first in line? Who was next? Where did he strike you? How high were you holding the sign?* I drilled them until each participant could testify to every detail. These were the first rank and file civil rights workers I had ever met and I was enjoying myself in their company. I also couldn't help noticing how curiously amused Bronstein seemed to be of my elaborate preparations.

A few days later my client and our many witnesses walked with me to the white downtown where the courthouse was located. Climbing up steep stairs to the courthouse entrance, I nervously observed police cars lining the streets. Police officers ran up the courthouse steps ahead of us with rifles in hand. Finally we stopped five paces in front of a state trooper who stood directly in our path holding his weapon with military precision across his chest.

Mustering my deepest voice to mask my fear, I demanded to know why the state trooper was "blocking a lawyer from entering a courthouse in the United States of America."

It appeared that he too was nervous.

"You can go in, sir," the trooper stammered, "but not, uh, them, uh, the demonstrators."

"They are not demonstrators." I said politely, pointing to my group as I spoke. "They're my client and her witnesses."

Watching his face relax slightly I added, "*Really.* I guarantee it."

Lowering his rifle and passing on my words with audible relief to the officers behind him, we were allowed to pass.

Having survived my first confrontation with Southern authorities and apparently winning the admiration of my young group, I led the way inside the building as we entered an impressive modern courtroom. The judge was already on the bench seated between the state flag of

Mississippi and the Confederate battle flag. If there was a United States flag I did not see it. After two mundane criminal cases our case was called.

Following testimony from the toughs I put the defendant on the stand. "And did you intentionally strike him with your sign?"

"No, after I was hit, I turned suddenly. . . ."

The judge interrupted and addressed me. "I understand your defense. Will your other witnesses confirm this story?"

Before I could answer the judge grunted, "Very well. Not guilty. Pick up your bail money at the clerk's office. Next case."

Thoroughly dazed at this unexpected turn of events I rushed to the clerk's office, picked up the bail money, and raced with my client to ACLU.

As we walked in Bronstein looked up from his desk and laughed. "Don't tell me you lost already?"

I responded by pulling out $200 in tens and twenties, thumbing through them like a bank teller. "What do I do with the bail money?" I asked innocently.

The surprised silence in the office was broken by my client giggling. "We won, I was dismissed."

Only the professor congratulated me. The others began an analysis —eliminating me as a factor—of why it happened and what it meant. Aware that civil rights cases were rarely won in Mississippi state courts (usually victories came on appeals to the federal courts), the lawyers speculated that the judge's motive may have been to provide a statistic for the US Justice Department, or to show that trials were fair in Mississippi, or perhaps to balance the next outrageous conviction, or maybe even to speed the calendar by avoiding so many witnesses. One joked that perhaps the judge rewarded the naive lawyer who took his court seriously enough to bring twenty witnesses.

Since no one asked my opinion and nor did I have one, I left with my client and headed down North Farish Street where she gushingly told everyone of our victory. She was asked: "You *won?*" "We *won!*" my client proclaimed. It was my first entrée into the world of "we." I was still an outsider in this world that rewarded only long-term commitment—not Summer Soldiers. Nevertheless the many pats on the back, slaps on the palms, and invitations to a few parties established that I at least had a toe in the door.

For my next assignment Bronstein sent me to monitor the same civil rights workers as they resumed their picketing at the supermarket where one of the group had been arrested. Within moments of my arrival I was engaged by an irate supermarket manager who, spying me as a responsible looking white adult in a suit, vented his frustrations by offering his opinions on slavery (favorable), lynching (unavoidable), integration (never!). I listened attentively until he ran out of steam and left. Then, beginning my watch of the picketers, I noticed a petite white woman in her early twenties severely limping from the effects, I would later learn, of childhood polio. It was incredible to me that anyone would come to Mississippi lacking the ability to run away from danger.

Because the summer heat was suffocating the picketers divided into two groups—one on the picket line and the other in the shade, from where I prudently conducted my surveillance. Happy to see me, those who had been at the trial began relating the entire courtroom story, telling it in the manner of minstrels and entertaining those who had not been present or had heard the story many times but were delighted to hear it again. This style of communication had a purpose beyond that of mere transfer of information: it was a mantra, a soothing sound designed to comfort, console, and reassure. In the retelling my role was much praised (if overstated), emboldening me to ask them about their lives as civil rights workers.

At first the incidents they related to me were lighthearted.

"Remember when we integrated that restaurant?"

"Oh, yeah, and we all went down."

"Right, and the waitress, pretending she was fighting mosquitoes, sprayed our table . . . and our food . . . with insecticide." (Much laughter.)

"She was fired," the speaker turned to me, "and now they're reasonably friendly."

Then more serious matters.

Some here had been arrested in Jackson a few months earlier and confined to the Fairgrounds—which Mike had shown me—imprisoned behind concentration camp wire. Although in their early twenties a number of them were veterans of many encounters: attacks with clubs, skull fractures, and serious concussions. They also told of being knocked off their feet from high-pressure water hoses. They discussed holding their ground while being beaten then awaiting the next round of abuse in Southern jails. Despite it all they knew they would remain in jail for a while, unwilling to pay a fine or post cash bail.

Yet, "everything, everyone is beautiful," said "Sally," the woman who limped. "The people, the cause, the picketing. I'm so happy, so thrilled.

I've never felt such emotions. But," she added, "I worry all the time, even on the line here. Will I be assassinated today?"

"Nah, don't worry," interrupted another, "it doesn't happen in Jackson."

"What about Medgar Evers?"

"Well, that's different. He was a big shot. Anyhow it usually happens in the rurals."

"I'm going to the rurals tomorrow . . ." I said, my voice expressing a fear I hadn't recognized until then. "I'm going to a county outside of Holly Springs to work on a case."

"Oh, you'll be alright," said Sally, unconvincingly.

"Oh, sure," someone else added, "just follow the rules and you'll be safe."

"Besides," Sally now added, smiling brightly, "I'll get you company. My friend needs a lift in that direction. Okay?"

"Good," I answered, immediately feeling better.

"YEAH! YOU'LL BE OKAY!" a voice suddenly boomed. It came from a tall, black civil rights worker standing near where I was sitting. His body language cried "hostile!" His accent identified him from the black ghetto, perhaps in Manhattan.

"HEY LAWYER!" he shouted as if I were yards away. "That's a great suit you're wearing!"

The remark was incongruous, especially considering it was a cheap suit I had deliberately brought to wear for these three weeks.

"Leave it on, man, that suit'll keep you safe!"

Translation: white professionals like me—dilettantes—are in no danger, unlike civil rights workers. I bristled. These last twenty-four hours I had felt so confident, a feeling of manly pride. Now this lout, somehow sensing my vulnerability, had scored a direct hit.

Before I could reply Sally spoke up for me.

"It's not a lawyer's job to take risks," she said. "We're lucky to have them."

My antagonist snorted. Then, as an obvious affront to me, returned to the line before his turn, presumably giving up his rest and the shade to avoid remaining in my presence. A few apologized for him.

When the picketing ended at sundown I told Sally that her friend who needed a lift should meet me at the ACLU house early the next morning. I said goodbye to the group, adding that I would see them when I returned from Holly Springs. A few of the men shook my hand firmly. Two women kissed and solemnly embraced me.

As I was walking away Sally called out, "I hope you're not bothered by that stupid 'suit' remark."

"Oh, no," I lied, smiled, and left. Of course I was bothered because the obnoxious one was right. I did—and was happy to—rely on the suit and my lawyer status to protect myself.

But I would soon discover that he and I were both wrong: out of Jackson, in the rurals, the suit would not protect this lawyer.

On the Road

The day I was to go to the rurals began at 4 AM when I was awakened by Sally's friend who had been told to meet me "early that morning." "Early" in New York City parlance meant around 8 AM; in civil rights country, as I was painfully learning, it meant before the rooster's first crow. "Sally told me you would give me a lift upstate," said "Peter," a white, twenty-year-old divinity student, smiling sheepishly when he saw that I was still half asleep.

"C'mon in," I grumbled.

My mood improved after I made us both a cup of coffee. Soon we were happily chatting away, and by dawn we were on the road.

Peter was heading for Okolona, a modest detour from Holly Springs. Okolona seemed a vaguely familiar name. Was that the county Bronstein had ordered another lawyer to avoid? Or did he say "Okahola"—southeast of Jackson? Since I was only passing through I thought *what's the difference?* The young civil rights worker was good company for the long drive as we traded civil rights stories. I told about my trial—my only tale—but his stories were about Okolona, a six square miles town of about 2,000, a 70 percent black population, and a dangerous area even by Mississippi standards. Beatings and shootings were commonplace, according to Peter, especially since voter registration efforts began.

In addition Peter was worried that his days in the Movement were numbered. It was "in the talk" that black militants, especially within SNCC, wanted a "blacks-only" movement led by local residents—not dominated, as they claimed, by white civil rights workers. The world of the Movement was changing, he said, somberly.

Before he could say more we left the highway, turning onto a dirt road that would take us into the black section of rural Okolona. This was my first lesson in "colored geography": where the pavement ends the colored folks' world begins. As my car hit the dirt for the first time the red dust permeated everything from shoes to nostrils. Even closed car windows could not keep it out.

I drove to a small wooden shack the size of a Manhattan living room —the "Freedom House" where civil rights workers could live and work. I was greeted by Peter's compatriots who were excited to encounter a lawyer. "We never get a lawyer here," the one woman among them complained. "Bronstein tells them . . ." She paused suddenly and exchanged a glance with the others. I pretended not to notice.

One of the group changed the subject to their work, including a trial concerning a black sharecropper scheduled in a few days. He was suing an important white merchant. "Would you represent him?" I was asked. "Winning this case is very important."

Knowing what Bronstein would say I declined, explaining that I had to be in Holly Springs that night for a very important court date the following day—and I then had other pressing commitments in Jackson. There was a moment of disappointment but then the civil rights worker who had asked my help said, "Anyhow, come and meet 'Harry Long,' the man who's suing. He's beautiful."

Soon I was walking with them, jacket off and tie loosened, to a sharecropper home: a shack with no running water (just a pump), not even an outhouse (discreet bushes were a few yards away), no electricity, holes in cardboard thin walls, and a large metal basin to squat in for bathing.

Then I saw the children and held back tears. They had open scabs and sores and were too listless to interfere with the flies sucking at their wounds. Most of the children had distended stomachs, which I had only seen in newsreels of starving youth in undeveloped nations.

Before I could regain my composure I was introduced to the first sharecropper: Mr. Long, a tall, very erect, black man wearing overalls, his smile interrupted by many missing teeth. We shook hands. When told I was a lawyer his face betrayed interest but he never commented on his need for legal help. It wasn't necessary. Still reeling from the sight of the children I volunteered to be his lawyer. Mr. Long thanked me; the others patted me on the back and smiled.

I soon learned that Mr. Long's case involved a seemingly insignificant matter: his purchase of inexpensive but defective merchandise from a town merchant. After we had talked for a half hour I was invited to join the noon meal. Over cornbread and Kool-Aid I plotted how *not* to tell Bronstein about my new case when I called in since he'd probably say "no."

Regretting that I had to leave Okolona for Holly Springs but assuring everybody that I would be back in time for the trial, I doubled back to the highway still stunned from the sight of the children.

HOLLY SPRINGS

Heading north I found myself driving through Oxford, home of the University of Mississippi or 'Ole Miss. There, just three years before, a massive mob, mobilized and incited by then-governor Ross Barnett and politicians of other states, had set out to block incoming black student James Meredith from integrating the university. White racists came from as far away as Alabama, Arkansas, and Louisiana. Two persons were killed and some thirty federal Marshals were wounded while protecting Meredith.

I continued due north to my destination, a sleepy Southern community where sharecropping blacks worked the fields and maybe supplemented their earning by working a bit in the off-season in nearby Memphis, Tennessee.

Holly Springs was the headquarters of the Civil Rights Movement in northern Mississippi. I glanced at my instructions: DRIVE DOWN MAIN STREET PAST A TASTEE FREEZ AND YOU'LL SEE THE FREEDOM HOUSE. *See the house? What house? Why the hell didn't they give me an address?* Then I saw why. Up ahead, under a huge poster of black and white hands grasped together, was the Freedom House.

I parked. As I began to walk toward the house I saw a small, intense white woman seated on the porch vigorously rocking in a dilapidated wicker rocker and eyeing me with ill will. This was Aviva Futorian—infamous in Mississippi both as a highly effective civil rights leader and as the daughter of a Yankee factory owner in Mississippi. It was said that her father had feared his business would suffer because of her civil rights involvement, but instead his customers had taken pity on him for having such a wayward daughter.

Because of my Okolona detour I was a half-day late, but since the court date that required my presence wasn't until the next day I had assumed no one would care. Aviva cared. She coolly explained that one of the reasons punctuality rules existed was to spare those waiting the anxiety of worrying that you might be dead. After I apologized Aviva relaxed, asked about my background and, of course, how long I was staying in the South.

Other Holly Springs civil rights workers appeared and pumped me for details of civil rights activities in the state—news which visitors from Jackson were expected to know and pass on. Knowing more than I realized, I satisfied their inquiries with hearsay reports of the latest successes, setbacks, and tragedies combined with scandalous gossip.

After my recitation Aviva invited me to a church meeting scheduled for that evening in next-door Benton County—her county—to discuss the impending hearing, not tomorrow's day in court. She assured me that the people would love to hear me speak. Before I could respond she added, "You should know there is a bomb threat."

In truth I was as frightened by the prospect of traveling to unknown Benton County, to a church filled with unknown people, as I was of the Klan and their bombs. I didn't want to go, but not wanting to appear faint of heart, I acquiesced.

The drive to the church was harrowing. Each headlight along the road became the imagined Klan, each detour sign a trap, until we pulled up at a large, one-room, wooden A-frame church. Aviva pointed out the protection: two of "our" security men at the dirt road entrance to the church grounds.

As we walked into the meeting Aviva spoke of the irony of civil rights meetings taking place in Christian churches. Christianity had been foisted on the slaves, she said, as a means of controlling them; now the former slaves used the church as an organizing domain for their struggle to end white supremacy. To a certain extent, I was later told, that had also been true during slavery when, for example, some of the spirituals sung were secret calls and instructions for escape: "Steal Away to Jesus" and "Follow the Drinking Gourd."

The meeting was already in progress as we entered but it would only really start now that Aviva had arrived. Since this was a weeknight during cotton season most of the men wore bib overalls, blue denim work shirts, and military-style boots all lightly covered with red dust, brown dirt, and cotton specks. Women were dressed in patched blouses and skirts. The atmosphere was good-natured anarchy: infants crying, giggling children running about, and parents whispering to neighbors. A hush fell over the room as Aviva was called upon to speak.

Welcomed and introduced by Mr. Rankin, a tall, erect black leader who possessed a tractor, a "herd" of two cows, a telephone, and indoor plumbing. His "wealth" allowed him to take a more public stance than some more economically dependent on whites.

Aviva began by invoking the dominant Movement slogan: "The Peoples are in charge!"

"Tomorrow," Aviva continued, "we resume fighting against the 'old man' behind this lawsuit." There were many appreciative snickers for brazenly attacking the county's leading white citizen and lawyer. Aviva's voice rose as she exclaimed:

"If you want to continue the fight . . ."

Yes! Uh huh!

". . . then no threats of violence will stop us."

No! No!

"We've been through so much but we'll go on fighting."

Yes! Yes!

Aviva smiled, the audience applauded, the chairman formally thanked her and then called upon "Mr. Jerrenenek?" to speak. Walking to the front, I invited all to call me Don, which was well received as much for my informality as for alleviating the problem of pronouncing my last name.

Every good trial lawyer must also be a good storyteller. The attorney has to assemble testimony and package it into a tale told dramatically and with enough intensity to hold the jury's interest. My New York peers rated me a good trial lawyer and an even better storyteller. Only a few knew I spent my college and law school summers as a waiter/standup comic in upstate New York resorts. These hotels in the Catskills were known collectively as the "Borscht Circuit," both for the Jewish clientele and the favorite dish. I was a poor comedian but with the slightest encouragement I could weave a yarn and hold an audience.

During the drive from Okolona I had silently rehearsed a short, boring explanation of the merits of the case I had traveled to argue, but after the excitement of Aviva's talk I couldn't resist attempting to also woo the audience. Drawing upon an anecdote told to me by my Piggly Wiggly clients, I told of a confrontation between a plantation owner, a local black farmer, and a white civil rights worker.

"And why don't you leave the nigras alone?" I mimicked the owner. "They were plenty happy before you came. No one was ever arrested or frightened. Isn't that true, Henry?" I acted out the haughty plantation owner talking down to his black Greek chorus.

"Yassah Boss, yes Sir." I exaggerated the response to much appreciative laughter.

"And you know," I added provocatively, "the white man was right. There was no trouble, or almost none, 'CAUSE nothin' changed."

Yeah!
"You were kept down, no right to even use a water fountain . . ."
Oh, yes.
"Forced to walk in the street, not the sidewalk . . ."
Ummmmh.

As I went through the long litany of humiliations the chorus of "Yeah," "True," and "Amen" grew louder and louder until it became a chant.

"Do you want to be 'happy' like before?"
No! No! No!
"Then I know why I'm here and I'll do my best for you tomorrow."

Receiving great applause and even an appreciative nod from Aviva, I spent the rest of the meeting basking in affectionate glances from the adults and blushing peeks from the teenagers.

I was very quiet on the drive back to Holly Springs. This time there was no fear of ambush, only a feeling that emptiness in my life had been filled in that church. I had experienced the "Mississippi High": the intoxication felt by white middle class civil rights workers who suddenly found themselves thrust into the idealism of the civil rights cause. Most had had hardly any prior contact with blacks and the poor; even less had had contact with danger and little experience with selfless action. That euphoria served to keep civil rights workers in the South, induced others to come, and made it difficult to retreat to normal living afterward. That night at the Freedom House, I fell asleep with unrealistic thoughts of staying in this mysterious and loving, yet menacing land.

The next morning I stoutly demanded, "Give me a large breakfast so I'll have enough energy for my one line in court today."

Everyone laughed.

I had traveled north to Holly Springs, eight hours round trip, all for a five-minute—but essential—appearance in court. The *Benton County Freedom Train*, a civil rights newspaper, had labeled a black school principal an "Uncle Tom." As if to prove the epithet the principal was prodded by whites to sue many black activists in the county and Aviva for defaming him. The lawsuit, part of a pattern of Southern psychological warfare, contained a message and ultimatum. The message was clear: These outsiders will get you into trouble and they won't be around or able to get you out of it. The ultimatum was direct: Accept segregation, get rid of the Movement, or face even more severe reprisal in the future!

Libel suits, although a legitimate remedy for damage to an individual's reputation, could be a sinister weapon when used to crush political dissent—especially where one side controlled the judiciary. As a lawyer I was familiar with the 1964 US Supreme Court decision in *New York Times Co. v. Sullivan,* which limited the scope of libel actions. That case was precipitated by an advertisement placed in the *Times* accusing unidentified white citizens in Montgomery, Alabama, of persecuting Rev. Martin Luther King Jr. The local police commissioner, asserting that the ad referred to him, asked for and received a half-million-dollar verdict from an all-white jury.

Following four years of unsuccessful appeals, the US Supreme Court reversed the court decision and issued a landmark ruling severely restricting the right of public officials such as a police commissioner or a school principal to successfully sue their critics for libel. The court held that a public figure could not win such a suit unless it was established that the offending writing was not only false but the writer knew the story was false or had recklessly disregarded the truth.

The *Times* decision would assure an eventual victory on appeal of the Holly Springs "Uncle Tom" verdict. But to launch the appeal process of a Mississippi verdict required the formality of filing a motion for a new trial—in effect asking the trial judge to reverse either himself or the jury. My job was easy: request a new trial, lose, and go home. The ACLU would then be free to begin an appeal process that could eventually end up in the US Supreme Court.

THE HEARING

After breakfast the many clients and I headed for the local courthouse situated in the center of a typical Southern town square. The antebellum white courthouse was surrounded by an expansive park which was ringed by offices, markets, shops, a movie theater, and a pool hall. In essence virtually the entire social, commercial, and civic life of the community was gathered in and around the square. Climbing the courthouse stairs with my clients, I entered what I later learned was a typical rural Mississippi steamy hot courtroom with its customary large black fan idly churning the stale, torpid air.

Immediately the local lawyers beckoned me with their good ole boy, just folks, country lawyer demeanor. As if I were in New York I left my clients on the audience side of the courtroom and crossed through the lawyer's gate to introduce myself and shake hands with the opposition. But as flesh touched flesh I realized my mistake. My sense of professional courtesy and the camaraderie of the bar was one thing, but in my clients' eyes I was fraternizing with the enemy.

"Good to have you here, Don," the leader of the Southern lawyers drawled. "Where y'all from? New York? Isn't a race riot going on there?"

Fortunately just then the judge entered the courtroom.

The judge graciously welcomed me but then fired his first volley. "I fear, Mr. Jelinek, that I am not permitted to allow you to appear before me in this case, no matter how much I would like to oblige you. You see, although we allowed Mr. Bronstein and a distinguished gentleman from Harvard to appear in this case without a license to practice law in our state, only *they* are the lawyers in *this* case, and only *they* can participate —unless you have their written authorization to replace them." He again apologized for inconveniencing me.

I had no such written authorization. No one had thought of it because such an authorization had never before been requested of a visiting lawyer. Since the judge was technically right, that I had no proof of authority to replace the other lawyers, I tried to neutralize the situation. "Could Mr. Bronstein authorize me by phone?" I asked.

"No, I'm sorry," said the judge, explaining that he would not be able to definitively recognize Mr. Bronstein's voice. To the delight of the local lawyers he confessed that he had a problem distinguishing between Northern voices.

"You have until the end of the court day," the judge offered. "Otherwise I fear I cannot hear or allow the motion for a new trial." I had three hours to produce the authorization and Jackson was four hours away. Panicking, I thanked the judge for the three hours and stumbled out of the courtroom to the snickers of my fellow legal brethren.

Glancing around the hallway, Aviva and frightened sharecroppers looked at me with ambivalence and forlorn hope, the euphoria of last night's church meeting forgotten. I sat alone on a bench attempting to calm myself. *There must be a solution!*

Half an hour later I knew what to do.

The judge's ploy wasn't so serious, I believed. No more so— actually less so—than situations in New York where, in one instance, the opposing lawyer "forgot" an agreement to postpone the trial and I found myself ordered to begin my case without evidence, witnesses, and preparation. In that situation—like other New York lawyers instinctively ready for a little treachery—I had alleged that the other side's papers weren't quite right, my major witness was ill, I was ill, and there were conflicts in my schedule for that day. The law, I believed, was a contest in which you fudged a bit, sometimes stretched a point, or even cheated a little. The other side did the same and the smarter one triumphed.

I lunged for my briefcase and walked briskly to where my clients huddled. I pulled out the legal papers with the title of the case (which named each person sued) and began calling roll. Each litigant answered, "Here."

"Well since you are all here," I said, "all you have to do is fire Mr. Bronstein and the Harvard professor and then hire me as your lawyer. Then I'll file the motion in my own name."

With a roar of approval from the clients we stormed the courtroom.

After leaning back in his swivel chair studying the ceiling where a large fly was in combat with the fan, viewing our jubilant faces, and hearing my plan, the judge concluded that a formal change of counsel was not necessary. He generously decided to "forgive" the authorization technicality. He then accepted me as Bronstein's representative, heard my brief argument, and denied the motion for a new trial. (The case was later won, as expected, on the authority of the *Times v. Sullivan* ruling.)

As I was leaving a much relieved and very friendly Aviva asked me if I'd like to visit again before returning to New York. "You could do some real civil rights work," she said, "live with the people and see what it's all about—without a suit on!" Dreading the thought of returning to routine New York legal work in that moment of triumph, I told her I was tempted, thanked her for the invitation, and said I'd let her know.

I knew I would decline the offer.

BACK TO OKOLONA

It was dark as I approached Okolona and attempted to retrace the route of the previous day. *End of pavement, okay, but which shack was the Freedom House?* I wandered and weaved in a hundred-yard circle between four houses. I didn't want to wake and frighten the wrong household, but it was 10 PM, I was tired and so hot even open car windows granted no relief. Finally selecting what I thought was the most likely house, I pulled into a makeshift driveway, tapped the horn lightly, and slid down into my seat to wait.

"DON'T MOVE!" voices commanded as rifles were thrust through the side windows of my car. I didn't move but whispered, "It's me, Jelinek," my voice rose in a singsong, *"the lawyer?"*

A pause, then nervous laughter. "Sorry, Mr. Jerinekel, we didn't recognize you in the dark. We're expecting some trouble. C'mon in, we'll hide your car."

Breathless and lightheaded, my heart bouncing inside my chest, I worked my way into the house and fell onto an over-patched, under-stuffed sofa. While I guzzled a cool drink Peter told me of a rumor that the Klan would attack that night. It seemed that one of his group mentioned in public that a civil rights lawyer was coming to appear in court the next day.

"We wanted to warn you to sleep in a motel but we couldn't reach you before you left Holly Springs. By now it would be more dangerous for you to drive out of here than to stay."

"So you will sleep in the rear house," advised the sole woman in the group. "It's behind the trees, never used, and no one will even know you're there."

She whisked me to the rear house with apologies for its sparseness. "Don't light the lantern," she gently ordered, "don't make any noise, and above all don't come out till morning."

I attempted a response but my voice cracked, "Of course . . . good luck."

Settling down on a thin mattress atop creaking springs, the bed without sheets, and the pillow without a pillow case, I tried not to move to avoid making any sound. All the while I tried to reassure myself that exaggerated preparation for danger was said to be an occupational hazard of civil rights workers. Fear stimulated camaraderie and *esprit de corps* for the front line troops. Modest about their accomplishments and bravery, civil rights workers spent much time buckling their armor in anticipation of the unlikely . . . or so I had heard.

Then the first shots rang out.

Oh my God! I thought. *It's real. I'm going to be killed!* Sitting upright on the bed as the second, third, and fourth volleys exploded, I realized that I was hearing shots over shots. Both sides were shooting. Then it was over and an eerie silence fell over the scene.

What if everyone on our side is dead? Twigs snapped. Was someone walking toward me? A slice of moonlight illuminated a broomstick in the room, the kind we played stickball with in the streets of the Bronx. Silently reaching over I grabbed the stick and laid it on the bed as my weapon. If they came through the door, what then? A broomstick against rifles and shotguns? Glancing out the window I thought I spied white-sheeted figures moving toward the door . . . or was it laundry on a clothesline? I was frantic.

I vowed that if I survived the night I would get on a plane for home the next morning. I clenched the broomstick so tightly that my knuckles ached. Chest pains began. Suddenly I was gasping for breath. Then everything went black.

"Don. *Don!*" I heard a voice as if through a drunken haze. The woman from last night was standing over me, shaking me. "It's early, but how about breakfast so we can talk and get ready for court?"

I stared at her, at the sun just peeking out of the earth, at the tiny room surrounding me. I was alive.

"What . . . ?" was all I said.

"They sometimes do that," she answered and smiled. "They drive by, shoot a few rounds high above our heads, and we fire back also high. Then they leave."

This, I learned, was ritualistic combat to satisfy Klan machismo. "No big deal," she said. Still although I hadn't done anything—I had not shot at anyone, I had not been shot at—I felt strong, brave, and proud of myself. I walked to the front house with a John Wayne swagger.

Self-deception was in command that morning. I assumed Bronstein had forbidden lawyers from working in Okolona and these civil rights workers knew why. The Klan had come shooting last night, yet all this trial involved was a black man unwilling to pay for a faulty piece of cheap merchandise. I never asked the basic question, *What's there to be shooting about?*

Had I asked, and had the workers fully understood their situation, they would have told me that Okolona was too tough to tame at this time. Past efforts had led to such bad results that veteran civil rights workers had moved on, leaving a vacuum filled by brave but inexperienced idealists.

The case concerned a defective item purchased by a black man from the store of a prominent white merchant. A demand was made for a refund or a reduction in price from the storekeeper. When this was refused a suit was filed against him—the first lawsuit, I was told, by a black man against a white man in the history of this community.

Had Mr. Long been a white man it would not have been a big deal, but Mr. Long was not a white man and suing a white merchant in Okolona was a very big deal. A strong black leader was now challenging centuries of white domination and black subservience in the courts controlled by their enemies. Peter, the man I'd given a ride to the day before, and his colleagues had intended to carry that challenge even without a lawyer, but now with a lawyer on the scene their dare threatened to turn the challenge into a *cause célèbre*.

In a few hours we were driving into the heart of "downtown" Okolona: wooden storefronts that faced a barely paved one-lane main street. Near a small house I saw a crowd of whites standing on a porch surrounded by sheriff's deputies with very visible guns and clubs. Near the porch stood white pool-hall types looking fierce and seemingly already half intoxicated.

"I'm going to park right next to the state trooper's car," I told the future minister, who was still pinning his hopes on brotherly love. "We're then going to get out of the car and pretend we're not frightened. Okay?" Peter nodded.

Climbing out of the car I shook hands with Mr. Long and asked him to identify the major characters. He pointed out the merchant standing on the porch conversing with the judge—a manual laborer when court was not in session.

I approached the judge and introduced myself. "My name is Jelinek and I'm the lawyer in this case. Shall we begin?"

No answer.

"Where will we hold the trial?" I tried again, wondering where the courtroom was. My question set off snickering among the deputies. "We usually use that there space under that tree over there," one said as he paused and pointed, "in case there be a hangin'." At this the deputies exploded with laughter. The judge, now ready to calm them down, addressed me.

"We'll use this ole porch if it suits you," he drawled.

"Sure," I said. "Who needs formalities? I love working out of doors."

Then I met the seller and became the professional. "Mr. Long believes he was sold defective merchandise," I said. To my relief, and after he debated the merits of the product with my client, the merchant agreed to a small price reduction. The whole procedure lasted less than twenty minutes.

Peter and I exchanged a few words with Mr. Long and his supporters, and then they drove off. Before we could follow the merchant invited us to his store for a cold bottle of Coke "to get the dust outta ya throats." This was exactly the brotherhood that divinity student Peter longed for. He accepted for us and I followed behind. As soon as we entered the store, however, the merchant's mood transformed into fierce belligerence.

"Why didn't you stay home and work in Harlem?" he bellowed, his face an unhealthy shade of crimson. "What about the Communists behind all of this?"

Outside the window I could see white toughs surrounding my car. I turned to the merchant, thanked him for the Coke, and told him I'd like to continue our conversation. Would he walk with us to our car so he and I could exchange a few more thoughts? As I hoped he had much more to say, and as we walked the group of toughs parted. Peter and I both entered my car from the driver's side. Promising to renew our conversation with the merchant on another visit, we drove off.

Fifteen minutes later we were on the highway to Jackson.

It seemed that all of North Farish Street heard of the Okolona adventures. For the next few days lower and middle echelon civil rights folks lavished praise on me but Movement veterans were not impressed. Although they gave me friendly "you idiot" shakes of the head, I was made aware that had I been a full-time civil rights worker I would have been severely castigated—and possibly sent out of the South—for my breach of the rules. Bronstein was so angry that he didn't even acknowledge me; he was obviously counting the days until my departure.

When I met up with Sally, the civil rights worker from the picketing case, she was with the antagonistic black civil rights worker I had encountered at the supermarket picket line.

"You remember George," Sally said.

I nodded. She had heard about Okolona, of course.

"It was way too risky," she chided me unconvincingly.

I gave her my best "itwasnothing" look.

"Aviva asked me to spend some time with her as a civil rights worker," I boasted, "but *because* of my job . . ."

". . . you've decided to go back home," George concluded for me. "Good idea. You got out of a big mess this time, but next time not even that suit'll save you."

I couldn't believe it. This man was intent on stealing my thunder at every turn. But not this time. Ignoring him, as well as my own rational side but maybe listening to my inner self, I "finished" what I had been saying to Sally.

"*Despite* my job I plan to accept Aviva's offer and return to Holly Springs . . . as a civil rights worker!"

I had allowed myself to be machoed into doing what I actually wanted to do. I stared defiantly at George who, to my surprise, grinned, slapped me on the back, and said, "I'll drive you." Then he left.

Wondering what I had done, I started to backtrack. "Of course I can only do it for one week. I'll send a telegram to my office in New York about an important case I have to complete." Sally nodded her approval.

"But what will Bronstein say?" she asked.

"No!" was what Bronstein said. "Absolutely not!"

I reminded him that he had no authority over me now that my agreed-upon three weeks were over, but Bronstein insisted that everything I did in Mississippi would be blamed on ACLU—that anything that happened to me, such as getting arrested, could jeopardize the fragile relationships between civil rights lawyers and the Southern legal establishment. I scoffed at the prospect of being arrested. In the face of my obstinacy Bronstein offered a compromise: I could spend my week with Aviva *if* I wore my suit and tie the whole time. I agreed.

Later that day, as I began telephoning Aviva to tell her I was coming, I imagined the Boss telephoning New York and shouting, "Don't ever send that *schmuck* to Mississippi again!" As I pictured Bronstein in his animated monologue, I pictured myself putting on overalls and joining the Movement.

4

Mississippi's Newest Civil Rights Worker

I began my first day as a civil rights worker on the morning of September 6, 1965, seated in a fast-moving ancient Pontiac. George, Sally's friend and fellow Piggly Wiggly picketer, was at the wheel. I was wedged between cartons of leaflets calling for voter registration and resistance to the Klan as well as invitations to community meetings.

I was already concerned about my rash decision to stay a little longer in the South.

"Don't worry," George said. "The worst is over." Then he told me his story, which I later juxtaposed with the final speech of Martin Luther King Jr. before his assassination.

Dr. King had been stabbed in 1958 and almost died. While in the hospital a doctor told a news reporter that his patient had to remain immobile—even "a sneeze could kill him." After recovering he received a letter from a ninth-grader. "I read that if you had sneezed you would have died. . . . I'm so happy that you didn't sneeze."

A decade later in a speech in Memphis, Tennessee, he recounted the little girl's letter and said, "I too am happy that I didn't sneeze. Because if I had sneezed, I wouldn't have been around here in 1960, when students all over the South started sitting in at lunch counters."[1]

It had all begun for George at a sit-in at Woolworth's "whites only" lunch counter in Greensboro, North Carolina. On February 1, 1960, four black college students sat down and asked to be served coffee and doughnuts. They were not surprised that their request was denied but were happy not to be arrested.

The next day other students, including George, were alerted via a telephone network to what was happening. Within three days the sit-ins were three hundred strong and soon one thousand. Ultimately the Klan reacted and beatings followed by arrests began. By the end of February demonstrations had spread to thirty lunch counters in seven states. By year's end 70,000 men and women had participated—3,000 of them arrested.[2]

"If I had sneezed," Dr. King also said in his speech, "I wouldn't have been around here in 1961 when we decided to take a ride for freedom and ended segregation in interstate travel."[3]

On May 4, CORE planned for Freedom Riders (seven black and six white) to travel on Greyhound and Trailways buses through Virginia, the Carolinas, Georgia, Alabama, Mississippi, and Louisiana. Many of the Riders were in their forties and fifties—two were young students from SNCC.

Five months earlier the US Supreme Court had ruled segregation in interstate travel illegal and that integrated travel on interstate buses and trains was a legal right. Separate bathrooms and dining rooms for interstate travelers were no longer allowed, and travelers had the right to use whatever facilities they choose and sit wherever they wished. The Freedom Riders would prove the noncompliance.

On May 15 more than a hundred Klansmen ambushed the Riders in Anniston, Alabama, attacked the Greyhound bus, smashed the windows, and set it on fire. The crowd held the door shut to burn the Riders alive, but the passengers tumbled off the bus—barely escaping with their lives—just before the gas tanks exploded.

In Birmingham, Alabama, Public Safety Commissioner "Bull" Connor incited another KKK mob to savagely attack the Riders, leaving them bloody and battered—so battered and so many jailed that SNCC members, including George, rode the buses and continued the rides.[4]

In 1962 and 1963 George was one of the young legions who walked the dirt roads of black Mississippi exhorting the descendants of slaves to register to vote. His leader and idol was Bob Moses, a twenty-six-year-old black New Yorker with a master's degree in philosophy from Harvard. As project director of the SNCC Mississippi project, Moses traveled to the worst counties in that state where he tried to recruit black sharecroppers to register at the county office.

For his efforts he was beaten almost to death, jailed, beaten in jail, and then released—and he returned to recruiting again, with the same results. He brought criminal charges against one man who had beaten him (a first!); an all-white jury acquitted the attacker. This led to Moses being escorted to the county line on orders from the judge who said he could not protect him.

"If I had sneezed," Dr. King added, "I wouldn't have been here in 1963, when the black people of Birmingham, Alabama, aroused the conscience of this nation, and brought into being the Civil Rights Bill."[5]

In Birmingham Dr. King's SCLC trained and directed elementary school, high school, and college students to participate in the demonstrations by taking a peaceful walk, fifty at a time, to City Hall to talk to the mayor about ending segregation. After over a thousand arrests "Bull" Connor called for the use of high-pressure water hoses and police attack dogs on the children and bystanders. On Sunday, September 15, 1963, four members of the Ku Klux Klan planted fifteen sticks of dynamite beneath the front steps of a church killing four girls ages eleven to fourteen —called by Dr. King as "one of the most vicious and tragic crimes ever perpetrated against humanity."[6]

Next came the Mississippi Summer of 1964. The one thousand volunteers recruited to provide support for black Mississippians were subjected to widespread terror; were shot at, beaten, and arrested; and became witnesses to the torching of black homes and churches. When three from their ranks were murdered, Bob Moses, acting as the main organizer of the Freedom Summer Project, gathered the shaken volunteers together (along with George) and told them that this was the risk they faced. He added that they had every right to go home and no one would blame them. All stayed.[7]

"If I had sneezed," Dr. King furthered, "I wouldn't have been down in Selma, Alabama, to see the great Movement there."[8]

George was also there during the carnage at the Selma Bridge on Sunday, March 7, 1965, when the protesters attempted to march across the bridge on the road to Montgomery. On the other side of the bridge a horde of state troopers halted the line. As the protestors kneeled to pray the troopers attacked, charging into the line of marchers with flailing clubs and drenching them with clouds of choking teargas. Sheriff Jim Clark's mounted possemen rode down on them, lashing out with bullwhips and rubber hoses wrapped in barbed-wire.[9]

George paused and said, "It will never get any worse than that."

By this time we had arrived in Holly Springs and George spied Aviva's station wagon parked alongside a café. He tapped his horn and as soon as she came out the two began a spirited, if almost coded, dialogue.

"Bob?"

"Recovering."

"The shooting in Canton?"

"Rumor, not true!"

"The Hinds County injunction?"

"Granted."

"The two in Columbus?

"Convicted . . . but we're appealing."

The greeting ritual finished, the two exchanged personal banter while George transferred my bags to Aviva's car. Then, with a mischievous smile, he wished me good luck and drove off.

WELCOME TO BENTON COUNTY

I had not yet spoken one word to Aviva. When I did she responded gruffly, "Get in; we've a good ride ahead of us." I did as I was told and we drove into the heart of Benton County.

Gone was the exuberant Aviva who had invited me "to see what it's all about." In her place was a veteran organizer well aware of the risks that she recruited people like me to face. I remembered a comment from an activist in Okolona: "If you never get too close to a fellow worker or volunteer, your heart will not be broken when they leave or die."

After Aviva reminded me that a lawyer should expect no special treatment from her or her fellow workers, she began a litany of the work to be done.

"First," she told me, "I'll teach you how to draft proposals for federal poverty grants. We desperately need money for two-row cotton pickers, fertilizer, and . . ."

As she launched into a list of basic needs I divided my attention between listening to her and focusing on the cotton fields we were driving past. Black people of all ages were removing specks of white from small plants and placing them in large sacks they dragged from plant to plant. It could have been a scene from *Gone with the Wind*—except that on the screen the black people sang and frolicked; here they just seemed hot and weary.

"Now as to the Voting Rights Act," Aviva continued, interspersing comments to me with waves and greetings to the sharecroppers in the fields. "Your job will be to obtain twenty signatures from our people declaring they have been denied the right to vote. Then we can get a federal man to come in and do the registering."

"Great," I said, my full attention recaptured. "That will give me the chance to drive around and meet everyone." Aviva smiled at my enthusiasm, but her smile faded when I added, "And I can easily get twenty signatures before my week is up."

She scoffed, "Shows how little you know about life around here. But you'll learn."

She resumed her monologue detailing my chores until we reached our destination: the home of an elderly black couple who had volunteered a bed for my stay. This home would be my base while in Benton County because of the "luxuries" it could offer me: an icebox, a pot-bellied stove, and a nearby outhouse. There was no running water but there was a pump. The couple acted nonchalant about my presence, but later I would overhear them discussing their concern about "sleeping the lawyer."

That first night I yearned for a few moments of solitude to adjust to my new surroundings but Aviva would not oblige. There was always more information to absorb. Over and over she hammered away about the rules of survival and what to avoid when dealing with the people. She continuously warned me not to flaunt my lawyer credentials. Eventually I fell asleep in a chair.

Early the next morning we drove to the first place where I was to begin collecting signatures. Aviva left me outside at what I was to learn was a luxurious home—equipped with electricity *and* a bathroom. Wondering who would introduce me here, let alone tell me how I was to get to my next destination, I knocked on the door.

"Ethel Shore" welcomed me, "C'mon in, lawyer, and don't let the children bother you." As I opened the door seven children jumped on me touching my white skin and bombarding me with questions. "How long you stayin'? Will you eat with us? Will you stay over? What's a lawyer?"

"Scat!" yelled Ethel in vain as she introduced me to her mother and her husband, John. The Shores told me about the local Klan and the latest arrests of civil rights workers; the children in chorus told me about the forthcoming school integration effort.

This barrage of questions and answers interrupted by offers of food ended when John announced it was time to go back to the field. Before I could ask the adults to sign the Voting Rights Act petition the middle child invited me to pick cotton with them.

"Oh, no," the grandmother said, "look how nice he's dressed."

"I'd really like to," I offered, "and I have work clothes in my brief-case."

Everyone laughed at a lawyer carrying a briefcase with work clothes in it.

Quickly changing I joined the whole family including their five-year-old in the cotton field that lay outside their home.

Picking cotton required knowledge of the plant, which the children provided me as I picked alongside them. The children were the best pickers in part because they were closest in height to the shrubby plants and did not have far to bend. Their value in the cotton field was the reason that Negro schools took recess during harvest season and why Mississippi was one of the few states without compulsory school attendance laws.

The plant I was shown had three leaves that formed a little container that held a seed surrounded by creamy fiber: the cotton. The objective was to remove the cotton along with the seed (the seed would be separated later at the cotton gin). After an hour I was working on my knees to spare my back as the children slipped some of their picked cotton into my sack to improve my yield.

"Hot 'nuf for you?" I was asked with sly grins. Periodically the grandmother answered for me that this 110-degree torture "could singe the eyebrows offa yuh." I agreed.

After two hours I was almost faint but I kept working, now sitting on the ground in front of the plants. When they stopped after three-and-a-half hours (for my sake, I believed), my sack contained enough cotton to earn me about $1.25.

Too tired to eat lunch I fell asleep in a rocking chair while waiting to resume work. I was still asleep when they returned from another four hours in the field. Nonetheless I gladly accepted their invitation to stay for dinner. Afterward the children went to sleep without complaint, sass, or backtalk, each kissing me and making me promise to stay over. I spent the evening listening to Ethel and John tell me how difficult cotton picking was (no argument from me), how he hoped for an automated cotton picker, how she planned to go to school, and how they both hoped the civil rights movement would get their children out of the fields. Then I was being helped by John to bed, barely able to undress before returning to a deep sleep.

Early the next morning I was awakened by Aviva shaking me. "So you think you're here for a vacation?" Get up," she chided. "You still have seventeen more signatures to go."

"Oh, my God," I gasped. "I forgot to ask them to sign."

Aviva looked away trying to hide her amusement. My suit went into Aviva's car. After obtaining the signatures of the two Shores and the grandmother, Aviva suggested, "While we're here, let's sign up the Brad-leys," a sharecropping family who lived a half mile away.

Aviva and I began to walk down a dusty road with her exchanging short "How-are-yas" with farmers along the way.

"You remember lawyer Jelinek, of course," is how she would pres-ent me. A few later confided that most whites looked alike to them at least for the first couple of times. As we passed a half dozen of Aviva's friends it was becoming apparent to me that in just a few hours she could easily sign up twenty people on her own. This apparently was not Aviva's goal. I later guessed that the main purpose of my assignment was to show off the lawyer she had recruited to work exclusively in Benton County.

Soon we were at the home of the Bradleys where we talked, picked a little cotton, talked some more, had dinner, and stayed over. It was be-coming clear to me that in 1965 *talking* was a major task of a civil rights worker.

The next morning Aviva took me back to my shack with instructions to spend time chatting with my hosts and drafting poverty grant propos-als. When she returned she drove me to the home of "Oscar Root"—one of her favorite people.

Root was an unschooled, somewhat gawky, beanpole of a black share-cropper with a gold tooth glowing from within an ever-present smile. Though blacks generally chose the better educated as their leaders, Os-car Root had achieved special status in the local Civil Rights Movement by his singular self-assurance. He could address a fellow sharecropper or New York lawyer without fawning, with clear ideas and perspective, and with a determination to press his position unless convinced to the contrary.

"Tell Don about the water fountain. How it affected your attitude about dealing with whites," Aviva said to Root, both of them already laughing.

"No, *you* tell him," he answered.

"Okay," Aviva began. "We were at the white school for a meeting with the white power structure regarding poverty program money. They called a break and we walked out into the hall . . ."

". . . where they had those low, white-kids-only water fountains," Root interjected.

"And," Aviva continued slowly, "I walked over to take a drink while the whites watched me. Oscar hadn't . . ."

". . . I had walked to town," he added, "and all the stores were white so I hadn't had any water and it was a day like today."

"So," Aviva resumed, "I noticed Oscar's parched lips and said, 'Why don't you take a drink?' And Oscar says to me, 'Oh, no,' and whispered . . ."

Root now acted out his part as he whispered, ". . . s'not for colored."

Aviva continued, "So I tell him, 'Oscar it's okay, DRINK!' Oscar looked at me, then we both looked at the whites, Oscar looked at the fountain and bent down . . ."

". . . way down," Root laughed, his gold tooth flashing.

". . . and DRANK!" they shouted in a chorus.

Root had never before used a water fountain and turned the handle too hard. The water splashed onto his face as well as his mouth and onto the freshly polished tile floors. She recalled with glee how the whites glared at him.

After a few more minutes of them trading tales Mrs. Root walked up with their six children.

"Oscar," she scolded, "aren't you goin' to invite the lawyer and Aviva in for a cool drink?"

Amidst more banter we entered the house, which unlike the Shores had no indoor plumbing; unlike the old couple there was not even an outhouse. Of course we stayed for dinner and ate what Aviva later told me was a better-than-average meal for the Roots: okra, greens, thick gravy, lots of cornbread, and Kool-Aid. They would probably have to cut rations for the rest of the week because of this meal, but it was important to them, Aviva explained, that they find a way to reciprocate for the work of the civil rights workers. Food provided a way. We talked into the night and then stayed over. I gained two more signatures.

For the remaining three days of my week as a civil rights worker I continued my assignment without Aviva, who had returned to Jackson. Lacking an automobile I usually walked to my first destination of the day, then a member of the family might drive me to the next home. It was a slow process. Only after many hours of visiting, answering questions, asking questions, picking cotton, eating, meeting neighbors, and talking some more would I be able to move on to my next destination.

At the end of the week (my suit now hanging on a nail in my hosts' shack) I had only eleven signatures. Obviously I couldn't leave without finishing so I got a lift to Holly Springs and sent my second telegram to New York: NEED ONE MORE WEEK TO FINISH IMPORTANT CASE. This would absolutely be my last week I told Aviva when she returned.

CONFISCATION OF THE COWS

"Before you go back to New York," she had said, "be sure to visit Harold Rankin," reminding me of the black leader who had introduced me at my first church meeting.

There were three advantages to visiting Mr. Rankin: a conversation with one of the county's policy makers, my next signature, *and* his genuine indoor-plumbing shower! After a week of sponging myself while standing in a small basin the attraction of a hot shower alone would have led me to Mr. Rankin's door.

It was when I was happily lathering that the sheriff drove up into the driveway and handed the Benton County leader a legal paper. Moments later, after Rankin's children burst into the room with the shower to alert me, I came bounding out of the house and bellowed: "What is this?"

Mindful that I was a lawyer and ignoring that I was only wearing a large bath towel, the sheriff explained that because the paperwork for the appeal of the "Uncle Tom" libel case had not been done properly he was confiscating property from the various defendants to pay the judgment.

Not done correctly? Had I made a legal error? I worried.

"That's impossible," I said, without conviction.

"No, it's true," the sheriff insisted.

I took in a long breath, looked him in the eye, and said, with all the righteous bravado I could muster while holding onto my towel, "Listen carefully to me, sheriff. Remove the stuff then, but take good care of it 'cause you'll be bringing it back by the end of the week." The sheriff smiled, removed two cows and a tractor, and drove off.

Putting on my clothes and racing to the phone, I called Bronstein who was appalled at the foul-up. It turned out to be nothing I had done, but he said he could easily resolve it.

Three days later, the problem resolved, several black residents and I stood outside the Rankin home as the cows and tractor were returned. This time I didn't say anything.

"Here's your stuff, Harold," the sheriff mumbled, fighting to save face. "Glad your lawyers straightened out the error."

Rankin answered civilly.

I had already learned that my lawyer's mystique worked both ways: not only did I receive blame for whatever went wrong, I was credited for successes I had nothing to do with. Still Aviva seemed impressed that I had stood up to the sheriff. She told me that my standing up to local authority was almost as important as the return of Rankin's goods. But she warned, "Don't let it go to your head. You still have a lot to learn."

With only a half week to go before my departure I began to more effectively structure my tasks. Arising at 5 AM I would begin the laborious process of visiting the outdoor latrine, shaving with cold water from the pump, and walking to my first destination. By 6 AM I would be in a cotton field usually talking more than picking. I talked about the sheriff, Rankin, and me; about voter registration; and the upcoming effort to integrate the schools, promising eventual success. After lunch it was back to the field. At dusk I would meet with other sharecroppers in the area, accept dinner, and likely attend a church meeting.

Exhausted but exhilarated by these near-perfect days, I found myself having trouble answering when someone would ask, "When are you leaving?" "End of the week," I would mumble, as if returning to New York was a betrayal—which I felt it was.

I did not have much to show for my time in Benton County. It was true that I had now collected twenty signatures, which could result in a federal official coming to register residents of Benton County, but otherwise nothing much had been accomplished during my two weeks as a civil rights worker—even the Rankin episode had been more bluster than action. Still I was increasingly reluctant to tell folks that I was leaving.

AVIVA DEPARTS

In the end the prospect of my return to New York would be entirely overshadowed by another, much more significant departure: that of Aviva herself. Having worked in Mississippi for more than two years, she planned to return home.

For veteran civil rights workers leaving the South ranked with the death of a friend or family as one of life's saddest moments. Yet for almost everyone in the Movement the time came when the urge to return to normalcy became overwhelming.

The very day I collected my last signature Aviva announced that for her that time had arrived.

"I must leave," she told me. "I have friends and relatives to be with. I want to go to graduate school, maybe get married. I need . . . I need to live a normal life."

"I know I'm abandoning the people," Aviva began chastising herself. "Harold and Ethel and Oscar and all the others. I won't be here when the schools integrate, I won't be part of the voter registration, but I have to go and . . ."

She paused and stared at me.

". . . and I want *you* to replace me."

Stay? Alone without Aviva? Though I inwardly balked at the thought, in the next instant I was cautiously euphoric. I hadn't really been prepared to leave Harold, Ethel, Oscar, and the others; now there seemed to be no choice but to stay—at least for a while.

"I accept," I announced to audible relief from Aviva. Leaving was difficult enough without having to tell her friends in Benton County that there would be no one to take her place.

"I accept," I repeated, "but only on a week-to-week basis."

Aviva ignored my conditional acceptance.

"Okay, Mr. Big-Shot-Civil-Rights-Leader, let's do some homework. You know almost nothin' now, and you probably won't know much more than next to nothin' by the time I leave, but let's try."

And so Aviva began my advanced indoctrination: how to run the mimeo machine, who to especially count on in the black community, who to especially watch out for in the white community, how to publish the civil rights newspaper (the *Benton County Freedom Train* of "Uncle Tom" fame)—and more rules for survival.

After a day and a half of intense instruction Aviva decided it was time to inform the black residents of Benton County of her imminent departure. I immediately saw that for me there would be no welcoming church gathering. I could see it in their eyes. *But for him* coming Aviva would have stayed. *But for him* as a replacement she would have stayed. *But for him* talking her into leaving she would have stayed. Aviva assured me this was a temporary mourning period, but in the meantime she said I must rely on a Movement maxim: "If you need rewards beyond your own internal satisfaction you're in the wrong line of work."

The black community of Benton County would not allow its beloved civil rights leader to leave without a grand farewell—to which Aviva persuaded her mother to attend.

The going-away party was in the grand style of the Movement in these waning days of its early integrated period—an era that was passing away. Within a year "Black and White Together" would give way to "Black Power!" and "Black Is Beautiful!" and minimal, if any, honoring of whites.

The party was set for 8 PM to allow sufficient time for the black farmers to virtually scrape the season's dirt from their skins. I heard my hosts express a sentiment that may have been repeated throughout black Benton County: "All I have is the one good shirt (or blouse), and the pants (or skirt) I wear to church on Sunday. Oh, how ashamed Aviva will be of us."

The gathering began with a grand meal: spare ribs (served only on special occasions), greens spiced for Northern tastes, cornbread (with more eggs and milk than usual), and punch.

The food was more abundant than the conversation, which as if by pre-arrangement excluded any mention of such unpleasant topics as racist whites, poverty, and Aviva's impending departure. Mrs. Futorian, Aviva's mother, was asked about her clothes, the latest books she had read, and the type of car she drove. In turn Mrs. Futorian, trying to be just-folks, asked about cotton gins, church meetings, and listened to stories Aviva had already told her.

Mercifully, Aviva cut the evening short observing that the next day was a workday for the farmers. She exchanged individual goodbyes with every person present: reminiscing, kissing, hugging, and crying. By the time it was my turn she was too choked up to speak and asked me to take a short walk with her while she composed herself. Then she berated me one last time for all the mistakes I was yet to make.

The next morning, witnessed by a small contingent, Aviva drove away.

5

Novice County Leader

Now I was in charge of the Benton County organization and my first order of business was personal. Unwilling to totally burn a bridge I sent a third telegram to my job in New York: UNUSUAL DEVELOPMENT IN CIVIL RIGHTS CASE/WILL PROBABLY RETURN NEXT WEEK. To my secret delight the job conflict was resolved for me with a "DON'T BOTHER!" response. With all ties cut but one (I would continue to pay for my New York rent-controlled apartment) I was free to begin work in earnest. High on the immediate agenda: preparing for the looming school desegregation and voter registration efforts—and implementing a plan I had devised to provide instant communication for a community mostly without telephones. I called it the "human telephone."

As I envisioned and as head of the network I would pass on information (or warnings) directly to an assigned district leader who, in turn, would pass it down the line until everyone was informed. When I first proposed the idea at a regular church meeting the "uhhuhs" and "hmms" were weak indeed, but in deference to my new position the sharecroppers agreed to try it. Despite the rigor of harvesting I called meeting after meeting and conducted test run after test run as if an invasion was imminent. I was readying my troops for battle. The community begrudgingly cooperated, but fewer and fewer residents showed up for later meetings.

Lacking formal Movement training I had unknowingly violated a cardinal rule of civil rights organizing: don't impose your style on a community that has its own historic methods to accomplish the same end. Southern blacks had managed to communicate with each other even during slavery. Their methods may have been slow but so was the pace of life. When an emergency occurred everyone usually knew in plenty of time, even without the aid of AT&T or my human telephone.

Within a month my plan had been scrapped and I heard mutterings that Aviva would never have undertaken anything so foolish.

SCHOOL INTEGRATION

One of the more significant civil rights projects was school integration, which was essential to the Civil Rights Movement—not least because it represented the only immediate means to upgrade the abominable level of black education in the South.

In 1942 Gunnar Myrdal, a Swedish Nobel Laureate economist and sociologist, described white-dominated Southern public education in his classic work, *An American Dilemma*. Segregated black schools, he wrote, were often overcrowded, dilapidated shacks in which one room contained the "whole range of elementary grades taught by a single black teacher." The teacher, herself, was

> . . . a poorly trained and poorly paid Negro woman [who] must control and teach a group of children from a poor and uncultured home background, in a . . . school house where she [is required to] perform at least some of the janitorial and administrative duties. She is also subject to unusual outside pressure.[1]

Social pressure, Myrdal wrote, dictated that the curriculum for black students be "industrial" as opposed to "classical" or "bookish." Because whites insisted that Southern blacks were destined to be "servants, farm laborers, and industrial workers," their education should be commensurate with humble status, daily duties, and the building up of character. In other words, noted Myrdal, it was believed that they should be "taught only to know the relative distance between two rows of cotton or corn"—not between two planets.[2]

In 1896, more than three decades after the conclusion of the Civil War, the US Supreme Court had ruled in *Plessy v. Ferguson* that segregated facilities were lawful and constitutional so long as facilities for the white and black races were of equal quality, i.e., *separate but equal*.[3]

That case involved a Louisiana law that required separate railway cars for non-white riders. Homer Plessy, seven-eighths white and one-eighth black, was classified as "black" and required to sit in the "colored" car. He was arrested when he instead boarded a "whites-only" railroad car and refused to vacate his seat; he demanded his Fourteenth Amendment right of equal protection. The 1896 high court ruled against Homer Plessy and upheld the constitutionality of state laws requiring racial segregation in public facilities under the doctrine of "separate but equal." This ruling legitimated segregated practices throughout the South for more than a half century.

More than forty years after *Plessy* the NAACP began a multiyear battle to overthrow the ruling. In 1935 black attorney Charles H. Houston began work full time for the NAACP where he designed a strategy to litigate and win legal precedents against all segregation, beginning with education. He was joined by Thurgood Marshall, one of his top students from Howard University Law School.[4]

In 1935, after health issues forced Houston to resign from the NAACP, Marshall led the organization's legal fight for civil rights arguing the lead-up cases which eventually were appealed to the US Supreme Court. As a black man Marshall risked his life traveling to the South to sign up parents of young students. There he met Oliver Brown and his daughter Linda, a third-grader; Brown became the lead plaintiff, joining thirteen parents representing twenty children. All of the cases were combined into one case: *Brown v. Board of Education.*

Marshall worked with Kenneth and Mamie Clark, prominent black psychologists already renowned for their "doll test." As part of the test black children answered questions about a white doll and a black doll that were identical except for skin color and hair. When the black children were asked, "Which one do you like best?" the children would inevitably point to the white doll. When asked, "Which is the bad doll?" the children pointed to the black doll.

"Which one do *you* look like?" was the worst question since by that point most children had already picked the black doll as the "bad" one. Many children refused to choose the doll they thought they looked like or started crying or ran off.

This research became the pillar of *Brown* and an important basis for the historic 1954 decision.

Of course Marshall knew there was nothing equal about "separate but equal" in Southern schools, but to contest "equality" would require that each school be evaluated separately. He ignored the "unequal" issue to get a universal ruling that would apply to all schools. The US Supreme Court reversed *Plessy* and unanimously held in *Brown* that "separate educational facilities are *inherently* unequal."[5]

Although *Brown* involved school segregation the precedent it set eventually spread to almost all forms of segregation.

In 1965—eleven years after *Brown,* twenty-three years after Myrdal's findings—little had changed in the Deep South. It was generally agreed within the civil rights community that only by sitting alongside white students in a "white" school could blacks obtain an equal education with equal resources. As a result of a long string of school desegregation victories by the NAACP LDF, school integration was beginning in communities across the South—including Benton County.

The night before integration began in Benton schools the Klan drove through the black community shooting out streetlights. In preparation for the big day I briefed the black students and their families about what to expect—though I didn't really know. I also kept in close touch with the US Justice Department, which was monitoring the effort.

In the morning angry whites and apprehensive blacks trailed school buses and cars to the schoolyard fence beyond which, by court order, no onlookers were to pass. Our black students who had never before attended classes with white children disappeared into the bowels of the white school while we returned to the black community to worry. That night two of the students reported back that they had been jostled a few times and heard a few "nigger" remarks, but there was no significant violence—except to their psyches.

At first the young black pupils were barely literate compared to their new white classmates and ill prepared for the school. In an attempt to bring them up to speed we set up tutoring sessions with volunteers from Holly Springs who gave the students crash courses in the basics. After a few months the academic performance of the black students improved and they were relatively well received by their white classmates.

Adults, however, were prepared to continue the curriculum of hate indefinitely: some white school bus drivers refused to drive into black areas to pick up children and the new black students were seated at the rear of classrooms, took segregated trips to the bathroom, ate at separate lunchroom tables, and often failed to receive textbooks. As quickly as I reported one violation to the NAACP LDF another would pop up.

If Southern governors had realized how many traps they could lay *inside* the schoolhouse door, I thought, they might not have worked so hard to block the entrance.

THE VOTING RIGHTS ACT COMES TO BENTON COUNTY

Dealing with school integration could easily have consumed all our time and energy but a second front was opening in the local civil rights war: the Voting Rights Act was coming to Benton County. The twenty signatures declaring denial of the right to vote had arrived in Washington and a federal registrar was soon to arrive, empowered to take over the voter registration processing from white local election officials.

The right to vote guaranteed by the Fifteenth Amendment to the US Constitution, adopted in 1870, provided that the "rights of citizens of the United States to vote shall not be denied . . . on account of race, color, or previous condition of servitude." But soon following the end of the Civil War and the departure of federal troops from the South black residents saw their recently acquired vote effectively taken away by terrorism, police harassment, and "voter qualification" formulas administered by white voter registrars. "Literacy" tests required black applicants—and *only* black applicants!—to correctly interpret obscure and intricate sections of the Alabama Constitution, poll taxes demanded a fee beyond the means of most black farmers, property requirements in some Southern states required ownership of forty acres of land (and few owned *any* land), and the so-called "character requirement" required black citizens to be vouched for by persons of high character.[6] Though federal court decisions declared many of these requirements unconstitutional the all-white Southern legislatures would quickly enact new ones.

Not surprisingly tactics like these ensured that Southern laws disenfranchised almost all black citizens. In 1960 a mere 5 percent of voting-age blacks were registered to vote in Mississippi.

Southern filibusters successfully blocked bills pending in the US Congress to counter these voting obstacles. Finally, a frustrated Martin Luther King Jr. threw his national prestige behind a registration drive in Selma, Alabama, and a march to the state capital in Montgomery. The carnage that greeted the march over the Edmund Pettus Bridge in Selma on March 7, 1965, sparked a national demand for federal protection of the right to vote.

Five months after the violence in Selma President Lyndon Johnson signed into law the Voting Rights Act, which provided that in any county where less than 50 percent of voting-age citizens were registered and where twenty qualified potential voters complained of discrimination state control of voting could be superseded. Also voter qualification tests could be suspended and federal registrars sent in to do the registering.

On September 25, 1965, the *Benton County Freedom Train* spread the word that federal help was coming:

All you have to do to register is to come down and sign your name or make your mark. Everyone should be prepared to come down and register even if you have to leave your cotton-picking. This is a big day for Benton County.[7]

The Klan began shooting almost immediately. Part of my job was to notify the FBI of civil rights-related violence, which I did after the first shooting into the home of a Benton County leader. Twelve years later I obtained my FBI file, which included a report of that conversation:

DATE: 9/25/65

At 12:15 PM on instant date, DONALD JELINEK telephonically contacted the Jackson [FBI] Office and furnished the following information:

* * *

He stated that he had just received . . . information regarding shots being fired into the residence of [a] Reverend . . . who is the Third District leader in the civil rights movement in Benton County . . .

* * *

He [Jelinek] advised me . . . that a federal registrar is coming to Benton County and that beginning next week, his organization will begin taking the Negroes to register. He stated that the bringing of the federal registrars into Benton County might trigger violence and he wanted the FBI to be aware of this fact. He requested that the FBI furnish protection for the people who will be registered in Benton County next week *and he was advised that the FBI could not furnish protection and that he should advise the local authorities.*[8]

Even before the arrival of the federal agent we had prepared for mass registration. Districts were created and blacks from each district were asked to organize carpools to the local post office—the only federal property in town—where the federal registrar would set up his operation. Each district leader had his date and time.

When I went to town to meet the newly arrived federal official he curtly informed me that he was not on a crusade—he was just a federal civil servant with a job to do. He didn't need to add the obvious: that he was a white Southerner—as expected. He then rejected all my requests to stay open evenings and Sundays, or any other plan I came up with to make registration easier. Even though he was not above playing verbal games with blacks asking to "reddish" to vote, he pledged to do his job well and sign up any eligible voter who came in. He would not be the problem; that would be local whites, especially plantation owners.

Because registering meant leaving the cotton field in full view of white plantation owners, at first it was mostly the elderly ladies dressed in their best clothes who came to meet the registrar. Then the male farmers, still understandably nervous, began to follow.

One day a civil rights worker driving a busload of farmers into town to register was challenged by the authorities for operating the bus without a proper bus license.

"Run to the Post Office building!" I shouted to him. "It's federal property!"

As he ran to the entrance I turned to the police and said, "This is federal property, you have no jurisdiction here!"

The response to my constitutional argument of sanctuary was a swat across the chest that sent me flying to the ground. The police then entered the building and arrested the driver. Subsequently I learned that I was wrong. Because the land was only *leased* from the state and technically still state property the police were within their right to make the arrest—not that they cared one way or the other.[9]

While there were frequent threats and occasional forays by armed night riders, most whites recognized that the federal presence represented by the registrar meant that it was a whole new ballgame in Benton County. Everyone who dared to register would be successful, while others could still register at a later time.

SOUTHERN JUSTICE

Still, unlawful arrests, intimidation, and harassment were far from over. As much as I yearned to leave my lawyer's license, suit, and tie in the closet, I quickly realized that it was my attorney's license and not my organizing prowess which was needed.

The Southern court structure informally comprised two systems: one for non-race-related cases and the other for civil rights cases. When it came to the cases where race was not a factor I had to begrudgingly concede that routine legal practice in Southern courtrooms compared favorably to what I had known of Northern justice, at least as practiced in New York.

In the play *A Man for All Seasons* the character Sir Thomas More states: "I know what's Legal, not what's Right. I'll stick to what's Legal . . . I'm not God."[10] In my experience the New York system virtuously proclaimed: *To hell with what's Legal or Right! Winning is what counts!* A New York lawyer quickly learned that not only did the highest priced lawyers with the wealthiest clients triumph most often, neither judge nor lawyer nor client cared who was right or wrong.

On the other hand, so long as racial issues were not involved, the rural Southern court system sought out justice. Small-town juries learned of matters which should have been kept from them, might have witnessed the event in question, or had a preformed opinion about a potential witness; lawyers were permitted to argue cases to members of the jury who were their clients. But despite lapses in procedural protections I had to admit that in most of these cases justice seemed to prevail. A small community which usually had one regular judge, two or three local lawyers, and townspeople who knew each other from cradle to grave would not tolerate corruption. Whether the reason was shame, community conscience, or reputation, a just—or at least honest—result was demanded.

Honor, the character trait most prized by Southerners, was considered essential to small-town morality and at times it even applied in civil rights cases. I once showed up in the office of a Southern lawyer bearing a written document I had prepared confirming a minor compromise we had negotiated. He was indignant. "My word is all you need!" he vehemently asserted.

Another time I presented an intricate injunction to a judge and he signed it with barely a glance. When I asked why he didn't read it for accuracy he advised: "Remember, young man, I'm the only judge in these parts. I'll see you again. This document better conform to what I ruled."

But in cases involving race there was not even the pretense of justice. Here the Southern court system proclaimed: *We know what Right is! And we'll ensure that Right prevails whether it's Legal or not!* New York money corruption was small change compared to the racist corruption to be found in Mississippi courtrooms. The entire legal system here—judges, lawyers, juries, and even the bailiff—seemed to be of one mind: anyone fighting for racial equality should be convicted or otherwise punished, fairness and justice be damned!

In these cases across the Deep South the Klan traded their white robes for black ones. Although the trials themselves were usually conducted "fairly" and "completely," in the end judges or juries would simply ignore the evidence and convict. The demands of small-town honor and decorum prevailed—except in the result. Although these verdicts would usually be reversed on appeal to the federal courts—most often on the grounds that blacks were excluded from the juries—the relentless arrests, chain of trials, convictions, and high bail consumed our time, energy and limited funds.

Most of my legal work took place in Holly Springs next door to Benton County, wherein sat the circuit-riding judge who presided over the Marshall County Circuit Court. The judge would be in town for only two weeks every six months and then would travel elsewhere on the circuit. If a matter could not await the judge's return (and rare was a matter in the rural South that could not wait), the lawyers would try their cases wherever the judge was then presiding. During the absence of circuit judges, justices of the peace—usually men with no legal training, some functionally illiterate—administered the law.

In Holly Springs this responsibility rested upon the broad shoulders of a pugnacious former deputy sheriff who was the town's used car salesman, mayor, and ex-officio justice of the peace. His name was Sam Coopwood but he insisted I call him "Coop" when he was off the bench—to which I reluctantly complied if no clients were around.

Most of the times when I appeared in Coopwood's court my adversary was the local prosecutor, who was intelligent, honest, despised the Klan, and disapproved of the White Citizen's Council. However he was also an avid segregationist and vowed to move to Omaha or "some such place where they don't have colored" if integration was enforced in Holly Springs. He usually had me at a disadvantage. Not only did he know all the jurors personally, some were his personal friends and some were his law practice clients. When I complained to Coop he reminded me that Holly Springs is not New York City. "Of course everyone here knows everyone else; you couldn't find a small town jury that didn't." But if I stayed long enough, he assured me, I would know all the jurors too.

I was relatively successful pursuing my civil rights cases in Holly Springs. Unlike most out-of-town civil rights lawyers who traveled from county to county, I remained in the same small court dealing with the same judge, lawyers, and courtroom personnel. Thus I was able to develop personal relationships and use them to my clients' advantage. On rare occasions I even won a case; usually I lost but I could arrange for low bail and a suspended sentence, or, in more serious cases, banishment from the South in lieu of a stiff jail term if my client consented.

But with the benefits came obligations. Unlike other civil rights lawyers I could not cross-examine too vigorously, embarrass or humiliate witnesses, or engage in dramatic outside civil rights matters. If I did I would risk losing my special status.

THE ELVIS ARRESTS

Sometimes I crossed the line unknowingly. For instance it had not occurred to me when I helped organize a demonstration aimed at integrating a Holly Springs movie theater that there would be unintended consequences. It was not a new fight after all. Ignoring the public accommodations provisions of the Civil Rights Act of 1964, the theater still required blacks to sit separately in an upstairs balcony.

As had happened several times before our integrated group refused to go upstairs and took seats on the main floor.

Our action seemed to be sparking a typical response: growls from the cashier, glares from the usher, a barrage of beer cans heaved at us, cries of "Kill the Niggers! . . . and the Nigger-lovers too!" Typical, too, was the mass exodus of whites demanding their money back. Untypical, however, was the reaction of the manager who was red-faced and sputtering. Unlike his reaction to other demonstrations, which I had seen him take in stride albeit unhappily, this time I knew something was particularly wrong.

I tried to calmly reason with him, but he wasn't rational. Finally he pointed out to me that the film that night was Elvis Presley in *Harem Scarem*. Sticking his face in mine he blared: "You came here tonight to ruin me because you know that the opening night of an Elvis film is my chief moneymaker!"

"No," I protested. I hadn't even checked in advance what was playing, and I certainly didn't know Elvis-economics. He didn't believe me and vowed to get even.

In the weeks that followed there was a dramatic increase in harassment arrests and heavy surveillance of Holly Springs civil rights workers. There was also an increase in alcohol-related arrests.

Though Mississippi labeled itself a dry state there was a bootlegger in almost every county and city. In Holly Springs the bootlegger was a policeman who sold liquor out of a booth in a parking lot behind a large house. I would often purchase bourbon from him and then join an integrated group drinking in the parking lot.

On September 15, 1965, at 5:30 PM I was in the Freedom House in Holly Springs when two police cars converged on the house. Three uniformed police officers entered through the front door with a search warrant. A fourth officer came in from the rear and walked to the front exclaiming: "Look what I found!"

What he had "found" was three-quarters of a gallon of whiskey. Sid Walker, the black project director who leased the house, was arrested and jailed for illegal possession of alcohol. I knew for a fact that there had been no liquor in the house before the police arrived because Sid and the rest of us had just searched the house hoping to find something to drink; we had been disappointed that our search was futile.

Three days later I brought eight witnesses who were in the house that night to the courthouse. A city policeman approached one of my witnesses and asked what she had seen before and during the arrest.

"You can't interview my witness," I warned him. "She was in the house and will take the Fifth Amendment."

"Are you advising these people not to cooperate with a peace officer investigating a crime?"

Recognizing a setup, I said I had to make a phone call before I answered. Hurrying to the nearest pay phone I dialed Bronstein who warned that although I would be on firm legal ground if I advised my clients not to submit to interrogation, I would likely be arrested anyhow. His tone reflected weary frustration: this could only happen to me.

"Why don't you go home?" he urged with frustration.

After the phone call I looked for the prosecutor who coolly warned me that I would be arrested if my clients and I didn't cooperate. Shooting him a look of disdain I returned to my witnesses.

The issue was both legal and political. Legally the Fifth Amendment barring self-incrimination would cover interviews with persons who were present in the house. But that was less important than the political imperative for noncooperation; I couldn't negotiate with the authorities while maintaining a position of strength and encouragement.

I announced to the group: "I direct you all to remain silent!" whereupon I was arrested for "obstructing justice." Each of the witnesses refused to answer and they too were arrested.

For a week the arrests continued to mount: drunk and disorderly, traffic infractions, old warrants, and driving an automobile with out-of-state plates.

Finally I sought out the prosecutor to reestablish the contact that had been broken with my arrest and asked what could be done about all this. "You shouldn't screw a businessman," he replied. He wouldn't elaborate but it was clear that he was referring to my ill-timed integration action on the opening night of the new Elvis Presley film. The white community had found me guilty not of obstructing justice, not of civil rights activities, but of a lack of honor—specifically honor among adversaries. The arrests were retribution.

As I continued my work in Benton County's black community into that autumn, I became nervously aware that on the white side of town my notoriety was inexorably expanding. My status as a lawyer within the court of law had previously offered some protection from racist backlash but my work outside the courtroom had increased my vulnerability. I was also increasingly being blamed by the white community for the rapid series of setbacks afflicting them including the integration of their school and the forced expansion of voting rights.

As my professional invulnerability faded my attention to basic survival tactics grew apace. When "Shelby," a young black Mississippi native in his early twenties, offered to teach me about defensive driving in the rurals, I signed on.

Morning after morning at 5 AM we practiced driving up to sixty miles per hour on winding rural dirt roads while jiggling the wheel creating a nearly impenetrable dust curtain in our wake. "Remember, white people rarely use these roads so *you* must learn them well," he said, "and remember that there is more traction on these dirt roads and you can make sharper turns on them than you'd ever imagine." In a crouching position he proceeded to demonstrate one screeching turn after another as I alternately cursed and prayed.

"Now you do it!" he said. When I got behind the wheel he issued a stream of calm but urgent instructions: "You can go faster . . . that's good. DON'T GRIP THE WHEEL! Now turn! Turn on two wheels, turn . . . THAT'S GREAT!"

By now I was shaking and drenched with sweat but we didn't stop until I could execute a turn at 45 mph—all the time reassuring myself that I would never actually need to employ this dubious skill. I would all too quickly discover I was wrong about that.

A month later I took a shortcut that would briefly take me through a sliver of a community known to be especially hostile. I was running late and convinced myself that I could drive through the area in the dark and be long gone before anyone had time to notice me. But within moments of driving my well-known station wagon into the neighborhood I was spotted by three local whites who immediately jumped into a red pickup truck.

The chase began. Speeding up I calculated I would be out of town and on a dirt road within minutes. Then the first shot was fired. Checking the rearview mirror I saw two rifles pointed at me: one from the passenger seat and the other from the back of the pickup. Then there were second and third shots as my rear window exploded. I felt liquid on the back of my head: it was blood.

Assuming the crouched driving position Shelby had taught me, I bounced onto the dirt road and began zigzagging, creating a veritable dust bowl behind me. I heard additional shots, but my pursuers—dust obscuring their vision—fired wildly while slowing down, unable to match my dirt road 45 mph. After making two sharp turns I was comfortably ahead.

Seeing an opening in a bush along the roadside, I hit the brakes and plunged the station wagon into the small opening. I shut off the engine and lights and waited. I assumed that if they spotted me I was dead, but they saw nothing as they whizzed by, still shooting blindly ahead of them.

For two hours I sat trembling until I decided it was time to brave returning to the road and drove to a nearby friendly black community. My hands were shaking and blood was dripping onto my face. The sharecroppers screamed when they saw my bullet-ridden car and the bleeding from my head. As I was helped from the car, a large woman laid me on the ground and placed my head against her as she sang children's songs to me. Others wiped the blood off my head and plucked the window glass from my scalp. Thankfully I had not been shot. My last thought that night was: "God Bless Shelby!"

After that I found myself under increasing pressure to be armed: "violent self-defense," civil rights workers called it. They paraphrased Movement leaders: "Where the law is unable, or unwilling, to enforce order, the citizens can, and must, act in self-defense against lawless violence."[11] A Mississippi black farmer, after returning fire against Klansmen, later warned Dr. King that, "This nonviolent stuff ain't no good. It'll get ya killed."[12] And a rebuff to the leader: "I don't know what the Lord told Martin Luther King, but the Lord's never once told me to turn the other cheek."[13]

Although I still refused to carry a pistol in my car I did agree to keep a rifle in my room. As the strain mounted I placed a mattress on the floor alongside my bed so I could roll off in an instant, land softly, and come up with my gun ready, thereby reducing my time as a potential target.

On the night of October 2, 1965, the Klan attempted to firebomb my daytime office by tossing a Molotov cocktail under the one-room shack. Fortunately the local KKK left too much space between the wick and the neck of the bottle. it burst into flames but did not explode and only singed the building.

"Get Don!" a teenager was told.

He ran to the back of the house where I was sleeping.

Hearing the sound of urgent footsteps running toward my room, I rolled off the bed and in seconds was lying with my cocked rifle aimed at the rear door. As the footsteps reached the porch and the door swung open I prepared to squeeze the trigger.

Then I saw a black teenager and, in a moment frozen in time, I managed to swing the rifle up in the air and avoid squeezing the trigger. There was no shot. The boy stood there staring at the rifle. He had come close to death by breaking another one of those many rules of survival: "Never enter someone's home at night without first identifying yourself." Panting with terror and horrified at what I had almost done, I got up and put my arms around the now-sobbing boy. After that I kept my rifle unloaded.

The damage to the office was minimal. Later that day a law enforcement official who was widely suspected of being one of the bombers came out to "investigate" the crime—which, to the surprise of no one, was never solved.

When I later told the story to George, who had first driven me to Holly Springs, he said, "You should have fired immediately even though you would have killed the boy. If he had been the Klan, you'd be dead now."

6

Time to Leave . . . and Return

fter being arrested, almost getting myself killed, and then nearly shooting a black teenager, I decided Bronstein was right: It was time for me to leave.

Although less than four months had passed since the August day I flew into Jackson, Mississippi—and a mere two months since the day when I first set foot in Benton County, picked my first cotton, attended my first church meeting, and ate my first meal in a sharecropper home— I was ready to leave and return home to long-time friends, a professional career, and an ample income. I looked forward to resuming the normal pleasures of middle-class life and the increased chance that I would stay alive for another forty or fifty years.

Yes, I would miss the people with whom I'd worked, but unlike Aviva I was not grief-stricken. I had not come intending to stay; I had only been dabbling and it was now time to return to my old life. Plus, I told myself, my basic work was done: our school integration effort was well under way and so far had gone relatively peacefully, and the bulk of voter registration in the county had been completed.

When I revealed my plans to the black community there was disappointingly little protest. Apparently the sharecroppers had balanced the advantages of having a live-in lawyer heading their civil rights efforts against the heightened scrutiny that my presence had brought them. The verdict was that my departure would maybe make their lives a little easier and safer. While they would not have asked me to leave, my departure was not resisted.

Still I had no doubt that I remained personally popular in the county—my recent arrest in the courthouse demonstrated the depth of my commitment—and I was given a church farewell evening filled with laudatory speeches and amusing anecdotes. It turned out that I had failed to disguise my distaste of the vegetables that were a major part of the meals they served me.

With conflicted feelings I rose to speak. Our time together, I told them, had truly been my life's greatest adventure and I would always remember them. I ended on a self-deprecating note: "I have given you something that not even Aviva ever gave you. Because I was so incompetent you now know you no longer need an outsider to lead your Movement."

Amidst appreciative laughter one ingrate growled: "Amen!"

On my last full day I visited Holly Springs to say goodbye to the civil rights workers who threw me a grand, drunken party. I also telephoned a farewell to Judge Coopwood and the prosecutor.

No sooner was I in the air, seated comfortably on a Delta flight headed north, than the feeling of excitement from my time in the South gave way, first to a feeling of loss and sadness and then to a rush of pride and satisfaction. The three months in the South had been an experience I would relish the rest of my life.

A group of friends greeted me at JFK airport and then fêted me at a party, during which I regaled them with stories of the South. As the evening wore on, however, I began to sense an almost imperceptible change: a distancing. It seemed as if with each story I told I was becoming less a comrade and more a conversation piece. The fight for civil rights in the South had previously been a major topic of discussion among these friends, but now it seemed no one wanted to talk about it in my presence. One week after the party my best friend confided that I no longer seemed like a peer to him. Instead I had become one of the people who used to impress us at cocktail parties. I was a veteran of the Civil Rights Movement and survivor of a world far apart from the New York existence of my friends.

Not only did I feel like I was losing friends, I also felt I had lost my way. In the days after the party, instead of looking for work I read books, watched TV, visited former girlfriends, and walked the old familiar streets of Greenwich Village chatting with merchants and longtime residents. Only later did I begin answering ads for well-paying corporate law jobs. To my surprise I discovered that I no longer had the stomach to be a "hired gun" representing the likes of sweatshop proprietors in the Garment Center or nursing home owners who warehoused the elderly—the kind of clients you rooted against even while representing them. I wanted something more.

I had lost my ambition and then the companionship of the lawyer colleagues with whom I had climbed the success ladder. I found I was not particularly interested in hearing about their achievements. Their pursuit of prosperity only reminded me of the desperate poverty that I had seen in Mississippi. They, in turn, did not want to hear about the South, seemingly considering me a fool for what I had done.

Since I had been culturally deprived for over three months I indulged myself by attending Broadway plays, the Metropolitan Opera House, and the New York City Ballet. But even as I watched a performance I frequently found my thoughts wandering elsewhere: I wondered what was being talked about at Benton County church meetings. Were the reluctant sharecroppers still being encouraged to register to vote? Were black students successfully attending the integrated classes? And what was the gossip? Any new demonstrations, boycotts, arrests?

Before I left for Mississippi I had expected my time to be a hiatus: memorable but brief. Yet now I found my life did not rebound as I had assumed it would. Also upon leaving I had hoped my three-month sojourn in the South would open doors for me, but I learned that while spending one's vacation in the South might make one an impressive applicant, extending that time for months made one a fanatic.

In pursuit of a job with the Civil Rights Division of the US Justice Department that might fit my new values, I secured an interview in DC, with an Assistant US Attorney I had met in Holly Springs. After greeting me warmly he asked what should have been a simple question: "Don, if you were working for us and a local white man was about to strike one of your Holly Springs friends—Sid Walker, say—what would you do?"

"I'd try to stop the attacker, of course," I answered. It was the wrong answer.

"You know," he smiled sadly, "we all wish we could enter into a civil rights fray—but of course we cannot."

We agreed I was not cut out for the job.

On the flight back from DC, I wondered if ACLU would give me another chance. With great misgivings I approached the ACLU civil rights administrator, Henry Schwarzschild, who scheduled lawyers for their two- to three-week excursions into Mississippi. I broached the subject over lunch:

"I might be interested in some additional time in the South with ACLU."

"You? After Okolona?"

"I can explain. You see, I didn't know it was off limits. I had heard of Okolona, but . . ."

"What about your movie sit-in? As a lawyer . . ."

"Well at the time I was more of an organizer than a lawyer. I . . ."

"What about your arrest?"

"You see, I called Bronstein first and he said . . ."

". . . and what about defying Bronstein by going to Holly Springs, and then replacing Aviva?"

"Oh, that. You see, she decided to leave suddenly . . ."

"I understand." Schwarzschild finished working me over and gave me a conspiratorial smile.

"I admire your style Don, but Bronstein's the boss in the South and he'd never accept you. You know what he told me?" Schwarzschild leaned over to emphasize the confidence: "You have no respect for the law."

"What? No!" I protested. "I'm against lawlessness as much as anyone. Ask . . ."

"Anyway," he interrupted, "no Mississippi for you, I'm afraid."

But he had a counterproposal. Since I was unemployed anyhow, why not work as an unpaid volunteer for ACLU in New York?

Well, why not? I thought. It wasn't like I had anything more pressing to do. And so I spent the next few weeks at ACLU's Manhattan office researching subtle points of law about the right to boycott, assemble, and picket in public places. Still I found I could only concentrate for a few hours each day. After that I would walk around outside the ACLU building staring blankly at passerby and wondering when I would snap out of my malaise, start earning a living, and resume my life.

A month of mundane work for ACLU passed slowly. Then one dreary day in mid-December Schwarzschild telephoned to tell me that a lawyer who had agreed to handle the Mississippi office for the holidays had backed out at the last moment. Bronstein's vacation depended upon a replacement and no one else was available. He asked if I was willing to go South for Christmas.

"To Mississippi?" I responded incredulously.

"Yes."

"Bronstein approves?"

"Yes."

"Salary?"

"Yes."

I agreed to leave within two days.

I hoped that this would provide the answer to my dilemma. Mississippi had become a fantasy larger than life, and I thought that only by experiencing it again could I finally make up my mind: Should I try harder to close the books on my Southern sojourn and remain permanently in New York or should I reopen the books and stay in the South for the long term? If my civil rights ardor continued unabated and I elected to remain, I would either attempt to convince Bronstein to hire me or I would seek work with other civil rights lawyer organizations working out of Jackson.

An appreciative Al Bronstein picked me up at the Jackson airport and earnestly thanked me for saving his holiday. After a two-day briefing he gave me several emergency numbers and left for his vacation.

The civil rights wars were also on vacation it seemed. The streets of Jackson were virtually empty: most "outside agitators" had returned to their "outside," local blacks prepared for Christmas, and even white segregationists seemed to accept an unspoken Christmas truce and stayed home with their families.

I had little to do but open the mail, take a few calls, and create busy work for my volunteer secretary. Walking around town I greeted the few friends who were not on holiday, exchanged old stories, made some unsuccessful job inquiries at the other law firms, and thought about my future. I realized Bronstein was my best chance for civil rights employment in the South. With this in mind—and using my Wall Street experience—I worked to upgrade the ACLU office: I simplified legal papers, expanded interrogatories, and wrote concise legal memoranda. I also tightened up office procedures, coordinated similar cases being handled by different lawyers, and suggested next steps in each case. I hoped all this would give me an edge with the Boss.

THE CANTON EXPERIMENT

At 6 PM on Christmas Eve while I was at the ACLU office anticipating the holiday party that night, I received a phone call: mass arrests were taking place in nearby Canton, Mississippi!

Bronstein had alerted me that there was a "Black Christmas" boycott under way in the city, twenty-four miles northeast of Jackson. Although the population of Canton contained a majority of black residents, restrictions on black voting ensured white control. But Canton's black population, long relegated to menial work and political isolation, was now fighting back. They were seeking economic opportunity and political freedom in this 75 percent black community by boycotting white businesses and picketing outside white-owned shops. As the holiday shopping season progressed neither side had yielded. Although black children would face empty stockings on Christmas morning Canton's white merchants were facing empty cash registers.

Now the merchants were retaliating.

When I heard the news of the mass arrests I issued an emergency call for volunteers, aborting the Christmas Eve festivities in the process. Civil rights workers poured into the ACLU office to offer aid and compile lists of those arrested.

I phoned the officials responsible for the arrests. Introducing myself to a deputy sheriff, I began my efforts to free the picketers:

"How about setting bail so those arrested can spend Christmas at home?"

"How about the Christmases of the merchants who are going broke?"

"How about a next day bail hearing?"

"How about white parents with no money for their children's presents on Christmas morning?"

"How about medicine for one of the prisoners who is epileptic?"

"How about white children with no money to see doctors, you damn nigger-lover!"

As he hung up on me I was reminded of the movie manager's anger during the Elvis demonstration. For all the claims by whites that they were fighting for separation of the races, it was when businesses suffered that the white community reacted with the greatest wrath.

Concentrating my efforts for now on the safety of the picketers held in the jails of an enraged community, I followed Bronstein's protocol for such matters and telephoned the FBI for help. Reaching the Jackson office, an agent told me they lacked the authority to interfere in such matters: "States' rights, you know." He suggested that I seek an injunction or contact the Justice Department. The Justice Department was no more responsive. I was advised that I must deal with the FBI—that only they had national police powers.

Lacking governmental assistance but aware that the glare of public attention often neutralized even the most maddened antagonists, I re-telephoned the jail and carried out a Movement ploy: I introduced myself as the world-famous CBS TV news anchorman, Walter Cronkite. Attempting valiantly to impersonate the TV commentator's neutral accent and sonorous baritone delivery, I inquired about the Christmas Eve arrests which "the whole country is aroused about." I was immediately told that everyone was safe, received a complete list of those arrested, and learned the general nature of charges and bail. The chief of police confided that he watched my show as often as he could but complained that its coverage of the South did not tell the whole story. I, as Cronkite, should visit there myself to see what is really happening. I assured him I would.

There were additional phone calls to make from there: the real media had to be apprised of the situation and the families of those in jail put at ease. I also assured other lawyer groups that the matter was under control with the aim of keeping them out of the way. This case was all mine! I did not even call Bronstein for help or advice.

Meanwhile the phone calls continued to pour in from Canton, most of them carrying news of more arrests. A pattern had been established in the besieged city: as a picketer was arrested and pulled from the line, another took his or her place. The picket line would not go away and the arrests continued. In the early hours of Christmas morning, with more than eighty demonstrators in jail, I began drafting the highest-caliber legal weapon in the civil rights arsenal: the federal removal petition.

The right to remove, or transfer, a case from the state to the federal system descended from a century-old, post–Civil War, Reconstruction-era statute. It had been designed to protect Yankee officials from sudden arrest and possible death in Southern jails.[1] Movement lawyers, organizers, and activists had revived the tactic and were now using this weapon in civil rights cases. Because all federal judges were appointed by the President of the United States, they were usually more sympathetic to arrested activists and demonstrators than state judges who could be the same people instigating the arrests. Thus the power of removal was crucial to the well-being of civil rights workers and local citizens accused of race-based charges and held in Southern jails.

To initiate the process was both simple and unique. There had to be an allegation in a petition that the state courts could not be trusted to enforce laws of the United States providing for equal civil rights. That was simple. The unique feature of the law was the manner in which it triggered the transfer to federal court: all that was required was a lawyer's signature on the petition—not that of a judge—and the transfer would occur.

Gratefully copying Bronstein's excellent models I began preparing the papers. I recited what had happened in Canton and tried to show that the state court would not follow federal statutes, nor prevent state officials from using Mississippi statutes for racist purposes.

After hours of composing, typing, and mimeographing, our bleary-eyed crowd cheered as I signed the last petition and announced that ACLU would purchase breakfast for the crew.

At Steven's Kitchen the levity was replaced by outrage as the weary civil rights workers voiced their anger at the federal government for once again refusing to intervene. Worst of all was the "betrayal by the President and his brother, the Attorney General," they charged. "They bribed us to ease up on confrontation," said one activist. "Our price was federal protection and funds for our work. . . . We sold out for it and then they didn't deliver!"[2]

In the early 1960s the federal government, long concerned about what they called "violent lawless" street protests, offered large foundation grants to advance civil rights work and promised federal protection *if* that work was primarily voter registration—not mass demonstrations which frequently resulted in bloodshed. Although many civil rights workers were convinced that significant gains could only be won in the streets, most were combat-weary, shell-shocked, and ready to take the deal. Desperate for funds for basic necessities like gas, car repairs, and bail, they also could not resist the offer of federal protection from murderous sheriffs and Klansmen.

Yet when peaceful voter registration efforts also resulted in bloodshed provoked by these same sheriffs and Klansmen, organizers found themselves abandoned and left to the mercy of their enemies. US Attorney General Robert Kennedy later admitted that the government promoted voter registration precisely because it assumed that protection would *not* be necessary. When calls were made for help, the government insisted that they lacked the authority to interfere.

The split between the Civil Rights Movement and the federal government had become a chasm. Civil rights workers, outraged by Attorney General Kennedy and FBI Director J. Edgar Hoover, fought back by asking William Kunstler and the NLG to sue to compel Kennedy and Hoover to provide protection from Southern violence. By "failing and refusing to perform such duties," it was asserted that Kennedy and Hoover were abetting the crimes of the Southerners.

The legal papers submitted to the court documented workers who were beaten for registering voters: one "barely escap[ing] from a white lynch mob," another forced to escape "by leaping out of a second story window," one "ambushed with firearms," and another "shot in the head." A civil rights worker was arrested for "sitting on the white side of a [Jackson, Mississippi] courtroom," then sentenced to jail "where he was beaten by guards."[3]

The lawsuit, a desperate cry for help without legal precedent, was quickly dismissed by the court because it sought "remedies which . . . the court has no power to grant."

This anti-federal government anger was news to me. Like many newspaper readers of the time I believed that the Kennedy brothers were loyal supporters of the Movement. Certainly Southern whites thought so, as did the sharecroppers. But the reality, I was told, was that the federal government had mostly turned its back on civil rights for eighty years and now begrudgingly reacted only when Dr. King or other high-profile leaders were involved or when a crisis sparked publicity. Then "the feds would quickly move in with the media, only to move out when the publicity abated."

By 7 AM Christmas morning, breakfast and diatribe concluded, I returned to the ACLU office. It was time for me as Walter Cronkite to call the jail once more and receive updated assurances of everyone's safety. A few days later all the prisoners were freed on bail—but that was hardly the end of the story.

Under federal law, once our removal petitions were filed in the US District Court, the counterstrategy for state officials was to pursue a motion to remand, or return, the cases back to the state system. The State of Mississippi filed for remand of the cases of those arrested in Canton and a hearing was scheduled. I undertook a frantic search of Bronstein's files for any model of opposition to the state's papers. Finding none I consulted other civil rights lawyers in town and then by phone in the East. I learned that none of their cases had ever reached this stage. Jackson civil rights lawyers told me that they were waiting to see my papers since they assumed that they too would soon have to prepare similar submissions.

The reason for the flurry of remand activity turned out to be due to a segregationist federal judge named William Harold Cox, appointed to the federal bench by President Kennedy.[4] For years Cox had fought against civil rights lawyers who sought to use the strategy to transfer cases to the federal court. At first he would not even allow the filing of removal papers. Later when he was so ordered by an appeals court Cox would stand at the clerk's counter ruling against the petitioners without a hearing—and apparently without even reading the papers. Again his actions were appealed and a higher court had now ordered him to conduct hearings.

We were facing just such a hearing!

In the days following Christmas Eve I visited the Canton defendants who were now out of jail. I ate with them, their families, and local SNCC workers. In doing so I was aware of the return of special feelings of warmth and purpose I had not felt since leaving Benton County. Any ambivalence about my future was over; I wanted to stay in the South. Unrealistic? *Perhaps*. A romantic reaction? *Certainly*. Economically unfeasible? *Surely*. But though I never thought of myself as a particularly happy person, I had found happiness here. So I made my plans. Since the ACLU continued to offer me the best chance of remaining in the South, the remand hearing was a godsend, offering the chance to impress Bronstein enough to hire me.

To quell the state's remand petition I had to demonstrate that my clients could not obtain a fair trial in a Canton court—easy to prove at Steven's Kitchen on North Farish Street but not under the stringent rules of evidence that applied in federal court. I had to present additional evidence since a single set of arrests was not sufficient proof of a pattern of racism. Initially my plan had been to simply show that racially motivated arrests had also occurred in Canton the previous year. But when I interviewed black residents I found them referring to incidents dating back years and, at times, even decades. Now I was considering the possibility that I could trace a pattern of racial discrimination in this one city almost as far back as the Civil War. This would be a massive undertaking that would require interviewing virtually every black resident in Canton and investigating a hundred years of city records. It would also require the support of most of the black community and its SNCC workers.

As this strategy took shape in my mind the civil rights worker in me saw implications far larger than just acquitting the defendants. Here was a hot-button political issue that could potentially further embolden the black community, educate Northerners, and place significant pressure on the federal government to intervene in civil rights matters.

It was also a very politically charged approach. I carefully tried to avoid being accused of crossing over the line from lawyer to political organizer, which would incur the wrath of both lawyers and organizers. So I hid my political goals behind my briefcase and began incorporating a style I would use in my work from that day forward: to organize in the guise of legal strategy and satisfy both arms of the Movement.

While activists began compiling a door-to-door oral history of Canton, I subpoenaed virtually every relevant book and civic record as well as major public officials in that city. Excitement spread throughout the black community as memories led to memories and long-lost documents were found behind newspapers covering holes in ceilings.

I coordinated this effort while shuttling back and forth between Canton and the ACLU office. I prepared legal papers to convince the federal courts not to remand the Canton case back to the state courts. A 1963 federal court decision had held that "the State of Mississippi has a steel-hard, inflexible, undeviating official policy of segregation."[5] To that observation I added a legal maxim I had often used in New York: "A state of facts once found to exist is presumed to exist until proven otherwise."[6] The burden, I would argue, rested on Canton officials to show that past discrimination no longer existed. We would rebut any evidence they tried to offer.

The hearing was to be held in Vicksburg, the scene of a major Southern defeat in as well as a turning point of the Civil War. Most of Canton would be there to see if history would repeat itself. Local black residents and the accused would arrive in rented buses and carpools. They would enter the courtroom alongside white city officials under subpoena.

Al Bronstein returned two days early and would serve as co-counsel. We polished the final brief together, and I was allowed to remain on salary an extra week. The night before the hearing I stayed over in Canton to review evidence and prepare witnesses.

The next morning television crews gathered as the black and white exodus from Canton began. I kept a low profile as Bronstein answered reporters' questions. When the case was called I rose to speak but the District Attorney cut me off.

"With all due deference to this court," he began in a slow, deferential drawl, "I am obliged to inform you that the People of the City of Canton have dismissed all of the indictments. There are no criminal cases for this court to review."

"*No! No!*" shouted someone in the audience's civil rights contingency. Turning I saw Canton blacks and civil rights workers with teary eyes. One black resident exclaimed: "No, we've worked so hard . . ."

"You can't . . ." I rose and shouted as Bronstein grabbed my arm, pulling me down to my seat.

"Of course they can," he smiled at me. "You've won."

"But the political impact . . ." I protested.

"I know," he said gently, "but you can't complain when you win."

After the court dismissed our papers as moot I explained to the audience that all of their work had not been for naught: their efforts had allowed eighty of our brothers and sisters to go free. Their bail would be returned. We had won, but everyone knew a great political victory had been snatched from us although I assured the gathering that this approach would be used in the future.[7]

That night Bronstein invited me to celebrate with dinner at his home and announced that he had directed Schwarzschild to find the money to hire me as a staff attorney. He then formally offered—and I formally accepted—the job.

A few days later I flew back to New York to give up my rent-controlled apartment and deal with my belongings. For reasons not clear to me even now I rid myself of most of my material possessions in order to be safer in Mississippi, as if I could run faster and duck quicker if I did not have a sectional sofa, three lamps, and pounds of books waiting for me in New York.

Then, saying goodbye to a career of upward economic mobility and looking forward to working for people I loved and believed in, I returned to Mississippi, this time to stay.

7

Full-Time Civil Rights Lawyer

I was now a full-time civil rights lawyer, which on North Farish Street meant I was fully accepted.

But if I had once imagined a swashbuckling career waging war in hostile courtrooms, standing shoulder-to-shoulder with a cadre of dedicated advocates, tempting violence and death in the fight for racial justice, the reality was much more mundane. The work was mostly dull and routine; most of the lawyers neither radical, dynamic, nor eager to innovate; and the legal organizations that employed them mostly concerned with budgets and image.

"Accept it!" Bronstein hollered at me. "The last thing we need is a bunch of self-appointed superstars and glory boys who come here for the cheers of the crowd and then depart leaving people like *me* to clean up their mess!" Bronstein insisted that our work was critical to the defense and well-being of black residents and civil rights workers—to relentlessly hammer away at Mr. Jim Crow with well-crafted, constitutional challenges. "This *is* the war!" he assured me, annoyed at having to discuss it. However I thought it was a war more frequently fought in law libraries rather than in courtrooms or on the road.

It is said each legal organization fell into a certain stereotype: ACLU attracted more aggressive and mostly liberal Jewish lawyers, the President's Committee appealed to the more conservative establishment WASPs, and the NAACP LDF was comprised of a cross section of the most proficient but least emotionally involved attorneys. I found civil rights lawyers, whoever they worked for, to be usually gentle souls eagerly searching for accommodation and reasonable compromise with the Southern establishment.

This may have been a war zone, but to me it more resembled frat-house collegiate life with intense friendships and preoccupation with sex. After mostly pushing papers all day the lawyers partied by night.

My colleagues were a diverse group: a personal injury lawyer from New York, a corporate lawyer from Washington, DC, and two new-comers to the bar from Florida and Rhode Island. Most ACLU lawyers lived together in a small house in a racially mixed neighborhood. The most prominent resident in the house was twenty-five-year-old Florida native Bruce Rogow—Civil Rights' Playboy of the Southern World. He was so good looking, intelligent, and charming that ACLU head Henry Schwarzschild confided to me: "You can't help hating someone like him."

When I saw Rogow for the first time returning from a week in Mexico with a beautiful British woman he had met in a bus station, he seemed a bronzed Adonis—I hated him too. But my impression began to change when I watched him stand up to a particularly infuriating judge who called him a Yankee. "Suh," he responded, greatly exaggerating his slight Southern accent, "I had to come north from mah home in Florida just to work in y'all's state." The judge grunted.

Rogow also seemed to be engaged in a one-man campaign against heroic pretension, insisting that the South was his home and he was just fighting to make it better. I would come to spend the best part of my Mississippi time with him laughing, talking, and almost shedding my sense of "how-great-I-am-for-being-here."

When not on the road my male colleagues and I spent our evenings at movie theaters, attending parties, or filling time with long dinners. In addition to the full-time lawyer contingent there was a constant in-flux of short-term volunteer lawyers who, during their vacation stints, offered an excuse for a party, a new audience to which to brag, and someone for the minimally paid civil rights workers to guilt-trip for meals and money.[1] Sex lives slackened when Rogow was in town; many of us, including me, focused our romantic lives on pursuing his ex-girlfriends.

Civil rights legal organizations in the South—like their corporate brethren—spent much of their time concerned with finances such as lawyers' salaries, rent, and automobile bills. Major expenses such as the cost of lawsuits and travel were funded by foundation grants, fundrais-ing parties, and, it was rumored, the CIA.[2]

If the people running civil rights legal organizations in the South were concerned with allocating resources and most effectively utilizing their lawyers, the stakes faced in Mississippi were frequently far higher and much more complicated than their counterparts in ordinary law firms. In civil rights such decisions could be matters of life and death: Would the lawyers dare go into certain counties? How many lawyers should be sent to defend arrested organizers? How long will they be needed? How should a mass arrest with hundreds jailed be handled? What if two mass arrests occur at the same time?

The heads of civil rights legal groups often performed the role of dispatchers coordinating lawyers who traveled up superhighways and down back roads from one end of the 400-mile-long state to the other. A lawyer would sometimes drive four hours to northern Mississippi for an early morning hearing, another three hours for an afternoon court date, and then finally to a distant motel in anticipation of a southern Mississippi appearance the next morning. Appealing a case meant either a flight or a four-hour drive to New Orleans, the seat of the federal Court of Appeals.

Although physical attacks on civil rights lawyers were rare, they did occur. Bronstein was once beaten while trying to visit clients in jail. Racist hoodlums chased Rogow into a local police station where he was assaulted as the police watched. Another ACLU lawyer was shot at while traveling in upstate Mississippi.

Fear was a constant companion to the lawyers' usually humdrum existence, and always being prepared for danger had medical consequences including insomnia, stomach disorders, and migraines. For some it produced early retirement. Civil rights workers and lawyers who remained on the job relied on the survival rules that had been meticulously developed as a result of countless encounters with angry locals. Rogow's beating, for instance, followed his eating with a racially mixed group in an infamous white café—a clear violation of the rules.

For those laboring for civil rights the knowledge that they were not alone was a major factor in addressing and relieving anxiety. By the mid-1960s the civil rights community had grown into a family of thousands in eleven Southern states. Good news about the fate of an endangered colleague brought a sigh of relief that could be heard across the South. After bad news civil rights workers and lawyers met and cried in hospitals and sometimes at funerals and memorials. Aware that lives could change or even end at any moment, most civil rights workers played hard, made love easily and passionately, displayed emotions quickly, and sometimes made stupid mistakes.

As I did when Mike Higson, a mini-bearded British civil rights worker, and I stopped on a trip back from a nearby county to go for a swim.

THE RESERVOIR

The place we chose was the Ross Barnett Reservoir, named for the former Mississippi governor who touched off a riot in 1962 when he refused to admit black student James Meredith to the all-white University of Mississippi.

We were aware that the reservoir was a place where white hoodlums were said to hang out and was considered off-limits. But there was no other beach nearby and we were desperate to cool off. We decided to take our chances. A half hour after we had spread out our blanket and removed our shirts, my dog ran off to frolic in the water with a friendly dog whose owner, a burly Southerner, decided to join us for "dog talk."

After we exchanged hellos and began stilted conversation he told us that what he hated most in the world were "niggers." He asked if we also "hated niggers."

"We don't hate anyone," Higson responded. At this point the red-faced Southerner demanded to know where we were from.

Higson, attempting to use his accent to our advantage, answered, "From England, visiting your state."

"Why y'all visiting?"

"Just seeing the whole country. Beautiful here."

Not knowing what role to play, I didn't speak.

At this point three other white men joined him and one shouted at us: "Sheet . . . you're nigger lovers, aren't you?"

We didn't answer. Higson was short and thin, and, although my size more matched that of our harassers, they had muscles that had probably been honed by farm work.

"Why you really here?" demanded one of the newcomers.

"Why you *really* here?" echoed another, threateningly.

Recklessly and needing to prove I was not intimidated, I whispered, "We're civil rights workers."

My mouth barely closed when I was struck with a punch that smashed into my jaw as if my attacker's arms had been coiled and my words released the restraining hook. When I fell he kicked me in the chest. As I rose up I was punched in the stomach, and then, as I doubled up, kneed in the groin. Never lifting my arms I caught a glimpse of Higson, his hands up, not striking but attempting to block and dodge punches.

"Shall we kill 'em?" one yelled to his buddies. "The sheriff says we can kill any nigger lovers we find and nothin' will happen to us."

Unfortunately this was probably true of Mississippi in 1966.

"Naw, why bother," my attacker laughed as he unleashed another shot at my already weakened jaw. Blood spouted from my mouth as I hoped I hadn't lost any teeth. With my hands at my side I thought about the handgun my civil rights worker friends had urged me to carry. If I had it I could have drawn it now. But then what? Point it? Fire it? No, I'd rather get beaten up and *probably* not killed than probably imprisoned for brandishing a pistol or *likely* killed. I recalled the black teenager I almost shot to death in Benton County and put the thought out of my mind.

Finally our tormentors finished with us and ordered us to leave their beach; we hobbled off trying to maintain some dignity.[3] Once in the car we checked each other's injuries and then drove to Higson's girlfriend for peroxide, sympathy, and condemnation for visiting the reservoir— something we would hear for weeks afterward.

In the midst of telling her the story Higson remembered my "confession." "Why did you say we were civil rights workers?" he asked and then broke into hysterical laughter, choking and then grimacing at pains made worse by the laughing.

I just shrugged. Any answer would sound as insane as his laughter.

His girlfriend, not sure which of us was the maddest, shook her head in disbelief.

THE MFDP CASES

Unlike movie characters who are beaten up one day and back on the trail the next, I did not bounce back quickly. I was aching and couldn't straighten up without great pain. I telephoned Bronstein, said I wasn't feeling well, and hinted that it was the flu. He was having none of it. "If you stayed out of the reservoir," he grumbled, "you'd be healthier." Besides, he added, "You don't have time to be sick. You are needed for a big case." I didn't ask for details but slowly dressed and then hobbled down North Farish Street, accepting the guffaws of civil rights workers.

When I arrived Bronstein explained his summons: It was the Mississippi Freedom Democratic Party (MFDP) and their coming Congressional Challenge. The roots of the MFDP lie in the work and philosophy of SNCC, which started its first voter registration projects in 1961 in McComb, Mississippi, and also worked to build parallel political structures to challenge the suppression of the black vote. In 1963 a shack-to-shack simulated "Freedom Vote" demonstrated the will of eighty thousand black Mississippians to vote if not terrorized and intimidated.

During the 1964 Freedom Summer SNCC decided to devote considerable resources to building grassroots political strength as part of the newly created MFDP. After numerous meetings in churches and homes four MFDP candidates were chosen to challenge the seats of the all-white regular Mississippi delegation (the "Regulars") to the National Democratic Party Convention in Atlantic City, New Jersey. The grounds: the Regular delegates barred blacks from their process and would not even support the certain Democratic Party nominee, incumbent president, Lyndon Johnson.

MFDP sought a viable coalition with Democratic Party liberal forces, and the delegations of New York, Michigan, and seven other states passed resolutions of support.[4] A legal brief was prepared for the credentials committee of the Convention detailing how the Regulars had maintained their position in the state and nation by imposing a reign of terror on black people. With the help of SNCC MFDP produced brochures, biographies of its delegates, legal arguments, historical arguments, and moral arguments—and then distributed them to all the nationwide delegates.

I followed the nationally televised credentials fight in the 1964 Democratic Convention between MFDP and the Regulars and heard the passionate speech of Mississippi sharecropper Fannie Lou Hamer to the Convention:

> They beat me and they beat me with the long flat blackjack. I screamed to God in pain. . . . They beat my arms until I had no feeling in them. All of this on account we want to register, to become first-class citizens, and if the Freedom Democratic Party is not seated now, I question America . . . .[5]

Despite Hamer's impassioned words the coalition of liberals at the Convention unraveled and the MFDP delegation was not seated.

President Lyndon Johnson, it was opined, feared that if the Regulars lost the Mississippi seats enraged Southerners might bolt from the Convention and wreck his plans for a massive victory in the South—where white votes were almost all there was! On the other hand he didn't dare openly oppose MFDP for fear of losing the support of Northern liberals.

The president and his followers attempted to craft a compromise: all Mississippi whites would retain their seats but MFDP would receive two nonvoting seats as delegates at large—their delegates already picked for them. As bait President Johnson held US Senator from Minnesota and national liberal hero Hubert Humphrey hostage by making clear: "No compromise, No Hubert for Vice President." MFDP's own lawyer, a prestigious attorney with impressive liberal credentials, folded and endorsed the compromise.

The MFDP walked out of the Convention maintaining that they had come to Atlantic City "to replace the racist Mississippi party, not to join it!" This ended the first stage in its attempt to challenge an illegal state political structure while *outside* that structure.[6]

Afterward MFDP challenged five white congressmen and the legitimacy of the 1964 election in Mississippi relating to the US House of Representatives. It charged that the election had been illegal and fraudulent since almost half the state's population was denied the right to vote, and those few black citizens who did manage to register were prevented from freely participating in the electoral process.

MFDP asked the House to set aside the congressional election results, to refuse to seat the state's white Congressmen, and instead call for new and fair elections in which every citizen can vote regardless of race. Legally the House had the power to refuse to seat, or unseat, any member for any reason it chooses.

But since under the rules only a *defeated candidate* could challenge an election in the House, three MFDP leaders ran for Congress in three of the state's five Congressional districts. And since they were not on the official ballot they ran on a "Freedom Ballot" asking supporters to cast unofficial ballots in churches and community centers.

On December 4, 1964, the MFDP filed official notice with the House of Representatives that they were challenging the results of the election in the Mississippi Congressional districts where the three candidates had run on the Freedom Ballot. Under the rules the challenged candidates were given thirty days to respond, bringing the matter to January 4, 1965, the opening day of the Eighty-ninth Congress.

A "fairness resolution" to unseat the Congressmen was defeated 276 to 149, but 149 votes to bar "elected" members of Congress, more than one-third of the House, was an astonishing number. The three who were directly challenged were only provisionally seated pending the outcome of the lengthy process.

MFDP had forty days to gather evidence in support of their challenge to the three provisionally seated Congressmen. With the assistance of Movement and volunteer lawyers, SNCC, CORE organizers, and MFDP activists fanned out across the state collecting affidavits attesting to the white power-structure's ruthless denial of black voting rights. Under House rules the MFDP was able to subpoena and force testimony from white officials.

Congress was compelled to address the issue. The MFDP eventually lost in the House of Representatives on a vote of 228 to 143, one-third had favored MFDP, but three thousand pages of testimony from the challenge became a vital part of the evidence in support of the Voting Rights Act.[7]

Having failed to expel the racist candidates, a statewide effort began to run black candidates for US Congress and Senate—all under the banner of the MFDP. A significant hurdle faced by MFDP was the Mississippi Democratic Party primary, which was now under federal supervision thanks to the passage of the Voting Rights Act.

For almost a century Southern whites had successfully used a mixture of violence and their own legal process to prevent blacks not just from registering and voting but also from running for office. While the Klan rode at night their lawyers toiled by day designing statutes to disenfranchise and disempower the state's black citizenry. Alarmed by the 1964 high-profile events in Atlantic City, these legal efforts went into an even higher gear.

This time the Mississippi Democratic Party sponsored rules decreeing that as a precondition to appearing upon the party's primary ballot, all candidates were required to pledge to support the party platform. The platform condemned the Civil Rights Act of 1964, called for the continued separation of the races, and declared that integration was a "direct threat to Southern womanhood, children, and all that is right, good, and true."[8] Of course, the MFDP candidates refused the pledge; my job was to file suit to have it declared unconstitutional.

This was a civil rights lawyer's dream: a can't-lose case of national importance. I limped over to Steven's Kitchen to share the news. But news of my assignment proved to be of little interest to SNCC workers. All that mattered to them was that Bill Kunstler was on the case.

"You civil rights lawyers are worthless!" a SNCC activist said angrily. "It barely matters if you win or lose because you ACLU types never fight the key cases . . . like *our* lawyers do—and are doing for us even now! The Kunstler team will handle the *important* MFDP case."[9]

Shock on my face, anger on his, he continued pouring out fury at "you" lawyers: "You make too much money, take too few risks, are low on commitment, high on compromise, and you're not at all bothered making deals with the racists. That's why we rely on William Kunstler!"

I knew that to Bronstein and Schwarzschild, Kunstler and his team were "probably Communists," couldn't be trusted, "shot from the hip," and favored "pie in the sky" lawsuits—but to SNCC activists they were the only lawyers who could be trusted not to sell them out, especially after the Atlantic City Democratic Convention.

Swallowing my distress and disappointment at their angry and unfair characterization of me and my colleagues, I tried to piece together from them why Kunstler was in our case. It soon became clear that there had been a split in the leadership of MFDP.

While a moderate faction had asked ACLU to secure their candidates' place on the primary ballot, a more radical faction brought in the Kunstler team to halt the entire election. Kunstler had filed a companion suit to ours which called for suspending all elections in Mississippi until more blacks were registered to vote; that the court should put the election on hold until satisfied that the end results of slavery and a century of racial discrimination had been reversed.

Pie in the sky indeed!

It was time for me to go back to the ACLU office and report to Bronstein what I had just learned: that Kunstler was pursuing a certain-to-be-lost suit that could undermine our solid chances in court. I conspired with Bronstein. The NLG no longer had a full time office or staff in Mississippi, so our on-the-ground assistance would seem to be essential to them. If we played hardball and refused to help Kunstler maybe we could encourage him to drop his case. Bronstein readily agreed.

Telephoning Kunstler in New York, I introduced myself and presumptuously explained why he couldn't possibly win, why his case would hurt ours, and why we could not help him in any way. Then I paused, waiting for the counterattack. Instead Kunstler told me he understood and respected my position, that he had heard about my exploits in Holly Springs, Okolona, and Canton, and looked forward to meeting me. Although he would have welcomed help, he said he and his team would figure out a way to somehow continue on their own.

I fell victim to the famous and genuine Kunstler charm. Affectionate to everyone, he would shake the hand of every man in a room like a politician running for office and kiss the lips of every woman in range. He could hold a group spellbound with his anecdotes about the great and notorious. No wonder Henry Schwarzschild warned me not to be taken in by him. But like Ulysses' crew hearing the songs and voices of the Sirens, I was enchanted.

Seduced, I ended up proposing a modification of our position. As long as Kunstler was proceeding anyhow, I reasoned that we could help him locate witnesses in exchange for his disassociating ACLU from his lawsuit. Bronstein agreed; Kunstler was grateful.

THE MFDP HEARINGS

On the eve of the hearing all the lawyers gathered in a northern Mississippi motel near the federal courthouse. That was when Kunstler, then 47, took me aside and confided to me his view of the state of the struggle both here in the South and nationally. He flattered me with a prediction that I had a great career in civil rights work. He himself wished he could stay in the South full time but there were mounting national political pressures.

Kunstler was undisputed dean of radical lawyers, the most famous radical lawyer in America, and the Bogeyman of the Bar—he himself recently sentenced to prison at a trial and out on bail pending his appeal. Born and raised in New York City, Kunstler had graduated from Yale University where he was an avid poet and represented Yale in a poetry competition. Next came Columbia Law School, followed by the US Army during World War II where he attained the rank of major and received the Bronze Star for heroism.

In 1961 he defended Freedom Riders who were beaten and jailed attempting to integrate Southern bus terminals and was a key advisor to Martin Luther King Jr. From there on he became a one-man legal warrior for those resisting the status quo: Stokely Carmichael, H. Rap Brown, the Black Panthers, Malcolm X, and many others less well known.

He became a household name when he was sentenced to four years in prison for contempt during his defense of the "Chicago 7," the anti-war demonstrators accused of causing riotous protests at the 1968 Democratic Party National Convention in Chicago. (Black Panther Bobby Seale had also been one of the accused—then known as the "Chicago 8" —until his case was severed from the others.) After Kunstler's sentence was pronounced he told the judge he was "most privileged" to pay with his liberty "the price of my beliefs and sensibilities."[10]

Taking advantage of the sense of instant intimacy that Kunstler engendered, I ventured delicate questions: "Why are you here? Why does MFDP need two sets of lawyers?"

"It all goes back to the betrayal in Atlantic City." He paused as if gauging my reaction. "You do know what I'm talking about?"

"Yes and no," I responded.

"The Democratic Party called Johnson's 'compromise' a 'symbolic triumph,'" Kunstler scoffed. Most of the Movement saw the offer as an "outrageous sellout by the white liberal establishment." MFDP rejected the "compromise."[11]

I had not realized the depth of the pain that had been left behind in the ranks of MFDP and SNCC.

This may have been the moment that ignited what became the Black Power Movement. In his memoir *Walking with the Wind*, then-SNCC Chairman John Lewis reflected back on the bitter events of that week:

> As far as I'm concerned, this was the turning point of the civil rights movement. I'm absolutely convinced of that. Until then, despite every setback and disappointment and obstacle we had faced over the years, the belief still prevailed that the system would work, the system would listen, the system would respond. Now, for the first time, we had made our way to the very center of the system. We had played by the rules, done everything we were supposed to do, had played the game exactly as required, had arrived at the doorstep, and found the door slammed in our face.[12]

After 1964, according to Kunstler, SNCC would never again trust liberals, including their lawyers. "Your lawsuit may be important," he said unconvincingly, "but SNCC believes a radical attack on the system is required and they will never again entrust that to liberal lawyers."

I was incredulous. "You mean that accepting a compromise to seat two Mississippi blacks in a formerly all-white Mississippi delegation for the first time in Mississippi history was a betrayal?"

"*Exactly!*" exclaimed Kunstler as if I had agreed with him. "As MFDP put it," he recalled, "we came to replace the racist Mississippi party, not to join them! We didn't leave the national party. It left us."

"But," he added, attempting halfheartedly to change his tone, "that was long ago. Now we're all friends."

I had many more questions but Kunstler, pleading the need for sleep in advance of the next day's cases, ended the conversation, shook my hand, and wished us both luck. We returned to our rooms. I lay awake much of the night troubled by the feeling that all was not well in civil rights paradise.

I had heard the complaints, of course, but had largely dismissed them as just griping. I hadn't realized the antagonism ran so deep—and that it was aimed at those who were the backbone of the Movement's political and financial support.

Moreover I recognized that had I been present in Atlantic City and attending the 1964 Convention with MFDP I would have happily accepted the compromise that so many disdainfully dismissed as a sellout and betrayal of trust. Where did that leave me?

Appearing before a federal judge the next day, I argued that requiring a pledge of support for racist principles to qualify for the Mississippi ballot clearly violated the US Constitution and the Voting Rights Act.

When I concluded my presentation the Mississippi Attorney General rose and stated that my lawsuit was a great waste of the court's time since his office had never intended to enforce the pledge. When I vigorously protested that this statement couldn't be trusted, the judge cut me off.

"Counselor," he said, apparently angered at my lack of respect for my adversary, "based upon the Attorney General's statement, there is no controversy and no need for an injunction. However," he added reassuringly, "if the State of Mississippi changes its mind before the election, I'll enjoin them."

I unhappily accepted "victory" and received congratulations from Kunstler and others in the courtroom. As in Canton I would have to be satisfied with seeing my adversaries choose not to fight.

Next it was Kunstler's turn. Where I had been logical and precise, he was dramatic and emotional, crying out for justice and compassion, recalling centuries of slavery and the need for amends. His witnesses were heartrending, his final statement sprinkled with biblical and classical references, so persuasive I found myself wondering why I had opposed his lawsuit.

Of course he lost. The court would not prevent a sovereign state of the United States from conducting a Congressional election.

"Great try," I told him afterward. "You were magnificent. I never dreamed you could present such a convincing case."

"Thank you," smiled Kunstler. "I think we'll win on appeal, don't you?"

"*Appeal?* Oh no, don't do that," I entreated him. "You'll lose and it will be a dangerous precedent."

"Okay, we'll consider that," said Kunstler, already turning to accept the congratulations of his supporters. They did appeal, of course. They lost, but the heavens did not crash in on us nor did the Movement collapse. That case was hardly heard of again, but for every ten of their cases Kunstler's team won at least one and made legal history.

If justice demanded Kunstler would strike, precedent and procedure be damned. If that was shooting from the hip I wanted to get out my lawyer's gun out and practice.

With Kunstler and his team departing the SNCC workers returned to their evolving militancy. I went back to many mundane cases—and one that was hardly mundane.

The "Rape" of the
Plantation Owner's Wife

Southerners had priorities of bigotry, I was learning: battling civil right boycotts rated higher than preserving whites only bathrooms, retaliating for economic losses of merchants was more important than enforcing separate lines at the local Tastee-Freez, and keeping blacks out of voting booths took precedence over keeping them out of the Holiday Inn. But what some whites would die for and kill to ensure: keeping a black man out of a white woman's bed.

In 1960, as the sit-ins were beginning in North Carolina, Alfred Windom, a black Mississippi laborer in his mid-twenties, invited a white woman to go to bed with him. She politely declined. It was a measure of how things had progressed in the South that Windom was not lynched for propositioning her; he merely was sentenced to spend the rest of his natural life chopping cotton in Parchman Prison.

I first learned of Windom's plight in 1966 when a SNCC worker passed on a note written, I was told, by a frightened black woman. It read: "Al Windom of Lamar County didn't do nothin' but he in Parchman cause a white woman say he rape her."

The SNCC worker asked if I would handle the case. I had to respond that ACLU policy forbids pursuing cases that are not directly civil rights related.

"You guys are worthless!" he snorted disdainfully.

As he started to walk away I yelled out, "It's organizational policy! I'm on their staff. *What can I do?*"

"*Lie!*" he hollered. "Say he was an organizer and that's why they jumped on him!"

Although I knew I was crossing a dangerous line, I did lie and ACLU approved the case.

A call to the court clerk confirmed that an "Alfred Windom" had been convicted and sentenced to life imprisonment after confessing to attempted rape of a white woman. In fact what he had "confessed" to was assault with intent to commit rape and burglary—the crime of entering the woman's home to commit rape.

I wrote to Windom letting him know I would visit shortly.

Windom was born in Mississippi, raised in Chicago, and streetwise enough not to be awed by a white lawyer—or by a white woman either, which was why he was in prison for life.

Inside Parchman Prison, after pleasantries were out of the way, I asked him to tell me about the rape charge.

"Nothin' happened," he said in response.

I gave him my best New York don't-bullshit-me-man look.

"Nothin' happened!" he repeated indignantly.

"Okay," I sighed. "Tell me why they charged you."

"I'd been working for the wife of the plantation owner. One day, after I had been drinking, I went over to her and said, 'I'd like to be with you.'"

"You actually said that?" I blurted out, omitting the end of the sentence that had formed in my head, *you crazy bastard.*

"Yeah," he answered, blushing slightly.

"And?"

"That was it. She said, 'Don't be silly, Alfred. Go home and sleep it off.'" He smiled and added slyly, "She wanted to. I could tell. I'd been with white women in Chicago."

"And then what happened?" I asked.

"That's all."

"No touching, tearing clothes, threatening? That's all?"

"That's all," he said.

"So why . . . ?"

"They said, 'Confess or you'll get what Mack Parker got!' He had been my friend. So I confessed."[1]

Many civil rights workers in the South had told me such stories. Still I was shocked and appalled.

I assured Windom that my office would represent him, but—I added with a wink—only because he was a civil rights organizer. After a pause he nodded knowingly.

Before going to Parchman I had confided in Bruce Rogow. "Be careful," he warned. "It happened just north of Pearl River County—Mack Parker's county."

Leaving the prison I drove back to Jackson, but instead of proceeding to the ACLU office I headed down the street to the offices of Jess Brown, one of a small number of black lawyers in Mississippi and one of the most courageous people I knew. Brown had been Parker's lawyer.

Although both lawyer and client had known the accused could never be acquitted by an all-white jury in Pearl River County, they hoped that Parker could obtain a reversal of the certain conviction by convincing an appellate court that he could not receive a fair verdict from a jury that excluded blacks.

One evening, after preparing for trial all day, Brown was asked by the judge if he was returning to Jackson, as he sometimes did, or if he was staying in town overnight. A strange question, Brown thought.

"I usually stayed over," he recalled, "but that night I had to go back to Jackson. I told the judge I would return the next morning."

That night Parker was seized from his cell, dragged away by a mob, and shot to death.[2]

"He was innocent," said Brown, who himself could have been killed that night, "but they murdered him."

A civil rights worker exclaimed that "sex is behind everything that goes on down here!" echoing economist and sociologist Gunnar Myrdal, whose definitive work about slavery and its aftermath in the Deep South, *An American Dilemma,* was required reading for Movement activists. "I have always understood that a Negro who touches a white woman must die," Myrdal quoted a white Southerner's words, spoken in 1934. "It is something that we learn in the South without knowing how or when or where."[3]

Sex between white men and black women was tolerated by white society, even by Southern wives if discretion was observed, but not between a black man and a white woman. Sexual race-mixing by a black man was a crime—the crime of miscegenation. It was usually considered rape since it was presumed that the woman's conduct had to be involuntary. The sentence could be court-imposed execution or mob-imposed lynching.

The penalty was the same for allegations of sexually provocative behavior such as flirting (real or imagined), sensuous smiling, or even lascivious looking. The most notorious of such Mississippi vigilante killings was the slaying of Emmett Till, a black fourteen-year-old accused of merely conversing with a white woman. He was brutally beaten and murdered, and his body dumped into the Tallahatchie River.[4]

It was clear to me that the name of Alfred Windom could be added to the names of Mack Parker and Emmett Till in this ignoble history.

We were granted a court date to try to overturn Windom's conviction. A hearing would take place within the foursquare miles of Purvis, population 2,000, within Lamar County, near Pearl River County.

"Don't go alone," Brown had warned. "Get Bruce Rogow to go with you."

It seemed like a very good idea so I walked over to the ACLU office and obtained Rogow's agreement to work alongside me. Preparing for the hearing, we already knew that it would be impossible to prove Windom's innocence in the same Southern courtroom and in front of the same local judge who had presided over the case. But if we could establish that black residents were routinely excluded from serving on Lamar County juries—and, in this case, that Windom had pled guilty to avoid being tried before an all-white jury—we could prevail on appeal.

What we needed were local black citizens who would review the lists of names in the county's pool of potential jurors to prove what we already knew: that only white names were on the rolls. We solicited help from the local black community, arriving in Lamar County a few days early for that purpose. We quickly discovered, however, that fear was so pervasive that no one would help us, not even Windom's family.

Nonetheless, on a torrid, shirt-drenching morning, Rogow and I drove into the white downtown and walked up the steps of the courthouse accompanied by the usual cries of "Nigger lovers!" and "Commies!" As we entered the courtroom we were introduced to Judge Sebe Dale and two prosecutors: one, the county's district attorney; the other, an elderly gentleman and personal lawyer for the alleged victim there to protect her from Yankee lawyers.

It must have justified their concern when I did indeed call the grand dame of the county's largest plantation as our first witness. A handsome woman in her forties, as she walked from the spectator's bench everyone, even the judge, rose in deference to her prominence, her whiteness, and her shame. As she walked past Windom to the witness stand, there was an intake of breath from the audience as if she might be "raped" all over again.

She was an appealing witness, neither hostile nor tense. After setting the scene I asked her what preceded the "incident." Alfred was ordinarily a good worker, she said. On that morning he was doing his chores when he suddenly approached her "under the carport."

Assuming I was mishearing because of her drawl, I asked, "Car what?"

"Carport."

"Pore?"

"*Port! Carport!*" she repeated, in an angry voice, assuming I was mocking her.

Panicked, I turned to Bruce: "What's a carport?"

With a faint smile he described a simple roof supported by four pillars to shield a car from the sun.

Everyone was now angrily shouting at me: the judge, the district attorney, and the elderly protector. Although rattled I began a lengthy apology using the Southern-style courtroom informality I had learned in Holly Springs, explaining that, to my knowledge, New York City had no such objects and that I had never heard of one.

"I had no intention," I beseeched her, "of embarrassing you or attempting to humiliate you. It was my ignorance alone that led to my confusion." She was seemingly gratified by my attempt at making chivalrous amends and, perhaps feeling empathy for my embarrassment, graciously accepted my apology.

Crisis over, I continued my questioning.

"What happened when he approached you under the . . . carport?" I asked, everyone smiling now when I used the word.

"He said, 'I want to be with you.'"

Hearing about this outrage, the audience again collectively held in their breath. Apparently this was crime enough for the spectators.

She continued, "Then I said, 'Alfred, you're drunk, go home.'"

I had been letting her talk on without much prompting, but now she stopped. Here it comes. Will she say he refused to leave and attacked her?

"And then?" I ventured, timidly.

"Then he left and I went inside," she said calmly.

"And then?"

"That night I told my husband."

I held my breath. Rogow was pale. She had confirmed Windom's version of the events. She was not accusing him of rape. I looked to Rogow for advice. He shrugged his shoulders; it was up to me.

I decided to continue.

"I apologize in advance for these questions, but I have to ask them. Did he touch you at all?"

"No."

"Above the waist?"

"No."

"Below the waist?"

"No."

"Attack you in any way?"

"No."

"Rape you?"

"No."

"Do anything but say those words, 'I want to be with you'?"

"No."

I looked at Rogow who motioned me to stop. "Thank you. No further questions."

I looked at Windom who displayed no emotion. I looked at the district attorney who was wildly whispering to the private lawyer. I looked at the sheriff who seemed equally surprised. No one knew the truth, I later surmised, except the witness and her powerful husband. Given the confession and guilty plea there had been no trial, no evidence, and no need for her to testify about what had actually happened that day—until this hearing.

"I have no questions for the witness," said the visibly uncomfortable district attorney.

Addressing the judge, I moved to dismiss the charges "because the victim says no crime was committed."

"Denied!" declared Judge Sebe Dale, who, although also surprised at the testimony, would never agree that *some* sort of crime had not taken place.

The prosecutor then proceeded to introduce Windom's confession into evidence. I jumped up and protested: "This is a confession to an act the victim just testified never occurred!"

But the judge accepted the confession as valid evidence of the attempted rape that had never occurred.

It was clear that this Alice in Wonderland proceeding was continuing. Now my task was to protect our client—and ourselves. Rogow, who had left the courtroom to call the ACLU office in Jackson, had now returned. I took the offensive.

The district attorney was about to introduce some additional evidence when I interrupted. I warned the judge that a full report had just been made by phone to J. Edgar Hoover (he glared at Rogow) and demanded that the judge assume personal responsibility for the safe return of Windom to prison after the hearing so that he would not become "another Mack Parker." I also demanded that the judge secure the stenographer's record and guarantee that no one will tamper with it.

All this was more than Judge Dale could tolerate. Over the advice and strong objection of his prosecutor, he insisted on personally recounting what he called "the true story" of this case. Before I could totally grasp what was happening he walked off the bench, sat down in the witness chair, and took the oath to testify in a case he was judging!

He then began his statement. Noting that he had been the judge in the original Windom trial, he wanted the record to show how the defendant had been treated:

> As the presiding judge in this case on the day that this defendant was brought into court [for the original trial] he was treated with the utmost kindness and caution and care as any human being can be given, and when he came into court he made the statement that he wanted to plead guilty. . . . He was advised then that he could not be sent to the penitentiary until some ten days after court had adjourned. He insisted that he wanted to go on [immediately],[5] and only one thing did he request and that was that he be permitted to see his family, and we thereupon made arrangements for him to see his family, and talked to him as kindly and gently as any human being has ever been talked to. *Not one single time was he ever referred to as a Negro or his color ever mentioned.*[6]
>
> It was as quiet and orderly and decent of a proceeding as has ever been held in any man's court, whether the civil rights outfit and the ACLU likes it or not or believes it or not.

Judge Dale continued:

> Of course what happened outside of the courtroom I have no knowledge of [referring to the threatened lynching] and I don't intend to say what happened but I do know what happened in the courtroom and I don't intend, regardless of what any court does about it, to be insulted about being that kind of crook and criminal to let a district attorney tell a man, 'We are going to send you to the penitentiary Negro and that is it.' It just didn't happen and it has

never happened in my courtroom and it has never happened in any courtroom that I have ever been in, in my life. It just doesn't happen down South regardless of what they say about it.

"Now," looking at me, the judge challenged, "do you want to examine me about any of it?"

While I had been listening to him, awestruck at this spectacular violation of judicial order and protocol, I had wondered whether he would subject himself to my questions after concluding his self-serving oration. To my delight he was offering me the chance to cross-examine him.

After a few preliminary inquiries about his background I hurried to the no-blacks-on-the-jury question before the prosecutor could convince the judge to return to the bench.

Judge Dale answered my question directly and arrogantly: "[No] Negro has ever served on any jury in this county since I began practicing law in 1924!"

I tried to suppress my delight at how this hearing was unfolding. With his last statement Judge Dale had guaranteed us victory on appeal. I asked the judge if he would have dismissed the case if "the victim" had told a trial jury the facts she related here.

"No, I don't think so," he said. "I think I would have let it gone to the jury."

But the judge was clearly anticipating where my questions were leading: that Windom's so-called "confession," the very confession of sexual assault that we had just heard the alleged victim repudiate, had been extracted under threat of death. He launched into a rambling defense of the original district attorney to whom Windom had "confessed."

> He and I rode to the criminal courts in this district for twelve years together. . . . He is a high-tone Christian gentleman and he accepted his duties and responsibilities as district attorney as a public trust. . . . I just can't conceive of any officer in any of these counties doing the things he [Windom] says has been done.

"Do you think," I asked, playing with the judge's sensitivity for his friend's reputation, "the officers in Pearl River County [where Mack Parker was lynched] are as high quality as [the former DA]?"

The prosecutor objected: "This is not Pearl River County!"

Ignoring him, I continued: "Has it been your honor's observation that Negroes in the South charged with crime involving white people, particularly white women, have not received as fair a trial as white people under similar circumstances?"

"I think they get just as fair a trial," the judge answered. "I think a Negro can get as fair a trial in Mississippi . . . as he can anywhere in the world. And I think another thing: one Negro is not going to let another Negro sit on the jury to try him. If you want to know the truth about it, we are having that experience because they know they can good time [deceive] a white fellow a lot quicker than they can one of their own color."

"Do you think," I persisted, "that a Negro can get as fair a trial as a white man without any Negroes on the jury?"

"Yes."

"Do you think Negroes in your circuit have been intimidated, to say the least, by what happened to Mack Charles Parker?"

"No. No, I don't."

"Do you think," I raised my voice, "a Negro arrested for a crime involving a white woman would not be in any way influenced by what happened to Mack Charles Parker?"

"No, he would not," flared the judge, angry at the constant repetition of Parker's name.

The prosecutor tried to stop the testimony. "Your honor, this is all outside and is going in the record."

Judge Dale now turned his wrath on the current district attorney.

"It is all outside but I would just like for the Supreme Court of the United States to know something about the truth about what is going on down here."

Then, turning back to me, he continued:

The crime rate is no worse in this state and the criminal condition is no worse in this state than it is [in] your state or any other state in the union, the Supreme Court and [US Attorney General Nicholas] Katzenback [sic] notwithstanding. . . . Anytime a circuit judge, or a presiding judge, gets so doggone scared of the Supreme Court ruling that he is going to kowtow to them, then he ought not to be circuit judge . . . I started out [ruling] on five cases [during] one court [session] and the Supreme Court reversed me five times in a row and when the sixth one came up I held the same thing and they affirmed it. Sometime maybe they will come to their senses. . . .

He then asked, "Are you ready for me to rule?"

"Yes," I said. I already had more than enough.

The judge began his ruling:

> I don't believe that any human being in the history of Lamar County has ever been dealt with any more fairly and kindly than this defendant has and it was all done in open court and open and above board and nothing hid from the public anymore than this hearing right now is being hid from the public. . . . I am of the opinion that this petition [for Windom's freedom] is without merit and I am, therefore, going to deny it.[7]

Judge Dale then proceeded to resentence Windom to life imprisonment. Rogow and I wished our client good luck, embraced him, and reluctantly surrendered him to a jail cell, not unlike the one from which his friend had been dragged and killed. We drove swiftly out of town and were relieved when later that night we learned that Windom was safely back in prison.

Thereafter the appeals process began. We communicated with Windom regularly and let the local court know that we were still monitoring his treatment.

Over a year later the federal courts finally freed him.[8]

TWO

Black Power Selma

A Crack in the Movement

From the time Alfred Windom was arrested and through his release, the Civil Rights Movement had assumed a radical new shape. Once rooted in racial harmony, the civil rights song "We Shall Overcome" was now being drowned out by cries of "Black Power!" which would dominate America and influence racial relations thereafter. The old Movement was now increasingly filled with emboldened, militant black civil rights workers who were more and more demanding of a segregated all-black movement. The position of white volunteers in the South was becoming less secure.

On a day I was to return home from my seemingly never-ending shuttle between Holly Springs and Jackson, Bronstein asked me to respond to a message from a civil rights worker in an upstate rural community. Using the WATS line (an early "800" number), the worker had called the ACLU seeking a lawyer to help with a case of "agricultural discrimination." Although no one understood what that meant I was asked to offer encouragement while emphasizing once again that there was little we could do in matters outside traditional integration cases. I decided I would stop by on my way down from Holly Springs.

Driving first on concrete then on asphalt and finally dirt roads, I pulled up in front of a tiny cabin so small from the outside it appeared that you would have to walk sideways once inside. In front, wearing the traditional civil rights uniform of overalls and denim work shirt, stood a fair-skinned, blonde-haired woman in her mid-twenties looking more Southern belle than civil rights worker.

"I'm Don," I began.

"Yes, I know," she burst in. "I'm Molly. Mr. Bronstein told me you would come. You're from New York and you got beat up at the reservoir."

She caught her breath and laughed at my obvious surprise that she knew about me.

"*I'm* from California," she raced on. "I came for the Mississippi Summer . . . and I guess I just stayed on."

Putting aside the official reason for my visit, we found ourselves quickly falling into animated conversation as we compared notes and traded tales.

Molly told me that her father had fought for the Loyalists in the Spanish Civil War, had been hit by shrapnel, and eventually lost a lung. Though Molly was raised to concern herself with the plight of others less fortunate than herself, when she decided to "Go South" in 1964, her father, bitter over his debilitating injuries, urged her not to repeat his involvement in other people's causes. Hearing this I told her about *my* father's disappointment when I gave up a lucrative career on Wall Street to join the civil rights struggle.

Molly then told me she had initially been a volunteer for COFO and the Mississippi Freedom Democratic Party. Now, two years later, she had trouble defining her status: she was no longer a part of MFDP and COFO barely existed. Like Aviva and her counterparts Molly had continued on as an unpaid staff member of a county-level freedom group spending her time on such projects as voter registration, school integration, and anything else the black farmers asked her to do. Rallying behind her and using her as their contact with the outside world, local sharecroppers believed that somehow this lovely young woman with blonde silken hair could help deliver them to a better life.

Responding to her description of growing up on the West Coast, I told her New York stories. We playfully swapped tales of who had been in the most danger since arriving in the South and, in the solemn idioms of the 1960s, traced the philosophical frames in which we placed our work. "Sometimes," she intoned, "you have to destroy something (she meant the South, of course) to save it. Like Howard Roark did!" She looked at me to see if I understood her remark. I knew the reference was to Ayn Rand's novel *The Fountainhead* about a Frank Lloyd Wright–type architect who destroyed his own creation because others had destroyed the purity of his design. When I told Molly that the book had deeply influenced me, she was delighted.

My own favorite novel, I told her, was *Martin Eden,* an autobiographical, idealistic work by Jack London. She hadn't read it so I acted out the plot for her. Suddenly, as if a dam had burst, we found ourselves reciting from memory passages from favorite books and authors.

Although less than an hour had passed I was in love and suspected the feeling was mutual—although, in hindsight, perhaps we were more in love with what the other represented than with the individual we barely knew. After over a year in the rural South Molly seemingly craved middle class conversation, discussion of books and ideas, and even the culturally familiar comfort of a white person. For me Molly represented the innocence of the young women I had met within the Civil Rights Movement: brave, dedicated idealists who I wanted to hold and protect from enemies outside the Movement.

"Why don't you come in the house?" Molly suggested.

"I have gonorrhea," I blurted out.

She might have replied indignantly, "I didn't ask you to sleep with me!" but instead said sweetly, "Come in anyhow."

"Actually I'm almost better," I added, making things worse. "All I have to do is visit my doctor once more to be sure."

Noticing that she hadn't renewed her offer, I asked if I could still come in.

"Yes, come in," she laughed, "but don't touch anything."

We walked into the little house, which was so small that there was no place to sit except the bed. "Sit down," she invited me nervously. We sat as far from each other as the little bed would allow.

Molly broke the silence by asking, "Are you with anyone?"

"No," I answered, "I was spending a lot of time with someone until recently. That's how . . ."

"I know how you get gonorrhea," she interrupted, with a look of exasperation.

"Anyhow, I'm not seeing anyone now," I said. "How about you? Are *you* seeing anyone?"

"No. It would be playing with fire," she responded, explaining that the only available men in this community were black and any relationship was sure to be disapproved of by black women.

"How about your ex-girlfriend?" Molly inquired. "Was she . . ."

"Negro? No. But before I began going with her I was seeing a black woman. She and I never experienced any racial problems. We went to Movement parties all the time, went out to black movie theaters, and ate in black restaurants."

"Probably because you're a lawyer," she interrupted. "You get special treatment." Then she asked why I was smiling.

"Maybe you could make everyone around here happy if you went with a white man," I suggested.

"Maybe," she grinned. "Do you know anyone?"

"Nope," I countered. "Just being theoretical."

Seated on her bed, I pulled Molly to me and kissed her.

"How about your gonorrhea?"

"Don't laugh," I growled, annoyed at life's little joke.

"Well, get better soon," she teased.

"I will," I assured her and kissed her again.

For an hour we lay in each other's arms speaking quietly about civil rights, our fear of death and injury in this strange and dangerous land, and the victories we were anticipating. She only hinted about the problem that had occasioned my visit, and we agreed to discuss it on my next trip—my excuse to return. I told her I would be back in three or four days when I'd again be on the way from Jackson to Holly Springs.

I drove away daydreaming of when I might see her again. First I would see my doctor.

DR. POUSSAINT

Dr. Alvin Poussaint, a thirty-two-year-old black Harvard psychiatrist, was the resident sawbones, shrink, and father confessor to civil rights workers. His official title was Southern Field Director for the Medical Committee for Human Rights. His job was to provide medical and psychological care for civil rights activists in Mississippi, to create and maintain a medical presence at demonstrations (bringing in doctor volunteers as needed), and to desegregate health facilities in the South by filing complaints under the Civil Rights Act of 1964. In his "spare time," he joked, he set up community-run lay health care clinics in black rural counties. He also sent battle-fatigued civil rights workers out of the South to friendly homes where they could be ministered to and helped to recuperate.

Dr. Poussaint's position clearly gave him a special vantage point from which to view the dynamics of the civil rights community. As he was examining me, which I really hoped would result in a clean bill of health, I asked him if he had noticed any recent conflict between black civil rights activists and white volunteers.

"You're right if you think that there's a conflict," he looked up, suddenly serious, "but you're wrong if you think it's recent. It's been going on since the first whites appeared in large numbers in 1964."[1]

It's a love/hate thing," Dr. Poussaint explained. The young civil rights workers are the first whites most local blacks have ever socialized with, eaten with, and shared a residence with. At first the whites were widely admired for having voluntarily put themselves in harm's way, but in time the good feelings lessened and some blacks began to complain about the whites' lack of commitment. After all, if things got too hot, *they* could always leave and go home to the relative safety and security of the North—not so for local blacks who had nowhere in which to escape. However committed they were, white civil rights workers were often seen as the children of those who had jailed, murdered, and enslaved them over centuries.

Even the skills of the whites were viewed with disfavor. The bureaucratically savvy, efficiency-obsessed whites acted, or were perceived as acting, "superior." They were accused of becoming instant, self-appointed experts and authorities on all matters concerning the Negro and civil rights.

They did a lot of talking and very little listening to local black people, it was said, and were impatient to direct programs and run project offices —even if it meant taking over from black people. They were accused of being paternalistic and condescending in their relations with blacks, as if they felt Negroes had little intelligence or capability. For example, if a white man taught a black person to use a typewriter, he was seen as flaunting his education and superior office skills. If a crisis occurred and the white civil rights worker (who likely typed much faster) impatiently took over the typewriter, he was accused of displacing and dishonoring the work of local blacks.

The anger of the blacks was further fueled, Dr. Poussaint said, by the actions of a handful of reckless white civil rights workers who caused breaches of security that threatened the safety of both themselves and members of the black community—a few seemed to consider being beaten or jailed as a badge of honor. "A white girl worker, while walking down a Mississippi dirt road, might reach out and affectionately take the hand of a Negro male worker," Dr. Poussaint noted. But if this was observed by police or white toughs, "the Negro fellow could receive a severe beating but the white girl would probably escape with an admonishment and an epithet." These reckless actions were interpreted as a lack of caring and respect for the black community.[2]

But even this paled in comparison with the most explosive issue of all: sex! "Negro girls were often resentful and jealous of the attention which Negro men showed to the white girls, and vice versa," he said. "During the Mississippi Summer a number of local Negro female workers came to see me acutely depressed because they were jealous of their boyfriends' attention to white girls."

Black men, meanwhile, were aware of the fact that by associating with white women they were violating the most sacred Southern taboos. They were often plagued by ambivalence, the doctor said. He recalled one young black man confessing: "Whenever I'm around one of these white girls, I don't know whether I feel like kissing her or punching her in the mouth!"[3] Eventually black men joined in the attacks on white civil rights women. "Black leaders with white girlfriends were embarrassed and were accused of selling out," Dr. Poussaint remarked. He himself had been labeled an enemy of black people because his medical care helped white volunteers remain in the South.

Distressed by what I was hearing, I related Molly's remark that as a lawyer I was immune from these problems. He agreed that as a lawyer I was probably receiving special treatment but that I shouldn't expect it to last.

"Lawyers are obviously vital to the Movement," he said, "but remember that most civil rights lawyers are white, highly educated, and capable of earning sizable incomes whenever they want. Only now is segregation breaking down so that in the future blacks will have a real chance to be lawyers and doctors. The poor and uneducated blacks in the civil rights movement are grateful but also angry at lawyers in general because they have used the law to cripple them."

"The tide is turning," he said and asked whether I had heard of black civil rights leader Stokely Carmichael.

"He's in Alabama now, isn't he?"

"Yes," answered Dr. Poussaint. "For some reason Alabama, and especially Selma, seem to be the hub of the black militant sentiment."

There was much I wanted to ask but other patients were waiting. As he saw me out he quietly announced: "Good news, you're cured!"

As I walked down North Farish Street to the ACLU office, as usual exchanging hellos, hugs, and handshakes with black men and women, I found I couldn't help scrutinizing their reaction to me, but I detected only the usual warmth and caring. Or perhaps it was because I was in Jackson with its cosmopolitan civil rights community.

Dr. Poussaint had said that the tension began in 1964 when white students came down en masse—but I later learned that it had occurred almost from the beginning of the Movement. SNCC's first staff in 1960, "on the whole [was] black, urban, and middle class in origin [and] primarily college students."[4] In 1964 SNCC workers coexisted with a thousand mostly white student volunteers assigned to work in Southern black communities during the Mississippi Freedom Summer.

SNCC members expressed alarm: the poorest people in the United States were to play host to the children of the most privileged. The family income of the Freedom Summer volunteers was 50 percent higher than the median family income in the United States—and just short of 300 percent higher than the median income of Mississippi black families.[5]

By the time I had arrived in 1965, one year after the white volunteers had come South for the summer, over one hundred volunteers remained, entrenched in small Mississippi communities and supported by grateful black farmers. Far from leaving, the white workers were actively engaged in bringing down even more white volunteers by inviting their friends, recruiting on campuses, and encouraging those already on hand to stay —including a white civil rights lawyer.

"[We] made a cardinal mistake, a disastrous miscalculation," SNCC Executive Secretary James Forman would later write of the time. After the 1964 Freedom Summer ended, "we did not anticipate that the [white] volunteers would either want to stay or would stay."[6] But when whites were around, Forman observed, blacks did less—and it was getting worse.

Despite the mounting complaints of black activists, white faces still dotted major Movement communities shielded by black sharecroppers who had decided that their white "guests" should remain. Although militant black civil rights workers were forced to back down, their smoldering resentment was not going away.

The bitterness was palpable in the cauldron of racial and sexual tension that was the South—a tension I would experience firsthand. Black Power arose in part, Forman said, from that misjudgment. The sweet multiracial sentiments of civil rights anthems were now increasingly being drowned out by harsh separatist rhetoric.

Three days later I eagerly began my next drive upstate. For once I did not begrudge the early rising or the long, tedious drive to Holly Springs because I knew that halfway there I would detour to see Molly. In record time I arrived at her little cabin. I was beside myself with joy when I spied her seated out in front.

Walking into her cabin and closing the door to keep out the sun, we sat down once again on her bed. Struggling for conversation Molly asked me what was new. I launched into a recitation of my three days away: a minor trial, a vigorous telephone argument with a Klan lawyer, a decision in the mail announcing victory in a voter discrimination case, *and that I was cured!* I left out my troubling discussion with Dr. Poussaint about race relations.

Suddenly my eye was struck by a ray of light, and then I noticed a second beam and a third. The beams were coming from the door, or rather through it.

"What are those holes?" I asked.

She didn't answer.

Walking to the door I stared at chest high holes that hadn't been there during my first visit. Then I stared at Molly whose eyes were filling with tears. Suddenly sobbing she told me what had happened only a few hours after my departure: she had heard a car approaching her shack and had walked to the door to greet the visitor thinking perhaps it was me having turned back. Then she heard the first shot. She dropped to the floor as bullets sprayed the door.

"That's the whole story," she said. "Then they drove off."

Returning to the small bed in the little shack, I held her tightly, the rays of light serving as a reminder of how I might never have seen her again or died myself had I remained with her. We made love in haste, swimming in the rich Movement mixture of peril and passion.

We didn't speak again of the shooting until dinner that night at a Holiday Inn restaurant, an impromptu celebration of Molly's survival. We feasted on the restaurant's "New Orleans" cuisine, overdid the alcohol, and concluded with an extravagant dessert. Bloated, we retired to a poolside table where the waiter brought us a pot of coffee. We sat holding hands and watching guests splashing in the outdoor swimming pool, but I couldn't block out the thought that I might have driven here only to learn that Molly was dead, slain at the hands of white racists.

"Why?" I blurted out, breaking the festive mood. "Why you? They don't usually go after white women. What have you been doing that so provoked them?"

"I really don't know," she answered solemnly, "but it could be the agriculture thing I mentioned to ACLU." She then told me of a local sharecropper who had visited her and complained he was not receiving his "cotton money" from the local agriculture office. She really didn't understand what the farmer was saying but suspecting there might be a bureaucratic snafu she agreed to go to the federal agricultural extension office and inquire on his behalf. Entering the office Molly encountered a more hostile reception than any she had encountered before, even from voter registrars. "I thought it strange—and excessive," she added, "so I called ACLU."

Equally clueless about what she had stumbled into but mindful of the bullet holes in her door, I assured her I would investigate before I left for Holly Springs.

Serious discussion ended, arms around each other, we walked about the motel grounds looking at the moon and mumbling to each other. The silly season was upon us.

I stayed over and the next day we ate again at the Holiday Inn, this time a Southern-style breakfast: heaping portions of tasteless grits which seemed to be alive and threatening to overpower the eggs and bacon it surrounded with corn muffins shaped like lizards lounged on the side of each plate. We laughed and loved the meal.

Dreading the idea of leaving her I asked, "Could you find time to come with me to Holly Springs while I handle a case? You could meet my friends at the same time. It's only for two days and I'd bring you right back."

She smiled. "No, I don't have the time, and yes, I'd love to come."

I was exuberant. While Molly went to tell her co-workers she'd be away for two days, I drove to the agriculture office in town. "I'd like to talk to someone about cotton money," I said to an elderly white lady sitting behind a desk in front of a Confederate flag.

"Well then," she said with a frosty smile, "I suggest you walk down the street and on your right will be an American flag and the US Department of Agriculture. *They* can tell you all about the Yankee program," she drawled, smiled, and dropped her eyes indicating I was dismissed.

A few minutes later I approached a small storefront office with an American flag and a photo on the wall of President Lyndon Johnson (in the Deep South you noticed such things). A gracious white Southern gentleman greeted me. (The fact that the office was federal didn't change the cast of characters: they were almost always white male Southerners.) He explained the program to me in simple terms: As a partial answer to the economic plight of farmers in the 1930s Franklin Roosevelt had created a program designed to keep excess cotton and other crops off the market and thereby raising prices. This was accomplished by providing government aid to those farmers who agreed *not* to plant a certain part of their acreage or to plow under some part of already-planted crops awaiting harvest.

"Is a lot of money involved?" I asked.

"I suppose it's in the billions," said the official as he chuckled, "but it's paid to farmers all over the country, even in New York, not just here in the South."

Is enough paid here in the South to justify shooting at Molly just for inquiring about it? I wondered what he would say if I asked but I did not. Answers to questions I did ask revealed that in addition to landowners black sharecropping farmers were legally guaranteed a certain amount of the money paid to landowners for crops not planted or dug up, especially cotton. The dollar amount was determined by a locally elected ASCS board.

Elected? By whom? Were blacks barred from these "cotton elections?" Did blacks ever get nominated? Elected? Serve? And why had I never heard of all this? Intrigued but cautious, I ceased my questioning and instead accepted a load of charts and pamphlets about the program. This would require more study; there would be no quick and easy answer for Molly.

An hour later, as we drove to Holly Springs, I sketched the details of my conversation and urged her to stay away from the USDA office until I knew more. She agreed.

Returning to Holly Springs was even more of a joy for me than usual. In addition to seeing friends I had Molly to impress. First a church meeting in Benton County with everyone turning out to greet me and meet my girlfriend to whom they told flattering stories about me. Feeling that it would be inappropriate for us to "live in sin" in a sharecropper home, we spent the night at the Holly Springs Freedom House.

The next day I took her to meet Judge Sam Coopwood in advance of a minor trial in his court. We traded pleasantries, including his account of my arrest for obstruction of justice, told to Molly as if it was a mischievous high school prank. Later, during the trial, I overdid my cross-examination of a hapless witness; an amused and tolerant Coop ignored my excesses, aware that I was just trying to establish myself in Molly's eyes as a dynamic litigator. He was in such a good mood that he even dismissed a few of the charges against my client—a hat tip to Molly, I believed. That afternoon I introduced her to many of my sharecropper friends, most of whom made a great fuss over us.

Everyone was having a wonderful time—except, as it turned out, Molly. She appeared increasingly despondent but I couldn't figure out why. She should be thrilled that her man was so well regarded, I thought. On the way back to her county we were silent until she tentatively tried an explanation:

"I'm somebody too," she began. "In my county, I'm important. People depend on me. I'm not going to trail behind you like a housewife. I'm sorry." She burst into tears.

I was confused. Why was our relationship going so badly? There seemed to be nothing safe to say so we remained silent for the rest of the trip. Then I left for Jackson, not staying over as I had planned.

For the next two weeks I immersed myself in office work and several trials in and out of Jackson. Though I was in Molly's vicinity a few times, I stayed away, fearful of forces I had somehow uncovered but didn't understand.

Molly, meanwhile, was experiencing bewildering reactions from another quarter: her black co-workers. After enduring days of cool silence from her colleagues Molly sat down with her closest friend among the group and asked, "What's going on?"

Finally the co-worker began to speak: "Molly, you're a dilettante. A rich, white dilettante. You dabble with the poor by day and then at night go off with your white boyfriend to live the good life. You go to places where *we* can't go—or afford to go—and do things that are way too dangerous for *us* to do. And you're going to leave us," she predicted flatly. "You'll leave us for your fancy white lawyer, go off with him, and sip wine by the pool. Good riddance."

When I heard Molly's account of this conversation, the illogical mixture of anger and dependency it reflected rendered me speechless. It was obvious now that I shouldn't have flaunted my money and our whiteness by eating in the white community. (I had been much more discreet when I was a civil rights worker in Benton County, indulging myself only occasionally when I visited nearby Memphis.) Still there were forces at work here that I didn't comprehend.

Although free of disease I again consulted with Dr. Poussaint, who had shown so much wisdom in these matters. I told him about Molly and asked, "What's happening here? I'm white, she's white. What's going on?"

He sighed sympathetically, shaking his head in sadness. "White civil rights workers, especially white *female* civil rights workers, just can't win," he said flatly.

While whites, he said, could not do enough to prove their loyalty, black civil rights workers were always waiting for a sign that the inevitable betrayal was about to occur—leaving represented the ultimate duplicity. For white women sexual tensions made it much worse. If a white female was romanced by a black male, her black female coworkers felt slighted, but if she rejected his advances it would be interpreted as racist. If she chose a white man she would be seen as retreating to her superior class and wealth—and, of course, race.

"The white woman can't win," Dr. Poussaint repeated. "She just can't win."

When it came to Molly, I was starting to suspect that neither could I.

Meanwhile life in Jackson was unfolding in what passed for normalcy, but that was soon to change. Arriving back at my office I was but one step inside the door when Rogow advised me that Henry Schwarzschild was in town and wanted to talk with me. I immediately called the ACLU administrator and arranged to meet him for dinner at a nearby motel restaurant.

Schwarzschild, a hard-bitten veteran of the bloody Freedom Rides of the early 1960s, confessed that he was happiest when he was in Mississippi. But now in middle age, he ruefully acknowledged, he would have to leave the fight to younger people. Not that running the ACLU office in Manhattan was easy, he hastened to point out, but he always looked forward to his trips to Jackson which "is our *only* office in the South."

"But," he added mysteriously, "that is about to change."

The ACLU leader was in high spirits. Always a good conversationalist and an entertaining gossip, he sported a hearty ego: "Rubberneck," Dr. King had allegedly dubbed him for his propensity of sticking his face into photos taken of civil rights leaders. Still he was especially enthused that night and kept looking at me waiting for me to ask him why.

When I finally did he told me that ACLU had obtained additional funding to expand ACLU's footprint in the South. For now he planned to open two new offices: one in New Orleans for which a high-level corporation lawyer from Washington, DC, had already been hired, and one in Selma, Alabama, for me to head if I was interested.

Barely able to absorb the message I asked, "Do you mean I'd be in charge of the whole state of Alabama?"

Henry nodded yes.

"My own staff and volunteers?"

He nodded again.

"And my own budget?"

"Yes," he smiled, amused at my incredulity. "But," he reminded me, "Bronstein will still be in charge overall, as chief of the whole operation."

Multiple unspoken thoughts competed for my attention, but one thundered to the front of my consciousness: *Now I can run away with*

Molly, away from our troubles! "It sounds incredible," I told him, but even as I spoke I wondered, *Why me?*

"The Movement in Alabama won't be as friendly as Mississippi," Schwarzschild cautioned, "but with your background as a civil rights worker with SNCC you have the best chance of being accepted by Stokely Carmichael."

"Why do I have to be accepted by him or anyone?" I asked. "Are there problems in Alabama of which I'm not aware?"

No answer.

"Black-white problems in the Movement?"

"It's too soon to tell. Carmichael was just chosen head of SNCC and no one knows what's going to happen. . . . Well?"

"Let me think about it tonight," I said. In truth I had made up my mind to accept until I realized I would be leaving Rogow.

Rushing back to the office I learned that everyone in town already knew of the offer.

"What did you tell him?" Rogow asked.

"I told him I couldn't possibly leave you helpless with every female in Jackson after your ass. And . . ."

Rogow cut me off. "I'm leaving, Don. Leaving Mississippi."

I was even more dumbstruck than when Aviva had announced her departure. I thought I knew him; there had been no hint.

"Remember the party we went to a few months ago with Jackson whites?"

I remembered well. A group of middle-class whites remarkably sympathetic to civil rights had invited us to a dinner party to show us that *some* Southerners believed in racial justice.

"Do you remember the daughter?"

"Yes," I interrupted. I was especially impressed that night meeting the daughter of the city attorney of Jackson, our archenemy. She attended with her husband and their four children. I had marveled at their courage in showing up at the party.

"Well," Bruce gave me a sheepish look, "I, uh, we, uh, we're in love and . . ."

"Her?"

Without emotion Rogow continued, ". . . and we're leaving to set up a home in Florida. No one knows," he warned me.

"I should hope not," I said. "So you're really leaving?" I asked as if I'd missed the point.

"Yes," Bruce answered. "If I stayed around I'd be shot for sure."

"Yeah," I agreed. "All these years they thought it was black super studs they had to worry about. They never guessed it'd be a Jewish civil rights lawyer who'd ravish their daughters." Bruce didn't laugh.

"Well, if you're *really* leaving," I said, "that just about makes my decision for me. So I guess I'll call Schwarzschild *now*," I said to suggest to Rogow that this was his last chance to come to his senses, give up this Scarlett O'Hara, and come to Alabama with me. Bruce offered no response, so I called Schwarzschild. When I returned from the phone we drank a farewell toast to the end of our days together in Mississippi.

"No," said Molly, a few days later when I visited and asked her to go with me. Although she said she was tempted to leave and start fresh in Alabama, she told me she'd had a taste of what it would mean to be "Don's girl."

"Even when I accomplished something everyone would think it was because of you."

She was determined to stay here and try to undo the damage she and I had done to her civil rights work.

We went on about the Movement, about love, and about the problems of love within the Movement. Slowly her real message emerged: It was not just "no to Alabama." It was also "no to Molly and Don."

I was not surprised, having caused her to spill so many tears. Nor was I inconsolable. In the two days since I had been chosen to head the Alabama office the power of it all began to intoxicate me. I wanted a loving Molly with me but not a perpetually depressed Molly. We spent one last night together, talking, crying, and making love. I cautioned her to be careful about the agriculture people and the cotton money, and promised I'd seriously look into it when I arrived in Alabama.

The next morning we said goodbye to each other. Although I returned to Mississippi many times, I never saw Molly again. However I did follow her progress and was happy that she and her local movement seemed to be flourishing.

The weeks of preparation to leave passed quickly and soon it was the night before my departure; it was also the night my Jackson SNCC friends chose for a farewell party. Much of the night was spent reminiscing about the decade of civil rights and the triumphs and defeats shared. My sense of nostalgia was real: the Mississippi Movement had been marvelous for me, but I could sense that it was changing forever. Looking back I could see how clearly that era as I had known it was almost at its end. In its place would come a period of disorder during which the Black

Power Movement would expel whites, call for black separatism, expand black militancy, and disavow integration.

The evening had been a euphoric one for me, and at its end we all embraced. One black civil rights worker whispered to me: "We all think of you as a black man." I was very touched, barely remembering the time not so long ago when those would have been fighting words.

As we all left I was given farewell advice: "Be careful about giving the impression that you know everything. Nothing rankles Alabama SNCC workers and Stokely more than a know-it-all, wiseass, white lawyer!"

10

White Lawyer in
Black Power Selma

Bright and early on the morning of June 16, 1966, I drove out of Mississippi and crossed into Alabama.

En route I passed the capital city of Montgomery where in 1955 the bus boycott began and Martin Luther King Jr. emerged as a national civil rights leader. To the northeast was Anniston where a Freedom Rider bus had been torched in 1961. To the north was Birmingham where in 1963 state troopers and local police had attacked peaceful demonstrators with police dogs and fire hoses and where four black children were blown up while attending Sunday school.

Ahead was my destination: Selma, a city of thirty thousand, the seat of Dallas County, and the unofficial economic center of western Alabama—in large part because the Alabama River flowed past it, irrigating cotton crops.

Crossing the infamous Edmund Pettus Bridge over the river and into Selma, I imagined I could see the specks of blood of those who had marched across it a year earlier to demand the right to vote.

Even though blacks made up over half of the population of Dallas County, less than one percent were registered.[1] It's little wonder given that attempting to register to vote required black citizens to line up outside the registrar's office to take a "literacy test" which was virtually unpassable for a black citizen. The retribution for even being on the line could be loss of a present job or future employment after being added to a "blacklist" maintained by the White Citizens' Council. Police or sheriff's deputies watching over the lines threatened anyone bringing food or water to those on the voter line. If someone left the line for any reason he or she would not be allowed back that day. On one occasion SNCC workers carrying food and water to those in line were attacked, beaten with clubs, shocked with electric cattle prods, and arrested.

"BLOODY SUNDAY" DURING THE SELMA MARCH

At dawn on Sunday, March 7, 1965, six hundred mostly black citizens of Selma headed for the Edmund Pettus Bridge to begin a march from Selma to Montgomery to demand voting rights and to memorialize Jimmie Lee Jackson, a twenty-six-year-old black military veteran and a deacon of his church who was shot point blank in his abdomen while attempting to protect his mother from the police. He died ten days later, a little more than a week before the march.

The march was co-headed by black civil rights leader and SNCC chairman John Lewis along with SCLC Executive Director Hosea Williams. One observer described the force that greeted the marchers when they crossed the bridge:

> From between nearby buildings [as the marchers approached the other side of the bridge] a line of horses emerged at the gallop, their riders wearing the possemen's irregular uniform and armed with bullwhips, ropes, and lengths of rubber tubing wrapped with barbed wire. They rode into the melee with wild rebel yells, while behind them the cheers of the spectators grew even louder. "Get those goddamned niggers!" came Sheriff Jim Clark's voice. "And get those goddamned white niggers!"[2]

Lewis would later describe that moment:

> The troopers and possemen swept forward as one, like a human wave, a blur of blue shirts and billy clubs and bullwhips. We had no chance to turn and retreat. There were six hundred people behind us, bridge railings to both sides and the [Alabama] river below. . . . The first of the troopers came over me, a large husky man. Without a word he swung his club against the left side of my head. I didn't feel any pain, just the thud of the blow, and my legs giving way. . . .[3]

One hundred of the six hundred marchers were so gravely injured that they were taken to Good Samaritan Hospital in Selma—among them John Lewis, who suffered a fractured skull. A young girl, eight-years-old at the time, later said that it was "like we were slaves after all, and had been put in our place by a good beating."

The massive brutality was seen on television by much of America and the world. On the night of the march a national television network interrupted a showing of the film *Judgment at Nuremberg*—in which Nazi horrors were documented—to televise the ordeal on the Selma Bridge. When the TV network broadcast fifteen minutes of "Bloody Sunday" footage, some viewers reported being confused, first assuming the images were of Nazi atrocities from the movie.

Rev. James Reeb, a white Unitarian minister from Boston who was in Selma waiting to march, was beaten with clubs by the Ku Klux Klan. He died two days later.

On Sunday, March 21, 1965, two weeks after the assault on the Selma Bridge, close to eight thousand people reassembled to begin the fifty-mile walk to Montgomery. Most were black, others were white, Asian, and Latino. Spiritual leaders of various religions marched alongside Dr. King, including priests, rabbis, and nuns. Four days later twenty-five thousand people marched to the steps of the state capitol building to present demands to Gov. George Wallace.

"The end we seek is a society at peace with itself," Dr. King told the crowd. "I know you're asking today, 'How long will it take?' I come to say to you this afternoon, however difficult the moment, however frustrating the hour, it will not be long."[4]

Later that night Mrs. Viola Liuzzo, a white Unitarian civil rights activist and mother of five from Detroit, was transporting marchers back to Selma when Klan members pulled up alongside her and shot her twice in the head, killing her.

THE MEREDITH MARCH

One year later another historic march took place in the Deep South, this one led by civil rights figure James Meredith, who set out to trek through the heart of Mississippi, from Memphis down Highway 51 to Jackson.

Four years earlier, in 1962, Meredith, a 29-year-old Air Force veteran, had become the first black person to attend the University of Mississippi. When lynch mobs formed outside the campus, President Kennedy sent in federal troops to quell the riot. Two people died and two hundred were wounded.

By 1966, fed up with what he described as the "all-pervasive and over-riding fear that dominates the day-to-day life of the Negro in the United States, especially in the South and particularly in Mississippi," Meredith organized his "March Against Fear."

On the second day of the march, barely ten miles into Mississippi, a white man stepped out of the roadside underbrush and fired three shotgun blasts at Meredith. Although initially reported dead he survived and was taken to a hospital in Memphis where doctors removed seventy pellets from his head, neck, and body. As Meredith recovered, civil rights leaders took up his march where he had left off.

One of those leaders was Stokely Carmichael, who had become chairman of SNCC a month earlier in what was *not* a seamless transition from the incumbent chairman John Lewis.

SNCC CHAIRMAN JOHN LEWIS

Born in Alabama to sharecropper parents, John Lewis had graduated from a Baptist seminary and then Fisk University—both in Nashville, Tennessee. As a student he led the Nashville sit-ins and was beaten, arrested, and jailed. One of the original thirteen Freedom Riders, he was on one of the buses attacked by white mobs and was then jailed again.

In 1963, at the age of twenty-three, Lewis was chosen as chairman of SNCC and that year spoke at the March on Washington where Dr. King gave his "I Have a Dream" speech. The next year he coordinated the SNCC efforts for the Mississippi Freedom Summer alongside then-SNCC chairman Bob Moses, who was also the organizer of Freedom Summer. In 1965 Lewis co-headed the Selma March.

His courage and tenacity was widely admired within SNCC and by the Movement. In 2010 Lewis would be awarded the Presidential Medal of Honor by President Barack Obama, who praised his "courage, fortitude, and purpose [which has] earned our lasting gratitude for a lifetime dedicated to the pursuit of equality and justice for all."[5]

However Lewis was not praised by SNCC for his devotion to Dr. King and what SNCC members called his "beloved community redeemed by suffering."[6] It was said that "Lewis viewed the Movement as a moral crusade, which conflicted with the dominant belief within the organization that the Movement was a political struggle."[7]

Lewis's actions also were disturbing to SNCC. He had marched in the Selma March after it was disavowed by SNCC as ill-conceived and disruptive to ongoing work. Stokely Carmichael, before he was SNCC chairman, opposed the March because he worried about the Selma people who would be marching. "My real concern," he said, "was what would happen [to them] once it got into 'Bloody Lowndes.' What security was SCLC planning for the people it was fixing to lead in there? Or, were they going to place their hopes on the intervention of the Good Lord and the federal government?"[8]

After the Voting Rights Act was passed that year, Lewis participated in a White House ceremony—the Conference on Civil Rights—which SNCC was boycotting because of the belief that it was a "transparent ploy to co-opt the new black vote for the Democrats." But the final straw was attempting to thwart SNCC efforts to form independent parties and run candidates in Selma and Lowndes County. Lewis encouraged black voters to vote for the Democratic Party candidates and, in effect, reject the indigenous local parties.[9]

The Stokely Carmichael who took over from Lewis as the new SNCC chairman was the very embodiment of the civil rights organizer: he had been part of the original sit-ins, the Freedom Rides, the early steps into Mississippi, the Freedom Summer of 1964, and the 1965 events at Selma—he was also a seasoned organizer. In 1965 he permitted white Seminarian student Jonathan Daniels, who he "knew and respected," to work in Lowndes County, Alabama, although Carmichael said working in Lowndes was "like operating behind enemy lines."[10]

In the summer of 1965 Daniels and Father Richard Morrisroe, a white Catholic priest, joined a demonstration in Lowndes alongside SNCC members and were arrested. After four days in jail they were suddenly released; a white man fired a shotgun at them and Daniels was shot dead, Morrisroe was severely wounded.

Mrs. Mabel Carmichael remembered: "I had never seen my son like that, silent, grim, like a heavy, heavy weight was pressing on him. Even when his father died, that had really hit him, but this was different."

At a SNCC memorial Carmichael said, "We ain't going to shed a tear for Jon, 'cause [he] is going to live in this county. We ain't going to resurrect Jon, we're going to resurrect ourselves."[11]

A month later during the continued Meredith March Carmichael made a fiery and historic speech, signaling a searing new chapter in the history of race relations in America.

On June 16, 1966, during a rest stop following the first day of the renewed march, Carmichael was arrested without cause by a deputy sheriff and placed behind bars. When he was released after six hours in jail he bounded onto a platform and roared to his comrades:

> This is the twenty-seventh time I've been arrested and I ain't goin' to jail no more. The only way we gonna stop them white men from whuppin' us is to take over. We been saying "Freedom" for six years

and we ain't got nothing! What we gonna start sayin' now is "Black Power!"

"BLACK POWER!" the crowd roared in unison.

What do you want?

"*BLACK POWER!*"

WHAT do you want?

"*BLACK POWER!*"

WHAT DO YOU WANT!?

"*BLACK POWER!! BLACK POWER!!! BLACK POWER!!!!*"[12]

ARRIVING IN SELMA

At about the same time on the same day that Carmichael was delivering those words in Mississippi, I was driving into downtown Selma. My new office was four blocks from the now-notorious Edmund Pettus Bridge, known in the Movement as the Selma Bridge. On one side of the street were the offices of Sheriff Jim Clark, his jail, the police department, the city jail, the mayor, and City Hall. On the other side of the street was a three-story building: the Alabama SNCC headquarters on its top floor, Miller's Funeral Parlor on the bottom floor, and, sandwiched in between, what was slated to become the ACLU office.

Instead of going straight to the new office I decided to first take care of unpacking and readying the newly rented residence. The new ACLU house, a mile away from the office, was not much to look at on the outside, nor on the inside for that matter—a broken-down two-story former whorehouse—but it did have lots of bedrooms for volunteers and visitors. But before I had a chance to settle in I received an urgent call from Henry Schwarzschild.

"Don't unpack," he instructed, "until we find out what Stokely Carmichael has in mind!" He then briefed me about reports emanating from that day's march. "Just wait and do nothing until the dust settles," he ordered. "We may pull you back to Mississippi."

"What do I do while I'm waiting?"

Schwarzschild shouted: "*Watch TV!*"

Then he hung up.

I plopped onto a secondhand sofa in the living room, turned on the twelve-inch black-and-white TV set, and watched for clues to my future. Carmichael's speech was *the* story on Southern television, discussed over and over again with new analyses, updated analyses, and inside analyses: What does "Black Power" mean?

Henry Schwarzschild (Donald A. Jelinek papers [M2225].
Department of Special Collections and University Archives,
Stanford University Libraries, Stanford, California).

THE PROBLEM OF DEFINITION

Stokely Carmichael expressed his conception of Black Power after the speech:

> When I talk about Black Power, I talk about black people in the counties where they outnumber [white people, working] to get to-gether, to organize politically, and to take over those counties from white racists who now run it. . . . And then you can talk about inte-gration. We are propertyless people in this county . . . so we grasp the political power now and then we see how we can work that political power to then achieve economic power.[13]

But critics of SNCC were poles apart in defining the new doctrine. Black Power was charged with highlighting racial divisions, eschewing coalitions with whites, and as anti-white, defeatist, and bitterly reject-ing the Civil Rights Movement's traditional goal of integration.[14] Roy Wilkins, Executive Director of the NAACP, considered the term and the movement it spawned "separatist . . . wicked fanaticism [pitting] race against race."[15]

Those supporting Black Power applauded its call for "self-determination," "self-help," and its cultural interpretations: the need to focus on the African historical experience and the impact of slavery, multiculturalism in the educational curriculum, the individual adoption of African names, and black consciousness on college campuses as students formed black student organizations and demanded their own dormitories and student centers, as well as more black faculty and black studies programs—the word "Negro" to be replaced with the commanding term "black."

It was the beginning of the end of hair straightening and skin lightening. Young people would grow comfortable wearing African-style dress and would become proud of natural afro-textured hair and their African roots. Black students would call for the institution of "black studies" curricula at their colleges. The slogan "Black is Beautiful" would come into vogue to counteract the self-loathing belief that African skin tone and facial features were ugly.

Black Power would bring forth the concept of "identity politics" which would greatly influence the emergence and "multiplicity of social justice movements," such as the women's movement, environmentalism, disabled rights, and the campaign for gay and lesbian rights.[16]

Integration and its successes had been relatively easy to measure—how many blacks registered and voting, black kids in formerly all-white schools, jobs for black workers—and how many black leaders elected to office. Black Power however was nearly impossible to quantify. It was a state of mind, albeit a revolutionary state of mind, intended to overcome the psychic oppression of three hundred years of state-sanctioned discrimination. The term, which superseded Dr. King's "Freedom Now," referred to a new value system rooted in this country's unique black experience.

But, no matter which definition of Black Power was accepted, it became indisputable that Carmichael's call launched a new era of racial politics in America. FBI Director J. Edgar Hoover was undoubtedly correct when he labeled Carmichael "the most likely 'messiah'. . . [who could] unify and electrify the Black Nationalist movement."[17]

AND WHO IS THIS BLACK POWER GUY?

The fiery new leader seemed to come out of nowhere. A native of Trinidad, Stokely Carmichael was educated at New York City's Bronx High School of Science (just as I had been seven years before him) and then at historically black Howard University in Washington, DC. While at

Howard in 1960 he took part in the first sit-ins in the South. The next year he joined the Freedom Rides to Jackson, Mississippi, where he was arrested and sent to the infamous Parchman Prison. But even Mississippi's "Devil's Island" could not temper him.

Carmichael was both militant and nonviolent, his sardonic humor hidden behind a warm enigmatic smile. In prison he was a problematic captive. In one instance, when guards tried to punish him by removing his mattress, he clung to it stubbornly while singing a spiritual, "I'm Gonna Tell God How You Treat Me!" When his fellow Freedom Riders were placed in solitary confinement, Carmichael demanded to join them, banging on his cell door until the guards acquiesced. Parchman Prison officials were reported relieved when he was released.

After the 1961 Freedom Rides concluded Carmichael's journeys matched that of SNCC: the advance party sent to Mississippi in 1962 and 1963; the Mississippi Freedom Summer of 1964; Atlantic City, New Jersey, for the "great liberal betrayal" at the Democratic Party National Convention; and Selma in 1965 at the time of the March.

He obviously did not come out of nowhere.

OPENING THE SELMA LAW OFFICE

The day after arriving in Selma I walked up the stairs to my stark office and said hello to a small welcoming committee of black sharecroppers.

I sat down in one of those high-backed, judge-type swivel chairs and turned in a slow circle, smiling nervously at the sharecroppers. They smiled back, a sign of their willingness to wait until I was able to work for them. A further swivel positioned me to stare out the window at the offices of the sheriff and his cohorts, and finally to boxes of office supplies strewn on the floor.

Suddenly a black SNCC worker named "Charles," a friend I had known in Holly Springs, burst through my office door. "Hi, Don," he blurted out and then he stopped before literally running back out the door.

An hour later he returned, greeted me warily, and sat down. "You heard about it?" he whispered. Though we both knew what "it" was, it was as if the words Black Power should not be uttered in my presence.

"Yes, but what does *it* mean?"

"I'm not sure, but it doesn't seem to mean . . ." he cracked a weak smile, "just power for black people."

He paused. I assumed he was about to tell me why he had returned to my office after his hasty retreat.

"There's a sign going up, uh, outside your door at the stairway to our floor. I told the folks upstairs that we should tell you about it first."

I couldn't guess the contents but I was certain it wasn't "Welcome, Don!"

"The sign says," he continued, now staring out the window and not at me, "NO WHITES ALLOWED UPSTAIRS WITHOUT PRIOR APPROVAL!"

He swallowed hard and I gasped. Even as a Jew I had never really been a target of discrimination. Charles appeared as pained as I felt.

"Oh," I mumbled, looking away to hide the hurt in my eyes.

"No one likes this happening to you, but until Stokely comes back from the march . . ." He paused and exploded, "I'm going crazy! The press is calling nonstop: 'What does Black Power mean? Are all whites excluded?'—I don't know what to say."

Warning me to stay out of trouble, he said he'd try to keep me posted and left.

I smiled, grateful to have heard a black person utter a friendly word. Was it only two days ago that I had been fêted at an integrated farewell party in Mississippi?

Confused and emotional, I left the office and drove to the ACLU house where I decided to hang out for the time being and ponder my future in Selma. After many hours sitting alone I came to the conclusion that if ACLU did not shut the whole operation down I would stay. I would work for other groups such as Dr. King's SCLC but I could not and *would not!* work for SNCC under these humiliating circumstances.

It took almost four days for SNCC to reestablish contact with me; Charles came to the ACLU house to tell me that "an important SNCC leader, H. 'Rap' Brown, is in jail and . . ."

"No!" I said, turning briskly back to papers on my desk. "I don't want to hear about it."

Unprepared for my reaction, Charles turned and left.

A few hours later he returned to ask me if I would take a call from Stokely Carmichael from the Meredith March "tonight at 8 PM?"

"Yes," I shrugged. It wouldn't make any difference; my mind was made up.

That night Carmichael telephoned me at the appointed hour. "Hi, Don!" boomed the charismatic twenty-five-year-old SNCC leader. "Glad to talk to you at last. Heard many fine things about you, as both a civil rights worker for SNCC and as a lawyer for SNCC."

"Thank you," I muttered.

"Sorry about the sign," he said, getting right to the point. "Whatever

Black Power comes to stand for," he continued, "it does not mean that we are planning to oust our white allies, especially one as essential to us as you."

"Tomorrow," he added, "we'll be in Philadelphia [Mississippi], where, as I know you well remember, three of our civil rights workers were murdered. One was black and two were white . . ."

"I'm sorry about Rap in jail . . . ," I interrupted.

". . . we needed a jolt to make us think out our priorities," Stokely laughed. But then his voice turned serious. "I hope you will continue to be our friend and represent us," he said. "And we really need you to help Rap as soon as you can."

When I paused he added, "There will be no more signs—and no more SNCC problems for you."

Once made, my decision felt good. "Okay," I said. "Tomorrow, first thing."

"Thank you," Carmichael replied. "And I'll expect you to call me if there is ever any trouble."

He then requested that I "wait ten minutes and then *please* go upstairs."

"I will." I said.

"Give 'em hell!" He hung up, leaving me to wonder if the "hell" he was calling down was for white racists or for the black power staffers upstairs.

As directed I waited the ten minutes and then walked into the hall just as Charles was taking down the sign. Then we both went upstairs to an initially nervous but eventually relieved and joyous reunion with my SNCC friends. Charles told me that Carmichael was impressed that I had initially refused to help Rap, that I "didn't take crap."

Carmichael said and wrote: "The goal of black self-determination and black self-identity—Black Power—is full participation in the decision-making process affecting the lives of black people."[18]

The SNCC chairman, who was chastised from within and from the media for having a "live-in" white lawyer, also wrote:

> It is our position that black organizations should be black-led and essentially black-staffed, with policy being made by black people. White people can and do play very important supportive roles in those organizations. Where they come with specific skills and techniques, they will be evaluated in those terms . . . [such as] white lawyers who defend black civil rights workers in court. . . .[19]

DEBUT IN SELMA

Now that Carmichael had given me the green light I was ready to begin work. Ironically the office I created in the heart of Black Power Selma started out with an all-white staff: a white secretary; a white volunteer lawyer from Toledo, Ohio; and two white law students from Harvard and the University of Chicago. Sharing space in the office was Shirley Mesher—also white—a former SCLC aide who was now a power in her own right among the grassroots blacks of Selma.

The Selma ACLU office was Southern-shabby with hollow separators creating small workspaces that did nothing to prevent every spoken word from being heard throughout the floor. One news feature described it as being "cluttered with leaflets, coke bottles, legal documents, boys from the street, civil rights workers and Negro citizens with complaints, all slightly agitated by a fan that fails to dispel the Alabama midsummer heat."[20]

That heat was the result of a "sweat-with-the-people" policy I inflicted on the office. It was my belief that clients without bathrooms should not have lawyers with air-conditioning. No one was happy about this policy—not Bronstein in Mississippi who resented the implication that his own air-conditioning somehow symbolized elitist privilege, and not my staff who begrudged scorching days too hot to work or to think. Even our clients hinted that they would have loved to have a cool place to come to.

While I also longed for a cool place to work, our sweltering office projected the image I desired: a People's law firm. My staff and I spent as many nights as we could outside relatively comfortable Selma, sleeping over in our clients' shacks and trying to become part of their community. However well-intentioned this effort might have been, the local sharecroppers later hinted that they would have preferred having a lawyer who dressed and acted like one. Though they appreciated having me stay over with them, they would have preferred a bit more reserve on my part. But having given up my New York career, I felt entitled to do it my own way, and I did.

Meanwhile the ACLU house was filling up with staff and hosted outside organizers working in the area. It was soon the civil rights center of Selma as SNCC workers visited and slept over—even Carmichael himself on occasion. The SNCC presence caused the FBI, always eager to assume that radical whites were in control of the Movement, to note in my FBI file: "_____ stated that SNCC has no organization operating at Selma, Alabama, and it appears the only contacts they have in this area are with JELINEK."[21]

The work in Selma was more often than not the same as in Mississippi: defense of criminal arrests, integration actions, brutality suits, and monitoring the various Civil Rights Acts. But it was a lonelier operation.

In Mississippi there had been three competing, full-time civil rights legal organizations. In Alabama I was the only full-time civil rights lawyer. I should add, even though this was true, saying it didn't endear me to local black lawyers who did part-time civil rights work in Alabama when they were not handling divorce and auto accident cases. Most had received their degrees in other states and were mostly paid by the NAACP LDF. Though I remained oblivious to their resentment of me, I would eventually pay dearly for my insensitivity.

There were other differences as well: in Mississippi civil rights money flowed freely but not in Alabama; in Mississippi the office was in the state capital, but in Alabama it was in Selma, population 30,000. In Jackson there was North Farish Street, bustling with civil rights organizing activity; in Selma the Movement occupied two floors of one building and one dilapidated house. There were other pockets of activity—SNCC also operated in Lowndes County, SCLC in Greene County—but there was no centralization and no "umbrella" for the Alabama civil rights community.

Was this it? Only a dozen SNCC members regularly in Selma and with SCLC almost gone? My confusion was based upon not understanding that in Alabama local blacks *were* the Movement, just as they surely were in Selma.

Still with fewer people I could more readily see and feel what was going on in town. Because almost the entire white power structure of Selma was located across the street I could often look at their faces and guess what kind of day lay ahead. If, as I approached my office, Mayor Joe Smitherman gave me something less than a snarl I could predict a good day; if Sheriff Jim Clark looked more menacing than usual I alerted our side to be careful and stay indoors if possible.

Meanwhile on my side of the street winds of change were continuing to blow. While I still worked for the integration of white institutions, Carmichael and SNCC were increasingly urging blacks to separate from the white world.

As the months passed my relationship with SNCC continued to evolve. My whiteness was never ignored but much of the attention to my race was lighthearted.

On one occasion I was working at SNCC headquarters in Atlanta, but as the day closed there was no mention of my being invited to eat and sleep over. When I hinted at my displeasure the SNCC workers gave in a little too easily. When it was time for me to go to bed, I was provided a cot from which the mattress had been removed, requiring me to sleep on a sheet covering sagging, creaky springs.

The next morning, stiff and aching, I awaited breakfast with a scowl until a SNCC friend started laughing. The laughter soon spread through the room as I joined in the merriment and received an extra helping of scrambled eggs.

Sometimes new SNCC workers would arrive and try to deploy their recently adopted black macho toward me. But the word was out: although white, I was a civil rights lawyer *and* a former SNCC civil rights worker —I was off limits!

THE ATLANTA PROJECT

My "safe passage" in the South came to an abrupt halt one end-of-summer day in 1966. I was driving to a small Alabama town where the following day black farmers and I were to meet a commander of the Alabama National Guard. We were to challenge a refusal to allow the use of the armory for a "black" event. On the way I gave a lift to a black SNCC worker who had a meeting of his own nearby.

It was dark by the time we approached a potholed driveway and saw a figure in the headlights. "It's Atlanta Project people!" my passenger exclaimed in alarm. "You shouldn't be here!"

Noting my confusion he quickly filled me in: "These are militant black separatists," he said, "who are demanding that all whites be excluded from SNCC. And they are also in opposition to Stokely Carmichael, who they insist is too sympathetic to whites."

Claiming white exclusion was what Black Power meant, they extended their criticism to black SNCC workers with white friends. These and other such efforts culminated in a SNCC policy that "discouraged" whites from functioning as organizers in black communities.

As the SNCC worker jumped out of my car I heard angry exchanges: "What's he doing here? You know no whites are allowed here!"

"He's a lawyer on a National Guard armory case," my passenger answered. "He's not staying here," he added. "He will be with the people who invited him."

As I drove off I heard an angry yell: "Drive out and don't come back!"

When I arrived at the place where I was to stay my annoyance at the incident melted away, replaced by much laughing, gossiping, and questions about goings-on in Selma. The day had been a scorcher so we ate our cornbread and greens on the porch as a dozen others, most still in field clothes, joined us for conversation.

It was a very enjoyable evening until four young black men drove up alongside the porch. One spoke from the car and ordered me to leave this house and community.

Before I could answer, my host yelled back that I was their guest, "a friend of the colored, and our lawyer who we need tomorrow."

"We don't need whites for anything," was the response. The folks on the porch murmured dissent but were clearly uncomfortable with the confrontation. I was getting angry but figured that once I explained exactly who I was the problem would pass. I left the porch and walked to the car.

I barely began speaking when the driver in a menacingly quiet voice whispered, "We *know* who you are. Now listen carefully! Get in your car and drive away—or you're dead!"

"No, damn it!" I yelled out. "I'm working for these people and no one is going to tell me what to do or where to stay or . . ."

That was as far as I got. The driver exited the car and put a gun to my head. He gave me until the count of three before he would pull the trigger.

A woman on the porch screamed.

Stunned and paralyzed with fear, I said: "I have a job to do and . . ."

The cocking of the pistol sounded to me like a clash of lightning. The driver quietly told me: "You'll be dead in seconds."

I could imagine the bullet penetrating my brain, which, if it would only function, would get me away from here. Then my host walked off the porch and begged me to leave *as a favor to him*!

"Okay," I gratefully said to everyone's relief, "if *you* say so."

As I slowly walked to my car I heard my host screaming at the young interlopers. I drove five or six miles, pulled off the road, and broke down sobbing uncontrollably from fear, humiliation, anger, and confusion. *Would he have pulled the trigger?*

I took a motel room and called Schwarzschild, who suggested I return that night to Selma. "No," I said. "If I am too afraid to do my work here I may as well leave and return to New York. I would never be able to function here again."

"Jean" with children (Donald A. Jelinek papers [M2225].
Department of Special Collections and University Archives,
Stanford University Libraries, Stanford, California).

The next morning only the sharecroppers appeared and we finished our work swiftly and successfully. Nothing was said but the extensive pats and hugs from my clients communicated their anguish.

I drove back to Selma, finding that the story had preceded me by at least five hours. Local SNCC workers were very upset for me, denouncing Atlanta Project people as dangerous militants.

I called Stokely—as he had invited me to, in case of trouble—but he didn't immediately return the call.

When I finally met up with him, he said, mock-fretting: "Can you imagine what would have happened to SNCC if that trigger had been pulled and resulted in the death of a white Jewish civil rights lawyer who identified with SNCC?"

"Not to mention what would have happened to me," I chimed in.

"Yes, there's that also," he conceded dryly. *True "black" humor,* I thought.

We laughed heartily.

The media learned of the encounter but I denied that anything had occurred, even to a friend who was a writer for the *New Republic*. He called me a liar and a masochist. We never spoke again, but SNCC workers commended me for "killing" the story.

Soon thereafter I heard that Atlanta Project members had been fired from SNCC.

By this time my white office secretary had left for home and I hired a young black woman named "Jean" to replace her. Soon we were working together and living together—along with her delightful children. Not surprisingly the development did not go unnoticed. We were very happy together, and I brought her to New York when I visited my parents.

On one occasion when I had work to do in Birmingham I invited Jean to come along with her children. Our first night in town we ate at a restaurant that catered to a black clientele.

After a half hour, a visibly agitated manager approached and told me that an angry black crowd had gathered outside yelling about this "white dude who took a black mama away from her old man." The manager feared they would break up his place coming for me and asked that I leave. Instead I telephoned a major civil rights leader who appeared and explained to the crowd that I was a lawyer working for the cause and that the woman was my secretary.

While I never again traveled with Jean in the South, in Selma, the very epicenter of Black Power, our relationship was accepted without complaint. We were invited to local parties, cafés and restaurants. We walked hand-in-hand through the black part of town, often to the movies.

Still, as militant Black Pride philosophy spread, it became more and more difficult for me to justify why I or any other white person should continue our role in the Movement. *Was white presence perpetuating the very dependency that black militants were talking about?*

Though Stokely had told me that Black Power was "not to oust our white allies," that's what was happening. Friction grew each day. Six months after my first conversation with the Black Power leader SNCC narrowly voted to expel whites from its ranks at a December 1966 retreat in upstate New York. Fannie Lou Hamer, one of the most notable figures in SNCC and the woman who had spoken so movingly on behalf of MFDP at the Atlantic City Convention, resigned in protest.[22]

Though the expulsions should have been expected, the reaction of white SNCC workers combined disbelief with hurt and anger. "We were good enough when we were beaten with you, jailed with you, and murdered with you," they lamented. Not to close the door completely, Carmichael called for some whites to work on a "volunteer contractual basis" in white communities in the South. Others could "organize the white community in the North around black needs, around black story, and the relative importance of blackness in the world today." Little came of this. It was essentially all over for whites in SNCC.

I, however, was not asked to leave.

With all this chaos I was grateful when fate placed in my lap a form of black power—in white cotton fields.

11

The Cotton Wars

O tis Blocton was a lean sharecropper in his early forties, living in a hardscrabble shack outside of Selma with his wife and seven children. During his first visit to my office he told me that though he had never made much of a living in the cotton fields, lately his meager earnings had taken a turn for the worse. He came to see me because he suspected he was being cheated.

Wondering if he might have made himself a target for retaliation, I asked if he had recently attempted to register to vote. "No," he responded. He had made an attempt earlier but he stopped trying after he was beaten by a deputy sheriff. But, he added with gumption, if he *could* vote he wanted it to be for something more than governor or sheriff. He wanted to vote in the "cotton elections."

Cotton elections. The phrase brought back vivid memories of the bullet holes that had riddled the walls of Molly's cabin after her minor inquiry into actions of the "cotton board." I had promised her that when I reached Alabama I would look into the connection (if any) between her question about federal cotton allotments and subsidies and the shooting that had threatened her life. That vow had been postponed in my hectic efforts to set up the new ACLU office, but now I would start.

According to a report by the US Commission on Civil Rights, the federal government had become involved with cotton farming in the South in the 1930s following "a drastic drop in world cotton prices . . . creating hardships more severe for Southern agriculture than for the country as a whole."[1] Southern landowners, notoriously bad farmers, had exacerbated the problem by cultivating cotton year after year while failing to rotate their crops. Severe soil consequences followed and made it increasingly difficult to earn a living from eroded and depleted land.

The Franklin Roosevelt administration legislated federal agricultural controls aimed at creating a better balance between supply and demand as a part of the New Deal. Laws and regulations limited the amount of land devoted to the production of cotton as well as corn, wheat, and peanuts, and paid farmers hard cash subsidies as an incentive *not* to plant. In addition mandatory emergency soil conservation programs were launched to encourage crop diversification.

Although federal law guaranteed income for cotton producers, essentially subsidizing the cotton industry, there was a troublesome snag. If crops were not planted and harvested there would be no (or less) revenue for the sharecroppers and tenant farmers whose income was based upon what they harvested. If the land they ordinarily planted sat idle, sharecroppers' income would be drastically affected and leave them unable to feed their families or pay their debts, leaving them vulnerable to reprisals.

The federal crop subsidy plan, therefore, provided that sharecroppers were entitled to a share of the subsidy allocated to the landowner. In theory, if it was discovered that landowners were depriving sharecroppers of their benefits, the USDA would withhold the owners' share of the payments. In addition a certain amount of land was *allowed* to be planted: the "allotment." Of course it was advantageous to plant a "cotton allotment" *and also* receive a subsidy for cotton not planted.

To implement these controls the federal government created the Agricultural Stabilization and Conservation Service (ASCS) administered by county committees, which determined how much land must lay fallow and the sum of money to be paid for cotton crops not planted. The size of the allotments was determined by the local ASCS whose members were elected in what was popularly called the "cotton elections." Of course, in the Jim Crow South, the "cotton vote" was denied to black sharecroppers in much the same manner as their vote for other public officials. Ballots sent out by the ASCS were received, cast, and counted locally, but despite black supermajorities in many rural counties no black farmer had ever been elected to a cotton board. Most often sharecroppers did not even receive a ballot.

Cotton was a very labor-intensive crop. Before the Civil War that labor had been supplied by black slaves; after the war it was mostly by black sharecroppers. The landed aristocracy may have lost the Civil War but never lost its sway over Southern agriculture. It did so by establishing a farm labor system that substituted debt for slavery. Sharecroppers were tied to white landowners who loaned them money to plant their crops, rent shacks, and purchase necessities at rates that ensured those farmers could never afford to leave the land: borrow, work, repay, and borrow again, a vicious cycle that reenslaved the sharecroppers after Reconstruction. And if they decided to leave the plantation they would be arrested for not paying their debt.

After harvesting their crop sharecroppers received "credit" for the value of their bales of cotton, often weighed by the plantation owner; they also received credit for their share of the federal subsidy for land not planted. But when the black farmers reimbursed the plantation owner for the "tab" they had run up in his store that season, the amount of the debt—also calculated by the landowner—was somehow always higher than the combination of the value of crop and subsidy. Sharecroppers would end the season in debt.

By winter their resources were usually exhausted, "slim rations" began, and the cycle would repeat. Under Southern control the New Deal agriculture laws served to make cotton production even more profitable for the landowners than it had been in slavery days. It was no longer necessary to purchase the slave laborers nor provide them with food, shelter, and supplies at the plantation owner's expense.

To protect this increasingly profitable system white planters enforced one-party Democratic Party rule throughout the region. Without two-party contests threatening their dominance and while benefiting from seniority rules, Southern congressmen and senators came to occupy strategic places on most of the powerful congressional committees, especially those dealing with cotton.

Although in its earliest years the Civil Rights Movement had been focused on fighting segregation and resisting racial brutality, it was soon realized that any struggle against economic racial injustice in the South would require a "Black Power" approach to federal programs such as those of the ASCS. In the fight for cotton parity each civil rights worker and lawyer stood on the shoulders of his or her daring predecessors.

During the Freedom Summer of 1964 an effort had begun to familiarize black farmers with the kinds of financial assistance available, help them win control of the ASCS, and then "divide the pie" much differently. Although threats and hostility against COFO and SNCC limited the 1964 effort, the cotton curtain eventually began to fray, if ever so slightly.

By July 1965 SNCC workers started holding local ASCS workshops with groups of ten to fifteen black farmers in six ASCS communities to explain the agency's programs and prepare for the upcoming ASCS election.

In Lowndes County, Alabama, an 80 percent black county, black farmers fielded a slate of candidates for the 1965 cotton elections. In response the all-white ASCS committee mounted a cunning resistance effort. Playing on the functional illiteracy of many black farmers, the whites nominated over a hundred candidates who had names similar to those on the black slate, effectively splitting the black vote and enabling another white victory.

Carmichael demanded that the election be reset and be conducted by federal officials: "If the government has spent billions of dollars to kill people in Vietnam to assure free elections, then they had better spend some of those dollars to assure free elections in Lowndes County ASCS."[2]

In June 1966 an embarrassed USDA voided the previous year's Lowndes ASCS election because white farmers had used fraudulent means to stay in power. New "make-up" elections were set for November 1966, although in the interim the same all-white ASCS boards remained in control.[3]

ASSIGNMENT OF THE ADVANCES

Before these elections could take place a federal bill was passed providing for sharecroppers to receive their government subsidy in advance. This seemingly minor change in the rules echoed throughout the white South like a thunderclap. If allowed to stand direct federal cash advances to black farmers would represent a full-frontal attack on the roots of the traditional sharecropping system. With cash in hand the farmers could purchase fertilizer, groceries, and other supplies at wholesale rates, bypassing landowners' commissaries. This would eliminate the necessity of turning to plantation owners for high-interest financing and could destroy the dependency upon which the whole oppressive system revolved.

Most black farmers in the Selma area worked under J. A. Minter, who owned over twelve thousand acres in Dallas County. The Minter family had been involved in plantation, mercantile, and ginning operations since the early nineteenth century. It was said that Minter managed his farm workers in the style of a late-nineteenth-century Bourbon planter: "He required his tenants to process their cotton at his gin, where they were paid in checks made out to him. When the tenants brought the gin checks to the Minter store, he paid them in scrip that they could spend only there."[4] In addition he made them purchase fertilizer from him at almost a third higher than the market rate.

Southern Congressmen quickly mobilized against the new "advance payment" bill. Before the first payment arrived the USDA added a "sweetener" for plantation owners: a right to exact a "prepayment" from the black farmers, who would then be forced to "assign" their federal payments to plantation owners to pay off the prepayment.

Shirley Mesher, the former SCLC worker, saw clearly that the forced assignment of the cotton money was a civil rights issue. In the spring of 1966 I joined a meeting she organized to discuss that situation with a visiting USDA investigator, who was to hear from local sharecroppers.

"I've lived on Mr. Minter's land all my life," one sharecropper said.

Another nodded. "Same with me, and now he's making us leave because we won't sign the paper."

A third man said, "I signed the paper, but it didn't make no difference."

Minter evicted twenty families who would not cooperate with him as well as those who had been working to integrate the white schools in rural Dallas County. If Minter could evict the farmers from the farms they would also be ineligible to participate in the ASCS program. Every black farmer at the meeting worked on Minter's land; the paper they were required to sign was an assignment of their subsidy advance.

The USDA agent promised to look into it. He believed that there must be room for reasonable compromise if we could all just sit down and talk to each other. The next day I called Minter's attorney, also the Selma City Attorney, who brushed me off.

Thus began my first agriculture litigation. I filed suit in Montgomery, Alabama—*Barlow v. Collins*—challenging the application of the assignment clause, using Minter's tenants as an example of the evils unleashed by the provision. Certain that the unmistakable injustice of the clause would result in it being quickly banned, I simply waited for the wheels of justice to turn.

Turn they did, against us. Alabama's US Attorney opposed the suit, which was dismissed by the district and appellate courts on the grounds that the farmers lacked the standing (the right to initiate or participate in a legal action) to protest the assignment clause. Minter had argued that the landlord has an absolute constitutional right to use and control his private property in any way he sees fit. Years later the US Supreme Court ruled in our favor, reversing the lower courts and declaring that the farmers had standing to challenge the assignment clause.[5]

I was quickly learning that successful litigation in the South could not be produced in the vacuum of a courtroom: publicity was needed with well-known figures recruited to offer their name and attend the proceedings so that the media—and thereby the nation—would pay attention. But resorting to the courts to address systematic Southern racism was not a strategy for the impatient. The NAACP Legal Defense Fund had famously waited decades for the favorable landmark ruling that became *Brown v. Board of Education.*

SWAFCA

Since the 1930s black farmers had become entangled in a wave of an agricultural transformation that had been working its way through the region. As agriculture began to be revolutionized by tractors, mechanical cotton pickers, and better herbicides, large landowners could plant, grow, and pick more crops without the aid of their black tenants. In many cases civil rights activity was the final straw, causing landlords to decide that it was time to send tenants packing.[6]

In 1966 the Southwest Alabama Farmworkers Cooperative Association (SWAFCA) was formed through the organizing work of Albert Turner, SCLC director in Alabama; Lewis Black, director of the Alabama Council on Human Relations; and Shirley Mesher.

The organizers of SWAFCA envisioned that the co-op would allow black farmers to buy in bulk at lower prices, avoid going into debt by not using the plantation owner as the county store, instruct on agricultural and farm economics issues, and have a general transformative impact on the self-esteem and confidence of its black member-owners. It also would instruct on better farming practices and give farmers the ability to shift out of cotton and corn and into more lucrative truck crops such as cucumbers that required less land. A vegetable producing and marketing cooperative started to take shape across the Black Belt by the end of July 1966.

In the co-op women "grew the crops more or less [while] the men would migrate out and try to find a job in the sawmill. . . ." For the first three weeks of June the co-op sold its members' cucumbers for 40 percent more per ton than they had received before joining the organization.[7] SWAFCA was seen as "the economic arm of the civil rights movement."[8] This economic foundation would keep people from having to move away and would also ensure the preservation of black voter strength.

DELAYING THE COTTON ELECTIONS

As the 1966 cotton elections neared Alabama's civil rights community and the National Sharecroppers Fund (NSF)geared up for a major campaign to elect black candidates in the coming September ASCS elections at the same time as the reset Lowndes County election. Their efforts would be augmented by summer volunteers from the North who would have two months to canvass voters, correct voter lists, obtain ballots and file appeals if necessary.

Then on July 10, 1966, Alabama's state ASCS board suddenly announced that it was moving up the date of the elections to August 16, 1966, with the day before as the deadline for mailing in ballots—almost a month earlier than the previously announced date. This would not be the first time the availability of summer volunteers had influenced Southern political actions. The Voting Rights Act, it was charged, was held up until the end of the summer of 1965 as a compromise with Southerners who wanted another year without a massive volunteer-generated black vote.

Soon a delegation headed by NSF leader Jac Wasserman was seated in my office, imploring me to force a delay of the ASCS elections and reinstate the original date.

I decided this was the moment to shift my strategic efforts from the courtroom to a wider arena and adapt a course of action that would expose corrupt manipulations by Southern federal employees: I would file a lawsuit designed to achieve a political goal as well as a favorable judicial position.

In order to attract national attention and the ear of US Secretary of Agriculture Orville Freeman, I decided not to file suit in Alabama where it would likely be given the back of the hand. Instead I would file in Washington DC, home to USDA headquarters.

I knew it would not be difficult to find black farmers to join the suit and that Carmichael and SNCC would sign on. But although Carmichael's reputation was growing exponentially around the nation, I also needed someone with exalted prestige. I needed Martin Luther King Jr. and the SCLC.

THE CIVIL RIGHTS LEADER

Born and raised in Atlanta, Georgia, Dr. King followed in his father's footsteps and became a man of the cloth. By 1954 he was pastor of the Dexter Avenue Baptist Church in Montgomery, Alabama, and a member of the executive committee of the NAACP. He rose to national prominence in 1955 as leader of the bus boycott in Montgomery that followed the arrest of Rosa Parks.

Dr. King had not sought to lead the Civil Rights Movement, but once leadership passed to him he devoted himself to promoting nonviolent tactics drawn from the ideas of India's Mahatma Gandhi. He promoted protests and demonstrations, which could (and often did) provoke a brutal response from local authorities. Violent acts that had been mostly confined to the dark of night or an isolated rural road now took place before the lenses of television cameras. As the horrors of the South became evening TV footage for Americans, it gave rise to a moral force to push for federal legislation to end three centuries of subjugation.

Although I had previously met Dr. King I had never had a substantive conversation with him. I had dealt with his organization in Mississippi and much more extensively since I arrived in Alabama. Many of my clients were highly regarded SCLC workers and I operated in Alabama counties that were very important to SCLC: Dallas, Greene, and Montgomery.

I decided to approach him by enlisting the aid of my friend Dorothy Cotton, who was a member of his inner circle and the highest-ranking woman in the SCLC. She had helped organize the student marches for the 1963 Birmingham protests, had marched with Dr. King on perilous Southern roads, and had accompanied him and his wife to Norway when he received the Nobel Peace Prize. As SCLC's education director, Cotton conducted citizenship classes throughout the South and often invited me to speak at her events.

When I nervously asked Dorothy if it would be appropriate for me to request a meeting with Dr. King, she said that it would not be difficult for her to arrange a meeting given my history. Detecting my anxiety about conversing with the man who embodied the hopes and dreams of the Civil Rights Movement, she was gently reassuring. "He is the kindest, most generous person you could talk to. You'll do fine."

I told her that I was uneasy because I thought of Dr. King as a celebrated man whom I had read about and watched on television—not

Dorothy Cotton
(Donald A. Jelinek papers
[M2225]. Department of
Special Collections and
University Archives, Stan-
ford University Libraries,
Stanford, California).

someone I might *actually* work with. She tried to be encouraging, but I whined, "Why would he listen to *me*?"

She gave me a hug and said he knew of and respected my work. According to Dorothy he "welcomed [Don's] participation with him in that great struggle for justice," and that "Don could have been with a great law firm . . . but chose to be with us."

Then she laughed, "Won't talking to him be easier than getting beat up at a reservoir or being shot at while driving on a Mississippi dirt road? You'll do fine," she assured me. "Let's go to the movies tonight and watch a white Alabama lawyer mop up the floor with Southern racists." I smiled. I knew she was referring to the revival in Atlanta of the film *To Kill a Mockingbird* with Gregory Peck as Atticus Finch.

When I left the theater that night I was ready for a meeting with Martin Luther King Jr.

As I prepared to meet the SCLC chief I thought of the contradictions of his life: a Nobel Peace Prize winner who witnessed death and violence under his leadership, a man who the FBI considered "the most notorious liar in the country [and a threat to the nation] should he abandon his supposed 'obedience to nonviolence,'" and a clergyman who was unsure about cooperation with fellow clergymen who wanted to "smooth the waters" on the eve of the Selma Bridge protest. He was scorned for diffusing the Movement by opposing the war in Vietnam and condemned for not opposing it sooner; he was beatified in life yet deplored by militant civil rights workers who thought he was too passive.

MEETING WITH DR. KING

Within days of the announcement that the state ASCS had advanced the date of the cotton elections, I drove to SCLC headquarters in Atlanta, located near the place of Dr. King's birth and the Ebenezer Baptist Church where his father still preached.

The SCLC office was a run-down storefront in a poor black section of the city. I had expected an orderly workspace to match Dr. King's quiet purposefulness, but instead I found chaos and anarchy. Various phones were ringing and only occasionally answered, mail was strewn over desks, and among the letters that had fallen to the floor was an unopened envelope from US Attorney General Robert Kennedy.

Everyone seemed to be yelling at the small stocky black man dressed in an open-collar white shirt and smart gray slacks—in contrast to most of the others who were wearing work shirts and jeans. Dr. King, then 37, appeared to be tracking everything that was thrown at him.

"Can you speak at [such and such] college next month?"

"Yes."

"On the sixteenth?"

"I think so."

"Will you endorse [so and so] for election?"

"I try not to endorse anyone; see if it's necessary."

"How about dinner tonight with Rev. [somebody]?"

"Ask Coretta."

"Will you do a guest sermon at [this one's] church, appear at a fund raising dinner, and meet [someone]?"

No one wrote down his answers, but as I had learned many times in the black South, New York-style efficiency was not the only way to get things done.

I was ignored while all this was going on except for "Hiya's" from the few staffers I knew. Finally during a break in the turmoil, Dorothy led me to Dr. King, who warmly shook my hand, congratulated my work with SCLC workers in Alabama, and asked what I wanted to talk about. I got three words out before his staff began pulling at him again.

This is his life, I thought, and the pulling was only getting stronger: Denounce Black Power! Endorse Black Power! Oppose the Vietnam War!

March! Don't march! Defy the injunction! Obey the courts! Call for calm! Release your people to retaliate!

It must have been an incredible pressure, I reflected, to be seen as the living symbol of morality. That day Dr. King seemed to me like Jesus of Niko Kazantzakis' historical novel, *The Last Temptation of Christ*—a man identified as the Messiah but with grave self-doubts. Maybe it was all a mistake.

I looked helplessly at Dorothy who, as an SCLC veteran, could yell at him.

"Martin! Donald's come all the way from Selma (*the magic word*) and you should talk with him. In quiet!" "Okay," he yelled back over the roar to Andy Young, his senior aide, and a few others.[9] "Come with me to the café. I want you to hear something."

Calm did indeed reign in the quiet "black" café as we sat at a rear table set aside for SCLC private conversations. Coffee and doughnuts were quickly placed and the waitress absented herself. There were no introductions. Asked to make a presentation, I began a laborious explanation of the cotton programs. In the middle of the subsidy part Dr. King was called to the front of the café to talk with another aide.

Discouraged, I looked at Dorothy who signaled for me to continue. I continued. Fifteen minutes later, upon Dr. King's return, he motioned for me to resume while Andy Young whispered in his ear, presumably delivering a summary of what he had missed. Twenty minutes later, Dr. King interrupted me.

"I understand. I like your plan . . . but why DC? Why bring the farmers? Do you have enough money, cars, food, sleeping accommodations? He paused and asked, "And have you provided for medical needs?"

I had not thought much about logistics and, while embarrassed, I was impressed by his humanity as well as his practical concerns. I admitted— and pledged to remedy—the lack of logistical planning.

"What is SNCC's position," he suddenly asked, "about joining in this with me?"

I knew Dr. King was scorned by SNCC for not having completed the second Selma march, for his late entry against the Vietnam War, and for his caution. He was mocked for his piousness and authority and called "Da Lord." I did not join in (or agree with) these attacks on him, but he knew I was aligned with SNCC.

"Stokely knows I'm here," I replied to him, "and will be present in the courtroom. He hopes that you'll join him in Washington, DC, for the hearing." Dr. King smiled, sensing my enthusiastic but subtle exaggeration, ignoring the tension between the two organizations. After a half hour I concluded with a candid admission: "I need the prestige of SCLC on the legal papers and your presence at the hearing to attract national attention to achieve our goals."

I believe he had made up his mind before I arrived based on Dorothy's advance summary; the meeting was to size me up. Dr. King announced approval for me to use the SCLC name and that he himself would appear "if possible and appropriate."

I thanked everyone, smiled at Dorothy, and left. I had other work to do in Atlanta: I needed to keep my SCLC/SNCC neutrality intact. I got into my car to drive to SNCC headquarters. Still I was so exhilarated at the prospect of working directly with Dr. King that I had to get out of the car and walk around the block to calm myself.

THE TRIP TO WASHINGTON

Time was working against us. Within days we needed a lawsuit to explain the federal program, document the abuses conducted within it, and plead for the postponement of the cotton elections—now just a few weeks away. I had already explained the lawsuit to the farmers, discussed their fears, interviewed them, and signed them up.

The final lawsuit, *William v. Freeman,* had thirty-six plaintiffs with farmers from twenty-three cities in eleven Alabama counties. Each was described in the legal papers as a "Negro, poor, a sharecropper or tenant farmer or small farm owner, and dependent on cotton farming for a livelihood."[10] Each farmer was prepared to testify that the ASCS routinely cheated them out of their benefits and denied them the right to serve on ASCS boards. Orville L. Freeman, Secretary of the US Department of Agriculture, was the lead defendant in our lawsuit asking the court to compel USDA to restrain their Alabama affiliate from holding premature elections. A court hearing was set for August 9 in DC, one week before the cotton elections.

Before I left Alabama I received a leaked copy of a secret USDA report documenting the department's 1965 civil rights activities. The report set forth many, many instances of USDA discrimination and contained "evaluations" which substantiated the charges in our lawsuit. The cover page read as follows:

January 21, 1966
To: The Secretary [of Agriculture]
From: William M. Seaborn, Assistant to the Secretary

Attached is the year-end report on civil rights activities in the Department in 1965. If you wish to transmit this report to the White
House, **you may wish to omit the sections entitled "Evaluation."**
/s/ Wm. M. Seaborn"[11]

Not tell the President? I was staggered. The report contained numerous instances of USDA discrimination—but it would be *better* if the
President was not told about them! The evaluations had been removed
from the Presidential copy.

I flew to DC to prepare for the hearing and to work on the logistics
of the housing and feeding of the witnesses and their families. Thirty-six
farmers with family members were driving to the capital, most on their
first trip out of the Deep South.

Once we were all in the courtroom for a prehearing conference, US
District Judge Howard Corcoran voiced his opinion that a conference
between both sides might resolve the issue with a compromise. I was
pleased. I had written to Secretary Freeman that the "real bad guys" are
the Southern racists hiding behind federal badges and federal payrolls—
that this should not be an adversary proceeding.

MEETING WITH USDA

On the eve of the court hearing eighteen top officials of the USDA sat at
a table of a length that all eighteen could face us directly. "Us" were two
local progressive lawyers acting as co-counsel, a black USDA civil rights
official who sat uncomfortably on our side of the table, and me. I did
not invite Stokely Carmichael or Dr. King, nor had I asked any of the
farmers to attend. This meeting, I envisioned, would go better if only we
professionals were present.

I had prepared a speech for the court hearing and decided to deliver it
here first.

"The problem," I began, "is poverty. It is poverty that keeps the Negro
in his place—poverty that keeps him from registering, poverty that keeps
his children in segregated schools, poverty that keeps him from enjoying
the comforts and privileges of white society. This poverty is enabling the
white Southerner to enter upon a new post-Reconstruction period, when
once again federal legislation is nullified and past gains are repealed."

"The federal government can cure the problem of poverty," I continued. "I don't mean welfare. I'm talking about providing the Southern
Negro with millions of dollars—in cash, rights, and services—that are

rightfully his but are taken away by Southern-born, Southern-bred, and federal-salaried employees."

The federal Agricultural Extension Service, I pointed out, is charged with providing technical assistance to all the nation's farmers but routinely deny help to Southern black farmers. "Your Soil Conservation Service will not service Negroes," I said. "The Farmers Home Administration will not loan money to Negroes to buy land."

I then argued that the only way this situation will change is if black tenant farmers gain representation on the local and state cotton boards—a move that white landowners are resisting with every tactic in their arsenal.

"We need time to get ready for the elections," I concluded. "We are here because the Alabama ASCS set the elections early this year so we could *not* be ready. In a memo to you to justify the new date, ASCS argued that 'the slack season between planting and harvesting is the best time for the election, and also that the farmers are transients who are not present after the harvest.' Nonsense! The ballot is mailed, so how could crop season affect marking five Xs and placing the ballot in the mail? And as to transiency, I have a memo here of a conversation with the Alabama State Employment Service which indicates that this is a minimal transiency period. The real reason for the new date," I insisted, "is so we won't be ready. We need your help so we can be ready. You must order the state agency to change the date back to the normal September date."[12]

I spoke for three-and-a-half hours rattling off specific events, names and dates, producing documents, and quoting the report of the US Commission on Civil Rights. I hinted at but avoided mentioning the secret USDA report.

When finished I was hoarse and choked up, but I thought my goal was in sight: I had brought our message to the center of power, the bowels of the government. Huge gains can be accomplished in this town by simply picking up a telephone. Surely by bringing USDA this information about injustices done in their name we could achieve a minor one-month delay of an Alabama agricultural election.

"Well, that's all I have to say," I said as I looked down at the mass of papers spread across our side of the table. I felt lightheaded as I accepted the congratulations of my co-counsel.

The eighteen men across the table exchanged glances waiting for their designated speaker to begin. That turned out to be a senior USDA official who also congratulated me for my presentation. "You're the type of young man we need, who keeps us on our toes." It turned out he was full of clichés that evening, each sounding more ominous than the last: "Rome wasn't built in a day" and "All things come to those who wait."

"There is a very delicate balance between the relationship of the federal government and the Southern states," he continued. "If we are ever going to bring about a change down there we have to go very slowly and very cautiously."

He paused. I held my breath. "We know most of what you've charged . . . and more. We've had our office of the Inspector General investigating the incidents you've described." He nodded in the direction of a pinched-looking man seated nearby with stacks of neatly piled binders in front of him.

Slowly and solemnly now, he continued, "Great changes have been accomplished, but *you* people can never have enough. Look how far we've gone. We must learn to live with the Southerners or else we can never deal with them. What does a year mean? Wait for the 1967 elections when it can be done right."

"But under no circumstances," he suddenly thundered, "will the USDA overrule a decision of a state ASCS and we doubt a court can, or would, order us to do so! I'm sorry."

The USDA men rose to their feet to leave. They had complied with the judge's order to negotiate. The answer to our request was an emphatic "No!"

I thanked my co-counsel; either more cynical or less naive than I, they were not especially surprised or upset at the result. Back in my room I poured out the story over the phone to Carmichael and then to Dr. King. Not surprisingly Carmichael gave me his "I-told-you-so" rejoinder, but in truth I thought he sounded more disappointed than he cared to admit. Dr. King thanked me for notifying him promptly; he later decided not to come to DC.

That night I called the wire services and angrily related the story of the secret report. Despite my intemperately calling Alabama USDA officials "crackers in federal uniforms," UPI spread the story across the country: "A super-secret Agriculture Department self-appraisal of its shortcomings in racial matters [is being used] in a ground-breaking federal suit." This forced a direct response from Secretary Freeman asserting that a delay in the ASCS elections "would disrupt efforts already made to run the elections fairly."

The ASCS, however, was uncomfortably reacting to its notoriety. On the morning before the day of the hearing in DC the state ASCS in

Alabama announced it would have "a member of its civil rights advisory committee sit in on all future meetings."[13]

THE COURT HEARING

The court hearing began on the morning of August 9, 1966, with thirty-six black farmers dressed in their Sunday best seated in a federal courtroom in the nation's capital. They were joined by their families, a dark-suited Stokely Carmichael, and representatives from various rural civil rights organizations, including the NSF. There were also a large number of reporters.

I began for our side by reciting my previous day's presentation accompanied by gentle choruses of "Amen" and "Ah hah" delivered so softly that the judge could not bring himself to silence the audience. Judge Corcoran, clearly annoyed by the failure of the negotiations and the reappearance of this case on his overbooked court calendar, was also visibly uncomfortable by the presence of the press, Carmichael, and the farmers themselves.

At one point he chastised me for keeping my clients from their crops. "Let's try to hurry things along so all these people can go home." I responded, "Only when the people come to Washington does the government listen."[14]

One of our first offers of evidence was a US Civil Rights Commission report on discrimination in federal agriculture programs. I then placed in evidence the USDA "secret" report with its cover letter cautioning that certain findings embedded in the report were not to be shown to the White House. I was pleased to see the judge sneaking a look at the cover letter to see if I had misstated its content.

The first in-person witness was a slim, black Alabama farmer in his fifties who had been a candidate in the previous year's ASCS elections. Peter Agee of Magnolia, Alabama, who had never previously set foot outside of his home state, was now swearing to tell the whole truth in the paneled elegance of a Washington DC federal courtroom.

He told the judge how a white ASCS county employee named Frank Shields had tried to bribe him and then threatened him. Agee described the day that he was returning to his house and hid when he saw Shields sitting on his front porch. "I dodged him," he said. "I went around through a corn field. I stood and looked at him, but he didn't see me."

"Why were you dodging him?" I asked Agee.

My witness looked askance at my foolish question. "When you see a white man sitting on your porch and you have signed something like what I have signed [candidacy papers for the 1966 ASCS ballot]. . . . Well, let's just say I didn't know what he had in mind."

Shields, Agee testified, persisted and eventually made contact. At first he offered an increase of Agee's cotton allotment. "He said to me, 'Peter, I will [also] give you ten acres of the best farming land and I will show you how to get loans for cows . . . if you just come out of . . . this election. That's ten head of the best cows and some land that would make two bales of cotton to the acre. You just come on down there and look at it.'"

"I looked him in the eye," Agee said, "and told him, 'I am going to hold on.'"

"Did you have a conversation about coming to this court?"

"They asked me not to go to Washington . . . but I came anyway. I don't know what the results will be when I get back."

The judge inquired, "*Who* asked you not to come to Washington?"

"That was this [ASCS] committeeman, Mr. Frank Shields. . . . '[N]o harm is going to come to you [he said], but don't go to Washington.'"

"I was a little afraid of Shields," Agee told the judge, "and shaking—just like I am now, but I didn't give in."[15]

Agee had been a strong witness and the press took feverish notes as he accused an ASCS federal official of bribery and intimidation. The stylized formal question and answer courtroom ritual had revealed something of the real world of white power and black fear.

After a long recess and before our second witness had a chance to take the stand, the government capitulated. They reversed themselves, agreed to overrule the Alabama ASCS and to extend the election for one month.[16] Carmichael said, "The extension will allow us to combine the momentum and organization of the November 8 [general] election with that of ASCS."

The farmers were ecstatic.

Soon a USDA truck brought boxes of blue pamphlets explaining the ASCS election process. There would also be a special financial grant for voter instruction. But despite the enthusiasm that had accompanied our victory in court, we were out-organized: the plantation owners mobilized and during that extra month and collected the ballots of the black farmers so as to save them the "trouble and expense" of mailing them.

In the end we lost badly. Not a single black farmer was elected to the ASCS.

Peter Agee returned home after his day on the witness stand and was working in the family store when some white men came in and threatened him. A few hours later other white men drove by and fired shots in the air. When white civil rights worker Dick Reavis called for the police to intervene, they instead arrested three blacks in the vicinity along with Reavis himself for objecting to their search of the Agee store without a warrant.

Agee knew his county. He would have to leave his lifelong home. He fled to Memphis a few hours before a group of white men told his sister to look behind the store, saying, "If you find a body there," one said, "it might be your brother."

I whipped off a letter to Judge Corcoran, enclosing a news clipping which detailed "the fate of a witness before your honor who dared tell the truth about bribery and intimidation."

I wondered if I had done wrong to take the farmers into such high risks: homes, livelihood and safety—in other words, everything. I was pained when that which I worried about occurred. Some of the farmers who traveled to Washington were evicted from land they had lived on for generations. They had no other work, no other place to go, and no other means to earn money. They were cut loose. They had shown great courage and now there was a price to pay.

Although bittersweet this *was* still a victory. In Washington DC we had demonstrated that we could overpower the USDA, at least under certain controlled circumstances. I also sensed we had a bit more muscle here at home: one Alabama farmer told a reporter that he had experienced some surprising improvements in getting information and help from the ASCS. "Something done shook 'em up," he was quoted as saying.

For their part members of the white agricultural establishment in Alabama had not been very concerned with the date extension. They had always known that a month either way would not change the results of the cotton elections. But they *were* concerned that the mighty federal agriculture department had been forced to interfere with the affairs of the ASCS—setting a precedent that they feared could affect the multibillion-dollar federal subsidy and allotment program. The earth supporting the corrupt system of Southern agriculture had not moved—but it definitely had trembled.

And within a few years black farmers began serving on the ASCS.

12

Black versus Black
in the 1966 Elections

The Voting Rights Act of 1965 ensured that there would be legions of newly registered black voters in the Deep South ready to vote in the next elections. By 1966 there were over 10,000 blacks registered to vote in Dallas County (which included Selma), a huge increase over the mere 335 who were registered at the start of 1965—but whites too had been registering voters and had 12,500 on the voting rolls.[1]

However it was also becoming clear that there were now deep divisions in the Civil Rights Movement which could undermine the impact of those votes.

Discord was not new in the fight for racial justice; the Movement had never been the cohesive entity that the media imagined. The reality was much more multifaceted than the simplistic view that the Civil Rights Movement was Martin Luther King Jr. leading his junior auxiliary of young civil rights workers into battle to fight the good fight. There were always multiple factions within the civil rights community, each claiming supremacy, some barely tolerating one another.

The 1955 Montgomery bus boycott had catapulted Dr. King to national prominence as *the* leader of the Civil Rights Movement with his then newly formed SCLC. But then came that moment in February 1960 when four black college students sat down at a whites-only lunch counter in Greensboro, North Carolina. They politely demanded the right to eat in this Woolworth's store *while seated,* and although they were denied that right, their defiant act ignited young black students in surrounding areas to take similar action. The arrests and beatings that followed triggered solidarity sit-ins in the Upper South and boycotts of Woolworth stores in the North.

SNCC was founded in April 1960 by black students who had emerged as leaders of the sit-in protest movement. It had originally formed to coordinate that protest but then later also joined it. Although King had hoped that SNCC would serve as the youth wing of his organization, the students remained fiercely independent of King and SCLC, generating their own projects and strategies.

The next year, these activists effectively replaced the Freedom Riders, most of whom were jailed or so badly beaten that they could not continue.

In his 1961 inaugural address President Kennedy told the nation: "Let the word go forth from this time and place . . . that the torch of freedom has been passed to a new generation of Americans."[2] The young SNCC civil rights workers began to vigorously assert that it was *their generation,* not the President's nor Dr. King's, which had received that torch—and they adopted their own, more aggressive approach.

The activist landscape was dominated by two civil rights groups: SCLC, with Dr. King focusing the national media spotlight on the ever-changing pageant of injustice in the South, and SNCC, which adopted a grassroots approach by organizing black sharecroppers, creating local movements, and slowly building indigenous leadership.

In the spring of 1965 the nation's attention was focused on Selma, Alabama, where SNCC had worked for two years to achieve significant breakthroughs in organizing all while facing Sheriff Jim Clark, one of the most violent and racist sheriffs in the Deep South. That year a local judge had issued an injunction forbidding groups of three persons or more from gathering publicly. This injunction, which effectively stymied SNCC, spurred the local leadership to ask Dr. King to bring his forces to Selma to take over an organizing struggle that they believed had stalled and which, they claimed, SNCC had proved unable to handle.

ELECTORAL RIVALRY

Thus it was no surprise then that the general elections of 1966 would spark sectarian tensions in the upcoming elections in Selma. As election day approached black activists in Selma fractured into two camps: the Dallas County Independent Free Voters Organization, popularly dubbed the "Free Voters," a grassroots, black-dominated organization independent of but aligned with SNCC; and the Dallas County Voters League, also known as the "Voters League," made up primarily of middle-class black citizens.

The prosperous members of the Voters League demonized the Free Voters, Black Power, and even SWAFCA. It was said that "many of the rural black elite saw the rise of any type of new political or civil rights organization as a threat to the carefully worked out race relations that existed in their particular county or region."[3] The Free Voters supported an all-black independent slate and received aid from SNCC organizers and Shirley Mesher, then in her early thirties, who had come to Selma from Seattle, Washington, for the demonstrations following "Bloody Sunday."

Because of her public relations talents Dr. King's forces had drafted Mesher out of the ranks to join the post-march planning committee as a $25 per-week SCLC "subsistence worker." With the departure of most of the media-savvy superstructure following the march, she began working with the coordinated grassroots effort that now had room to emerge and which eventually organized itself into the Free Voters.

A maverick within Dr. King's ranks, Mesher found herself caught in the crossfire between the two black political parties. King could not discharge her because of her grassroots popularity, yet he could not fully endorse her efforts and risk antagonizing the local established black leadership. Eventually Mesher herself resolved the tension, deciding to resign from SCLC but electing to stay on in Selma, sustaining herself with food and lodging from her new grassroots community.

Meanwhile the two opposing parties of black Selma residents matched the conflicts between SCLC and SNCC begun during the final stages of the Selma campaign. SCLC opted to link up with traditional local black leaders while SNCC hoped to develop leadership among individuals who normally had no say in their communities.

The split had a strategic component to get rid of the savage Jim Clark who was running for re-election as sheriff in the upcoming election. The Free Voters recruited a slate of black candidates, including their chosen contender for sheriff. The Voters League believed that since a black candidate could not prevail in the election for sheriff, they would attempt to defeat Clark by backing a white moderate opponent: Wilson Baker, a former public safety director who had previously headed the city police. To achieve that end the Voters League felt a pragmatic necessity to support the *entire* Democratic Party slate even though that ballot was headed—embarrassingly!—by Lurleen Wallace running as a stand-in for her term-limited, segregationist husband, George Wallace.

Shirley Mesher and Don Jelinek at Selma office (Donald A. Jelinek papers [M2225]. Department of Special Collections and University Archives, Stanford University Libraries, Stanford, California).

Most of the longtime leaders of the black community called for participating in the Democratic Party primary to vote against Clark despite the fact that anyone who participated in the Free Voters nominating convention was barred by law from casting ballots in the primary. This was an either/or situation, leading to a bitter debate between the two factions: the mainline black leaders argued that so long as white voters are in the majority black candidates cannot win regardless of what party they belong to, and so it was claimed the supporters of the Free Voters would be "wasting" the votes of the black community. It would be a needlessly provocative act for new black voters to break entirely with the Democratic Party and vote for an all-black slate in Selma's first integrated election. Black residents were urged to vote the straight Democratic party line slate although that would mean no votes for any of the black candidates

The Free Voters, on the other hand, argued that this "lesser-of-two-evils" electoral strategy simply guarantees the triumph of racism in one form or another, and they accused the elder leaders of seeking to preserve their power and influence against poorer and more radical upstarts.

The May primary race was tight and bitter even though Baker was on the Democratic Party ballot and Clark ran only as a write-in. With solid backing from middle-class blacks and partial support from town whites, Baker held a small lead. But when Clark challenged 1,600 votes from three predominantly black precincts, the election was thrown into the courts and fiercely contested. The ruling went against Clark; Baker won the primary nomination as the Democratic Party candidate for sheriff and Lurleen Wallace was nominated for governor.

THE BOYNTONS

By the time I received the green light to work in Selma, a racial scorecard was needed to track all the players: Black versus Black, White versus White, Black versus White, SNCC versus SCLC, and Sheriff Jim Clark's people against just about everyone else.

I could see why I had been warned by Schwarzschild to avoid getting involved in the local elections, but he had also given me a conflicting piece of advice: to court. Amelia Boynton (Robinson), a leader of the Voters League, and try to win her good will.

The Boyntons were a prominent and politically active well-to-do local black family. Amelia Boynton, called the matriarch of the Voting Rights Movement, was born in Savannah, Georgia, in 1911 and as a child traveled with her mother by horse and buggy to pass out leaflets advocating women's suffrage. At age fourteen she entered what was then the "Georgia State Industrial College for Colored Youth" and then transferred to Tuskegee Institute where she studied under George Washington Carver.

She spent decades beginning in the 1930s attempting to register black voters in Alabama at a time when the practice was considered fruitless and quite dangerous. In 1963 she became the first black person since Reconstruction to run for the US Congress from Alabama. Boynton had met Dr. King in 1954, and her home was a meeting ground for civil rights leaders in the area; the Selma-to-Montgomery marches were planned there and an early draft of the Voting Rights Act was written there.

In 1965 she was in the front ranks of the Selma March and was clubbed unconscious by a state trooper; there was fear for her survival. But she was a guest of honor at the White House a half a year later when President Johnson signed the Voting Rights Act into law, an event seen as a direct consequence of the marches.

By 1966 she was a leader of the Voters League in vehement opposition to the Free Voters, which she believed would result in Sheriff Jim Clark being reelected. Boynton operated a real estate office located in a storefront in Selma; she occupied the front room while her son Bruce conducted his law practice in the back of the office. Bruce Boynton was best known as a test-case plaintiff in a lawsuit that established the right to integrate bus terminals—a case that became the rationale for the

Freedom Rides.[4] He was also to be the legal sponsor I needed to practice in the Alabama courts as Jess Brown had been for me and others in Mississippi.

When I introduced myself to the matronly well-groomed Amelia Boynton, her greeting was cool. After a few moments of ritual weather talk she asked if what she heard was true: that Shirley Mesher was sharing space in my office. Pausing briefly for my affirmation, she launched into a denouncement of Mesher who, she asserted, was compromising efforts to defeat Sheriff Clark by supporting a "virtually illiterate Negro" for sheriff.

And, she added with venom, she'd heard that Mesher referred to her as "bourgeois," and to her son Bruce as a "no account, sellout lawyer." Mrs. Boynton produced a leaflet put out by the Free Voters, accusing the Voters League of "trying to mis-lead Negroes and SELLOUT for Personal gain. They have SOLD THEIR SOULS . . . YOU need not sell yours . . . DON'T BE TRICKED BACK INTO SLAVERY. DON'T BE FOOLED!"

Boynton stated that I was empowering Mesher by allowing her to use my office—in effect sabotaging the work of the true Negro leadership in Dallas County. I continued my bad start when I rejected her ultimatum that came in the form of a question: "Do you plan to allow Shirley to remain in your office?"

Although I barely knew Mesher at that time, I tend to bridle at ultimatums.

"Absolutely," I said firmly.

"Well," Boynton replied archly, "this will make our relationship less productive than I had hoped."

"I hope that when I better understand the situation here, we can be good friends," I said cheerfully as I headed for the door, my smile locked in place. In little over five minutes I had earned the enmity of Boynton, her son, and by extension most of the ministers and middle-class blacks in Selma.

Each side was certain that its position was on the "side of the angels": the Free Voters were convinced that the real message of their opponents was that "dumb, lower income blacks" should remain in their subordinate status; the Voters League believed that supporting a third party candidate would reelect Jim Clark.

As I walked out the door I was startled to come face-to-face with the infamous Sheriff Clark whose posse had beaten Boynton. Life in Selma would be far from uncomplicated.

INCITING A NON-RIOT ON THE EVE OF THE ELECTION

There have always been potential black voting majorities in certain counties throughout the South—those counties where slaves had been clustered because plantations were located where the soil was richest. To encourage a high turnout of those recently registered to vote under the new voting rights law, a SNCC sound truck traveled through the black downtown a few days before the election.

The newly registered citizens were exhorted to vote for the grassroots slate and against the wife of George Wallace and the elite blacks who support her. The driver would shout: "Vote the Free Voters Organization!" and then attack the Voters League using words similar to those in the leaflet Boynton had shown me.

From my window I could hear the sound truck when it came down our street; I could see the heads of white officials in their windows across the street, peeking out from offices in the jail, police department, fire station, and city hall.

Driving the sound truck was Thomas Taylor, a tall, lanky black militant in his late twenties who had traveled from Pennsylvania for the elections. A SNCC volunteer with a daunting presence, he was wearing a Muslim cap, beads, and jeans. He double-parked the truck on our side of the street at the edge of a large, multiple-lane, virtually empty roadway. He planned to run upstairs to the SNCC office for further instructions.

As people learn to listen to silence as well as sound, so did the tenants of the Selma Movement offices react to the turning off of the sound truck amplifier. From my window I saw a city policeman approaching the driver's side of the truck.

Told he was "blocking traffic," Taylor was ordered to move the truck, but before he could do so, according to eyewitnesses, a policeman struck him through the open window.[5] Taylor rolled up his window as his attacker ran to his police car and grabbed a shotgun. He then returned and smashed "the closed window . . . with the butt of his shotgun and ordered [Taylor] from the truck at gun point." Taylor was then "struck . . . with the muzzle of the shotgun" and "further assaulted by city policemen and firemen," as he was taken to the jail through an alley across the street.

Hitting the street at the same time, Carmichael and I saw Taylor being led away. Two police on motorcycles roared across the street to get in on the action, joining the officer with the shotgun who was now threatening onlookers. As a crowd of black farmers in town for Saturday shopping

Selma police cruiser and SNCC sound truck, Selma 1966 (Donald A. Jelinek papers [M2225]. Department of Special Collections and University Archives, Stanford University Libraries, Stanford, California).

Police officer with shotgun approaching SNCC sound truck, Selma 1966 (Donald A. Jelinek papers [M2225]. Department of Special Collections and University Archives, Stanford University Libraries, Stanford, California).

SNCC volunteer Thomas Taylor being arrested, Selma 1966 (Donald A. Jelinek papers [M2225]. Department of Special Collections and University Archives, Stanford University Libraries, Stanford, California).

watched silently, one could hear the shutter clicks of SNCC photographers present for the elections.

Although Carmichael was chairman of SNCC, Stu House was the SNCC leader for the Selma area and was present when the police officer arrested Taylor. It was he who stepped forward and urged the crowd to vote for the grassroots candidates to end such police abuse.

Police officials immediately demanded that he cease orating "because it might cause a riot." House boldly responded that the people were orderly "as always," and it was "only the city police which continuously rioted." House was given one more chance, but he refused to stop speaking and was arrested for inciting to riot. He too was led away.

Before anyone could move, eager to up the ante, the police announced they were seizing the sound truck. This would be overtly illegal but instead of words of protest, I froze. Filling the vacuum, Carmichael spoke softly, even timidly to the police: "I'll drive the truck away, sir," he said, meekly, "so it won't block traffic." Without waiting for an answer, he serenely walked to the truck. The police looked at each other but Carmichael's logic and calm had rendered them immobile. He climbed into the driver's seat and drove slowly away down the street. (He later told me he blessed the presence of keys still in the ignition.)

(left) SNCC activist Stu House imploring gathered crowd to vote, Selma 1966 (Donald A. Jelinek papers [M2225]. Department of Special Collections and University Archives, Stanford University Libraries, Stanford, California).

(below) SNCC activist Stu House speaking to assembled crowd, Selma 1966 (Donald A. Jelinek papers [M2225]. Department of Special Collections and University Archives, Stanford University Libraries, Stanford, California).

Stu House being led away by police, Selma 1966 (Donald A. Jelinek papers [M2225]. Department of Special Collections and University Archives, Stanford University Libraries, Stanford, California).

This police encounter was a bad blow to our posture of courage and fearlessness, undermining our message to potential black voters that things had changed and that it was now safe to vote—also my passivity weighed heavily on me. Suddenly the static of the speaker system broke the silence. "BLACK POWER!" boomed Carmichael's amplified voice. "BLACK POWER!" The crowd came to life, first with sly smiles, then shouts of delight at Carmichael's audacious act. "Now you know," he bellowed, "why you must vote for your black brothers and sisters!" He whizzed around the corner and parked the truck.

I was filled with admiration. No matter what eventually happened in the election, this day was ours.

The dumbstruck police still had not taken any action as Carmichael walked back and formed a picket line around the jail.

When the picketers were warned they would be arrested if they didn't cease their activities, Carmichael asked his supporters to permit him to picket alone. He was soon stopped at the steps of the city hall by the mayor and chief of police. When he refused to leave, he was arrested for inciting to riot.

The police report filed that day was relatively accurate: "CARMICHAEL, STOKELY, RACE C . . . MADE REMARK IN FRONT OF CITY BUILDING ABOUT BLACK POWER & MADE PROVOCATIVE MOVE TOWARD POLICE [the only

Stokely Carmichael and others protesting for voting rights, Selma 1966 (Donald A. Jelinek papers [M2225]. Department of Special Collections and University Archives, Stanford University Libraries, Stanford, California).

falsehood!]—ALSO WAS ON LOUDSPEAKER URGING A LARGE GROUP OF NEGROES TO GO TO THE JAIL AND SEE ABOUT THEIR BROTHERS ALSO YELLING BLACK POWER."

Carmichael was relaxed when I visited him in his jail cell that evening, joking that I could use a night in jail myself to get some rest.

The local court attempted to set the trials for Election Day, but even the Selma white establishment did not and could not pull that one off. A later date was scheduled. The day before the election I filed for removal of the "sound truck" arrests from state to federal court and then waited out the election results.

On Election Day November 8, 1966, even though Baker was on the official Democratic Party ballot with Clark only as a write-in, Wilson Baker defeated Jim Clark by merely five hundred votes: 7,249 to 6,742. But although the majority of whites voted for Clark, the majority of black voters honored the instructions of black leaders. As a result none of the black candidates on the Free Voter ticket won.

As daring as the SNCC leader's electoral effort had been, the strong law enforcement reaction had been a powerful reminder that the black

Stokely Carmichael speaking with Selma's chief of police, Selma 1966
(Donald A. Jelinek papers [M2225]. Department of Special Collections and
University Archives, Stanford University Libraries, Stanford, California).

farmers still had to live the rest of their lives in white-dominated Selma.
Also the internecine wars between blacks discouraged many who felt "a
plague on both their houses."

Into the early 1970s Selma blacks were not able to elect a candidate
of their choice to the city council because its members were elected at-
large by the entire city, meaning the white majority still controlled the
elections. But threatened with a lawsuit under the Voting Rights Act, the
Selma City Council decided to elect its ten members from single-member
districts. After that change five black Democrats were elected to the city
council.[6]

LOWNDES COUNTY ELECTION

Nearby Lowndes County, Alabama, often referred to as "Bloody
Lowndes," was an especially evil district. It was there that Viola Liuzzo
had been murdered in the aftermath of the Selma March. It was also
there that Seminarian student Jonathan Daniels was shot to death. It was
also a place where even attempting to register to vote could be fatal to a
black citizen.

Stokely Carmichael being placed under arrest, Selma 1966 (Donald A. Jelinek papers [M2225]. Department of Special Collections and University Archives, Stanford University Libraries, Stanford, California).

Although blacks constituted nearly 80 percent of the county's residents, they always represented a negligible percentage of the vote. On the other hand whites typically turned out one-third more votes than they had registered voters—a phenomenon widely referred to as the "graveyard vote."

Spurred by the Selma demonstrations and Dr. King's presence in Selma in early 1965, seventeen brave people rallied around John Hulett, a lifelong resident of the county, to attempt to form a local party. They believed they could mount a successful organizing effort in Lowndes County. As a sign of SNCC support Carmichael rode throughout the county on a borrowed mule wearing a large floppy hat so that he could conceal his face from whites; he met with and talked to black farmers, encouraging and assisting them to get registered. In addition the SNCC research staff discovered an unusual Alabama law which permitted a group to organize a political party on a *countywide* basis, and in March 1966 the Lowndes County Freedom Organization (LCFO) had been born.

Assembled crowd watching police after Stokely Carmichael's arrest, Selma 1966 (Donald A. Jelinek papers [M2225]. Department of Special Collections and University Archives, Stanford University Libraries, Stanford, California).

Of course there was danger for participating sharecroppers who were subject to being kicked off the land for political activity. Some twenty families were evicted in 1965 and spent the rest of the winter living in tents with temperatures often below freezing. Carmichael and SNCC set up a tent city in Lowndes County for families who were evicted for ASCS activities, for trying to register to vote in the general elections, or for attempting to enroll their children in white public schools

When the time arrived to put up black candidates, SNCC helped organize workshops on the duties of sheriff, coroner, tax assessor, tax collector, and members of the board of education—the offices up for election in 1966.[7]

Since every political party in Alabama had to have a corresponding logo that voters could recognize, LCFO took a provocative stand and chose a snarling black panther as its party symbol. The new independent, all-black political party became popularly known as the Black Panther Party. Carmichael saw the black panther as "a bold, beautiful animal," representing the strength and dignity of black demands today." Hulett described it as "a vicious animal that never bothers anything unless it is cornered."[8] Comparably the Mississippi Democratic Party had as its logo a rooster with the emblem "White Supremacy for the Right."[9]

In a speech on the eve of the Lowndes elections, Carmichael summed up what they all had gone through, and why a new and independent political party was necessary. He thundered:

> We have been beaten, killed and forced out of our houses, but to-night says that we are right! When we pull that lever we pull it for all the blood of Negroes spilled . . . to stop the beating of Negroes by whites [and] for all the black people who have been killed. We are going to resurrect them tomorrow . . . We have a lot to remember when we pull that lever.[10]

Whites used every weapon in their arsenal to defeat the Black Panther Party: ballot boxes were stuffed, blacks were given ballots already marked for white candidates, blacks who could not read (and some who could) were "helped" to cast their vote by their plantation owner, and truckloads of blacks were driven in from the fields by their landlords and told for whom to vote.

The night of the voting an LCFO worker who spent the day driving voters to the polls was severely beaten while on his way home. An Election Day driver and poll watcher couple were kicked out of the house that had been their home for eleven years—along with their nine children. Another black family's home was destroyed by fire, leaving two adults and fourteen children homeless and penniless.[11]

On Election Day in Lowndes County, as in Dallas County, every black candidate was defeated—but four years later in 1970 John Hulett was elected sheriff and other black candidates secured local office.

13

The Dark Side of
Two Federal Judges

J ust as the Civil Rights Movement in the mid-1960s South was divided between stately incremental efforts—as exemplified by the NAACP and the brash impatience of SNCC and other black power advocates—so too was the division within the civil rights legal community. It was split between those who believed lasting change would only come about slowly, step by step, case by case in the courts rather than the streets and those who promoted direct action and at times civil disobedience.

JUDGE JOHNSON

The Honorable Frank M. Johnson Jr., the most famous and revered federal judge in the South, resolutely believed that all Americans deserved equality. However he detested any efforts to achieve that equality by methods outside the court system—even the peaceful passive resistance advocated and practiced by Martin Luther King Jr.

Judge Johnson grew up in Winston County in northern Alabama, a region often out of step with the rest of the state in part because the county's infertile soil virtually eliminated the need for slaves. Winston County opposed secession from the Union, but when it happened anyhow the county seceded from Alabama; many county residents, including Johnson's forebears, fought for the Union. Thereafter the county became a Lincoln-Republican outpost in the otherwise Democratic Party "Solid South." Johnson's father at one time was the only non-Democrat in the Alabama legislature.

Johnson, who became an active part of Dwight Eisenhower's successful bid for the presidency, was appointed US Attorney in Birmingham after completing a combat command tour in World War II. In 1955 President Eisenhower chose him to be the youngest federal judge in the country. His court was in Montgomery where the bus boycott would launch Dr. King's career as a civil rights leader.

Johnson went on to become the most prominent desegregationist judge in the nation. He was one of a three-judge panel that, on the authority of *Brown v. Board of Education,* declared segregation of the Montgomery bus system unconstitutional—effectively ending the need for the bus boycott. For the next two decades, either alone or in combination with other judges, he desegregated 107 school systems, buses, bus terminals, parks, museums, mental institutions, jails and prisons, airports, and libraries.

But he paid a high personal price for his rulings, which were widely reviled by Southern whites. His mother's home was bombed, he received innumerable death threats, crosses were burned on his lawn, and he warranted around-the-clock federal bodyguards. In addition he and his wife were socially ostracized; Johnson gave up teaching Sunday school when no one came to attend his classes. He reluctantly left his church altogether when people moved away from his pew as he sat down.[1] His son Johnny was constantly badgered by classmates *and* teachers, and he even received death threats. In 1975 Johnny committed suicide after prolonged mental illness aggravated by the harassment.[2]

Still Johnson remained a tough law-and-order man with sentences longer than the national average. He was an autocrat described on the bench as "peering down from Olympus," his demeanor so fierce that a Justice Department lawyer once fainted while appearing before him. When "respectable" civil rights lawyer organizations came before Johnson, such as the NAACP LDF, they were well received—the same did not apply, however, for the lawyers he felt were choosing to pursue justice by extralegal means.

Johnson despised the concept of Black Power as much as he did the beliefs and tactics of the Ku Klux Klan. He denounced the philosophy that "a person may, if his cause is labeled 'civil rights' or 'states rights' [an equation of SNCC with the Klan], determine for himself what laws and court decisions are morally right or wrong—and either obey or refuse to obey them." According to Johnson, these beliefs are entirely foreign "to our 'rule-of-law' theory of government."[3]

Dr. King and Judge Johnson, whose celebrity began in the same city, were to have an epic clash in another Alabama city: Selma.

THE SELMA MARCH AND THE JOHNSON COURT

After the first march in Selma had ended in March 1965 with the savage events of Bloody Sunday, Dr. King and the civil rights leadership petitioned for a federal injunction to protect the marchers in a second march planned to take place two days later. "The State of Alabama," said Carmichael, "temporarily relinquishing its states' rights rhetoric and posture, went into the hated federal courts seeking an injunction against the march. *Which they got!*"[4] Judge Johnson issued an injunction *forbidding* the next march, which exacerbated the tensions within the civil rights community and presented Dr. King with a set of thorny alternatives.

If King obeyed the injunction, the magnitude and intensity of the throngs already assembled in Selma—and still arriving—could be dissipated. Also SNCC might march no matter what he decided. On the other hand if he challenged Johnson Dr. King would be defying the most renowned civil rights friendly judge in the nation as well as the power of the federal government itself at the very time landmark civil rights legislation (the Voting Rights Act) was pending before Congress.

Dr. King eventually decided to march but with a reservation few were aware of: when the marchers came to the scene of the Sunday carnage he led the gathering in prayer but then turned the crowd back. Dr. King, whose successes had been based on both legal and extra-legal nonviolent resistance, chose not to overtly defy Judge Johnson. And even though King was brought before Johnson on contempt charges for even beginning the second march, he was vilified by many SNCC activists who denounced his backpedaling as "Turn Around Tuesday."

According to Carmichael, "We discovered later that there had been some agreement with [Attorney General] Robert Kennedy, with the government, that the march was not to proceed."[5] When Johnson subsequently dismissed the contempt charges against King—which civil rights activists considered proof of a deal—the judge succeeded where almost every Southern sheriff, legislator, and governor had failed: he discredited Dr. King in the eyes of his followers, especially with the more militant civil rights groups.

Meanwhile James Forman, SNCC executive secretary, labeled Judge Johnson's injunction as "legal blackmail." He resolved to never again see "movements destroyed by placing the question in the courts." Forman demanded the marches resume. To underline the point he led a SNCC march the next day *from* Montgomery—the other end of the intended route of the Selma-to-Montgomery march—in direct defiance of the judge and his injunction. Forman and his fellow marchers were arrested by local police.

A petition to remove the cases of those arrested from the state courts to the federal system came before Johnson, who should have disqualified himself given the personal attacks on him especially from Jim Forman. Ignoring evidence in the SNCC papers that "county police charged into our small group on horseback: hoofs trampling, the cops whipping people . . . with long sticks," Johnson ruled that "county police were discharging their duty and responsibility *to keep the sidewalks open* and reasonably available for normal use."[6]

He denied the removal petition and remanded the Forman cases back to a state court in Montgomery for a "fair trial." A year and a half later in November 1966 the cases fell into my lap.

THE FORMAN CASES

I had arrived in Selma after those events which indelibly seared that town's name into the nation's conscience, but I had yet to meet the lead defendant, who was well on his way to becoming a civil rights icon. A bear-like man in both stature and disposition, James Forman was gifted with a dazzling mind and amazingly clear organizational vision. In 1961 he had been chosen as SNCC's executive secretary at the relatively ripe age of thirty-three in an organization that prized youth.[7] Accepting a salary of $60 per week, he went on to create a semblance of order in the perpetual anarchy that was SNCC.

"One hundred sixty-seven defendants!" I mock-moaned to William Kunstler who had asked me to handle the cases of the arrested marchers. "And how," I asked him, "do we get the cases back to federal court given that Judge Johnson has denied the removal petition?"

"No problem," Kunstler said. "Just ask the 'super-lawyer!'" We both laughed at this description of Anthony G. Amsterdam, professor at the University of Pennsylvania Law School, former law clerk to the celebrated US Supreme Court Justice Felix Frankfurter, and a legend in legal circles.

To most, Amsterdam had earned his legendary status with his bravura performance in an argument before the DC Court of Appeals. He cited page and volume from memory as he quoted an "ancient" US Supreme Court case as the key to his presentation. When the judge told him that there was no such case in the court library under that citation, Amsterdam responded, "Your honor, the court's copy of the volume must be misbound." It was.

To me, however, he was the law professor who was willing to drive seventeen hours from his Pennsylvania home—nonstop and without sleep—to arrive at the Mississippi ACLU office in the morning to advise us on how to proceed with difficult civil rights cases. We eventually came up with a plan to try to convince Judge Johnson to throw out all of the cases. The approach was based on an 1886 US Supreme Court decision *Yick Wo v. Hopkins,* a relatively obscure ruling but one of a handful of decisions in American jurisprudence that I truly admired.

That ruling had come in a case involving a San Francisco ordinance requiring a permit to open a laundromat. But it was enforced only against Chinese laundries, not "white" laundries. The US Supreme Court ruled that such selective prosecution of one group but not another is unconstitutional *even if the prosecuted group is actually guilty of violating the ordinance:* "Though the law itself be fair on its face and impartial in its appearance, yet [it may not be] applied and administered by public authority with an evil eye and an unequal hand. . . ."[8]

Yick Wo v. Hopkins had previously been used either as a defense *during* trial or *after* trial as a basis for appeal. We would now ask that the case be used preemptively to stop the state prosecution *before* trial by using evidence of discriminatory enforcement. I filed an injunction suit that painted the full picture of the Montgomery march and argued that *even if* citizens, both white and black, were involved in disruptive activities, only blacks were charged.

The suit documented numerous instances where "local whites in Montgomery ran wildly through the streets, screaming obscenities and racial epithets, assaulting, threatening and intimidating the peacefully demonstrating [black civil rights workers] and, in certain instances, attempting to run down the demonstrators when they crossed the streets." Further, although local whites were "flagrantly guilty of all the crimes for which [the marchers] were charged, these local whites were ignored by local law enforcement officers who made no attempt to deter, arrest or prevent this unlawful conduct."

MEETING JUDGE JOHNSON

I brought this request for an injunction before Judge Johnson. Despite the enormous contempt SNCC and especially Forman felt for him, I admired Judge Johnson and looked forward to meeting one of the few "good" jurists in the South. I met Johnson in his regal, walnut-paneled chambers, bringing with me my new local "introducer," Charles Conley, who was replacing Bruce Boynton. Conley was a black Montgomery attorney not admired in civil rights circles: SNCC staffers had warned me not to trust him in part because he was more interested in money than civil rights. I told them I needed the man's license, not his soul; in fact his pragmatic interest in money was a language I understood from my New York days.

The judge was as formidable as his reputation had suggested, looking down on lawyers appearing before him from a desk that was exceptionally high off the ground. Tall, stooped, wearing half-moon glasses on the bridge of his nose, he silently offered the customary chambers handshake—but it was a weak gesture, his hand barely touching mine. In an abrupt departure from the Southern style of civility to which I had become accustomed, he brusquely asked our business.

The main business in Conley's mind was to get me admitted to practice in Johnson's court under my own name; he did not wish to put *his* name on a controversial SNCC case. Conley promptly offered me for admission, praised my record, and listed my credits, including admission to practice before state and federal courts in New York, the Fifth Circuit Court of Appeals in New Orleans, the federal court in Northern Mississippi, and, most important, the nearby Birmingham federal court—an equivalent of this court. Johnson accepted my credentials and admitted me to practice in his court under my own name.

That accomplished, we proceeded to my request for a temporary injunction; perhaps presumptuously I reviewed the facts as applied to our new lawsuit.

"This is the same case I already ruled on," Johnson loudly interrupted me, jerking his head so vigorously that I expected the half-moon glasses on his nose to take flight.

I was knocked off balance as much as his glasses. I was in the chambers of the most anti-segregationist judge in the South, but the atmosphere was as tense as it would have been with the most hostile of Southern judges. Johnson labeled my version of the facts as "dubious" and described this lawsuit as an attempt to "bypass" his previous removal ruling and "slip" the case back into the federal system.

I asserted that the *Yick Wo v. Hopkins* precedent represented an entirely different argument than my previous request for removal but to no avail. The next day he denied the injunction and refused to stop the trials.[9] We filed an appeal of his ruling, but in the interim the trials would begin in state court.

AN UNLICENSED LAWYER

Adding urgency to my desire to avoid trying the Forman trials in state court, a new and unexpected development occurred which threatened my ability to defend these cases at all.

A few months earlier, shortly after returning from the successful ASCS case in Washington DC, I had appeared in a local state court on a minor case: a civil rights worker charged with disturbing the peace. While I was waiting to begin someone in the audience challenged me: "Jelinek . . . not licensed . . . state bar . . . improperly appearing in this court."

Before I could fully register what was happening the judge announced: "Under the circumstances we will postpone today's hearing." After a signal from the judge I followed him into his chambers. Before I could ask what had just happened he apologized. "I'm sorry. It wasn't my idea. He's from the Alabama Bar Commission in Montgomery."

"But what is this all about?" I protested. "I've been trying cases all over Alabama and Mississippi for a year, dozens of cases. How can they object now?" My plaintive complaint sounded as if it had come from one of my most unsophisticated clients: *That's not fair; how can they do this to me?*

The judge shrugged his shoulders, but he gave me a clue. "I hear you did real well in Washington," he remarked casually. I instantly realized it was not a change of subject.

"Oh my God," I whispered as realization dawned upon me.

"Y'all watch yourself," he said in parting.

Could I be barred from practicing law in Alabama state courts?

It *was* true, as I later explained to my concerned clients, that I was not a member of the state bar in either Mississippi or Alabama. But I told them that out-of-state lawyers were allowed to practice in these courts *if* they were associated with a locally licensed lawyer to "introduce" them to the court. That out-of-state civil rights lawyers were allowed, even welcomed, to practice law in the South was not a case of collegial graciousness or mannered gentility; Southern lawyers *needed* us outside civil rights attorneys in their courtrooms! The Sixth Amendment to the US Constitution required that "in all criminal prosecutions, the accused shall enjoy the right . . . to have the assistance of counsel for his defense."

In March 1963 the US Supreme Court required that state courts also must provide counsel in criminal cases to represent defendants who are unable to afford their own attorneys.[10]

Obviously at any given time there were many civil rights workers accused of crimes throughout the South. If local lawyers were forced to represent these "outside agitators" they risked their standing in the community; actually winning a case, perish the thought, could end a career. Plus civil rights lawyering was low-paid (or unpaid) and time-consuming work. Given Southern ironclad local control of the bench and the jury pool, Southern lawyers had nothing to lose and everything to gain by allowing outsiders to handle these cases.

Conversely *we* needed access to the state courts even though the likelihood of winning favorable verdicts was remote. Our goal was to establish a forceful presence in the state system, a presence that announced to our clients: *You will be protected from start to finish! We will arrange your bail, cross-examine your accusers, demand that you be treated with respect, stand by you when you are found guilty, negotiate your sentence, and eventually free you on appeal!* The Southern state court system was the arena within which our contribution to the struggle for racial justice played out.

For me, attorney Boynton, as my introducer, had held the key that provided me access to Southern courts, and the ACLU office had been paying him well to assist me. But on September 12, 1966—a month after the ASCS hearing in DC and two months after my confrontation with his mother—he notified me he would no longer serve as my local counsel. Charles Conley replaced him.

Four days later on September 16, 1966, a grand jury made up of plantation owners and other prominent whites encouraged local courts to take action against any "unlawful practice of law in Dallas County [where Selma is located]." It was noted that the crime carried punishment of up to six months behind bars and a fine of up to $500.[11]

THE FORMAN CASES

When the case of *City of Montgomery v. James Forman, et al.* began on Friday, November 11, 1966, in a Montgomery state court three days after the recent statewide elections, I was far from sure I would be permitted to practice. I rose and was able to speak about two words before I was unceremoniously barred from participating and ordered to remain silent. This time, however, the now-routine tactic had a new wrinkle: I was informed that as an out-of-state lawyer I was required to be recommended by an *officer* of the Alabama Bar Association, not just a licensed local lawyer like Conley.

When the judge then asked if Conley would defend the SNCC leaders in my stead, he declined stating, "I do not feel I could represent these people without compensation." The court would not pay him and so the defendants were left without counsel.

When I insisted that the defendants needed a lawyer and I was the only one available to defend them, Judge Eugene Loe ordered me silenced. The trial would proceed.

Anticipating this turn of events Forman and I had prepared a not-very-impressive strategy: I was seated in the front row of the spectator section when the arraignments began. As each SNCC defendant was asked his plea (in addition to Forman six other SNCC leaders were among the accused), he would walk over to me and, in a stage whisper, ask me for advice. After the third repeat of this ritual Judge Loe exploded and shouted, "You are impeding and harassing this court, and I will not stand for it!"

I explained that I was now "acting as a friend to the defendants, granting them advice."

Forman was next. He walked over to where I was seated and in a booming voice asked, "Don, could you explain what 'disorderly conduct' means so I'll know if I'm guilty or not?"

I answered equally as loud and in dialect, "It's doin' what the MAN don' like!"

"That does it!" the judge shouted. "You are in contempt!"

A bailiff came running over and dragged me to a holding cell connected to the courtroom and locked me in. Thirty minutes later, apparently to mollify me, the judge released me and announced that I was no longer cited for contempt; he said I could sit in the audience if I remained quiet. When I told him "I could not possibly remain quiet under these circumstances," he had me ejected from his courtroom.

Listening by an open door, I heard a rare performance by Forman who, for an hour and a half, spoke extemporaneously of his own history in this city and state. He vigorously denounced the courts, segregation, and racial violence in Alabama; he told of being jailed and beaten while attempting to register voters and while organizing protests in lawless communities. Then he began telling the story of the SNCC march in Montgomery.

When the prosecutor interrupted him to note that it was past the lunch hour and he was hungry, Forman pounded the table, "I'm hungry too—but for more than food." He roared, "I'm hungry for freedom! *Freedom! Freedom!*"

There were no surprise endings. The defendants were all convicted and given suspended sentences of thirty days in jail plus a $100 fine which they refused to pay. When the judge learned I was still on the premises he sent for me, scolded me for my outbursts, and, forgetting that the contempt charge had already been withdrawn, suspended a sentence he hadn't imposed upon me.

I obtained bail and had all my clients out late that night.

THE REAVIS CASE

On November 17, 1966, the court calendar in Marengo County, Alabama included a black youth charged with homicide arising out of an automobile accident; a white SCLC worker, Dick Reavis, charged with vagrancy and obstructing justice; and a local black civil rights worker, Charles Saulsberry, charged with breach of the peace for wandering after dark in a white neighborhood. The latter two cases were mine.

The court was convened in an Alabama National Guard armory building. No American flag was visible although a framed copy of the Prisoner of War code was prominently displayed in the hallway.

I sat through the first case and observed the sixteen-year-old black driver assigned to a white lawyer who just happened to be present in the courtroom waiting to see the judge on an unrelated matter. I then watched as the accused and his involuntarily drafted lawyer held a five-minute conference after which the lawyer announced that his client would plead guilty to negligent driving resulting in the death of his friend and passenger. He accepted a sentence of two years in prison. Judge E. F. Hildreth approved the plea. I moaned and wished I could have intervened.

The case for my client Dick Reavis was next. Born in Oklahoma and raised in Texas where he was a University of Texas undergraduate, the twenty-one-year-old Reavis was the most arrested civil rights worker I knew. He spent so much time in jail and out of the sun that he was considered the only truly white man in the South. He had a Texas-style crew cut, a red-chin beard, was fearless, and was a friend.

Two days earlier Reavis had been found guilty of driving without an Alabama driver's license, ignoring a state law that permitted recent arrivals to use their homestate license for a period of time that, in his case, had not lapsed. Since local authorities also refused to allow him to take the Alabama driving test, he was arrested virtually whenever he turned

Dick Reavis with Don Jelinek (Donald A. Jelinek papers [M2225].
Department of Special Collections and University Archives, Stanford
University Libraries, Stanford, California).

on his ignition. By the time his court date arrived Reavis had collected twenty citations. For the first six he had been fined $350, which he would not pay, and was jailed.

Among the courtroom spectators for his vagrancy trial and other matters was his wife, Becky. Incensed at testimony of the police chief against her husband, she jumped up and loudly accused the chief of being "the best liar I've ever known!" When the judge demanded she apologize Becky asked me if she *had* to. I told her it was her choice, but she would likely be jailed if she declined. Nonetheless she would not apologize; Judge Hildreth held her in contempt, fined her $50, and sentenced her to five days in jail.

As his wife was being moved to a cell, Reavis' charges were heard. The first one was vagrancy: that he was without funds and spent his time simply loitering. In rebuttal I called a series of witnesses: his SCLC boss, who testified to his industrious work and produced cancelled checks for his pay during that period; his unhappy father, a conservative newspaper editor from Texas, who had flown to the trial to testify that he sent money to his son during that same period; and finally a local black woman who told of Reavis' fourteen-hour-a-day work schedule. *Impressive evidence,* I thought. *Too bad he'll be convicted.*

A lunch recess was called, Reavis was taken back to his cell, and I went for a quick lunch with civil rights workers. At a nearby Dairy Queen, the 1964 Civil Rights Act notwithstanding, the counterman would not serve our integrated group. Although I would have preferred to let it pass, eat somewhere else, and get some rest, confrontation was required. I sought out the police chief, who was with the sheriff that had just been defeated for reelection, in large part due to Reavis' efforts. When I demanded they enforce the law and remedy this injustice, they laughed and walked away. I made notes for a later challenge. With no lunch or rest, I returned to the courtroom.

Judge Hildreth, having "pondered the evidence" during the break, found Reavis guilty of vagrancy and sentenced him to six additional months in jail plus a $100 fine. However, in deference to his father, the judge offered to suspend the sentence *if* Reavis agreed to not appeal the judgment. In open court the judge was offering Reavis freedom if he accepted the unjustified conviction without complaint.

Reavis, of course, refused. Hildreth expressed disappointment, telling the dazed father that he was saddened that "such an intelligent young man will sacrifice himself for so questionable a cause." I expressed my outrage at both the sentence and the attempt to "bribe" Reavis to give up his constitutional rights. I also looked at the father, who seemed to be reconsidering his sympathy toward Southern institutions.

While I was putting the case file away I heard the voice of prosecutor T. H. Boggs informing the judge that I was not licensed to practice in this court. He demanded that I take the stand to be questioned under oath as to my status.

I should have immediately demanded to have a lawyer present because there were criminal consequences to these charges, but I defiantly agreed to take the stand. I proudly stated that I was a New York lawyer, admitted to federal courts in three states, and that I was associated with Charles Conley. I added that I had tried many cases in Alabama: Carmichael, Forman, and Reavis among them. The terse recital lasted fifteen minutes.

Judge Hildreth was unimpressed with my credentials. Since I was not licensed in Alabama he declared, "Never again will you try a case in my district!" The judge then granted a recess for me to talk to Reavis about finding new counsel.

"What kind of candy bars do you like?" Reavis asked once we were outside in the hallway "What brand cigarettes do you smoke? You're about to be arrested."

"Nah!" I stated emphatically. "They're afraid of me and the ramifications of arresting a civil rights lawyer. And besides, if they are going to arrest me, why am I still in the hallway?"

Reavis gestured that I should look behind me, where I saw Marshall T. Wilmer Shields walking toward me. He produced a warrant charging me with practicing law without a license, told me that I was under arrest, and hoped I would come peacefully.

As I was being arraigned in another courtroom Reavis was refusing to accept other counsel, telling Judge Hildreth that he didn't trust anyone else. As his father looked on he was tried and convicted again.

Next was Charlie Saulsberry's turn, a black civil rights worker I had also been representing. Without a lawyer Saulsberry received a $50 fine and was locked up for twenty days in the "blacks-only" portion of the jail.

JAILED

As these proceedings were going on I was being escorted to a cell in the county lockup. Two scruffy whites watched me as the door to their four-bunker cell was unlocked. Was this going to be one of those setups where "drunken" cellmates beat up a civil rights worker and then he is quietly released from jail? I tensed and sat down on my bunk, making sure neither of my cellmates could get behind me.

I couldn't have been more wrong about them. Welcoming me heartily, they told me that "ole Dickie" had told them that "this ole lawyer was raising hell and would sure enough be locked up before the day was over."

When Reavis arrived he summarized all that had happened since my arrest. "Three's a crowd in Linden Jail," a reporter wrote. "After two trials, not only was Reavis behind bars, but so were his wife and his lawyer."[12]

I settled in for the long stay because I had advised my staff that if I were ever arrested I should receive no special treatment. In solidarity with cash-poor sharecroppers, civil rights workers were refusing to post cash bonds. I had told my staff that I would refuse as well.

In about an hour I ran out of conversation with my jail buddies and began to feel the confinement of the ten-by-four cell. I wanted to pace, an undefined anxiety having come over me. *What was it?* I was no longer afraid of immediate physical harm, nor was I afraid of the confinement itself. I realized that it was the Samson/Deliah haircut syndrome: I had lost my power—white state officials were no longer afraid of me.

Noticing my growing anxiety, my cellmates took action. "Okay," one of the scruffies announced. "We were going to save it for after dinner, but it seems the attorney can use some brew *now*." The three of them laughed. Eager to be distracted, I watched with awe as they began to prepare the locally famous "Marengo Jail Moonshine." They placed water from the jail cell toilet into a plastic pitcher and then added Kool-Aid, coffee grounds, and three opened Contact antihistamine cold capsules. I was high in no time, giggling and giddy when dinner arrived. I laughed myself to sleep by 9 PM, comfortable now after five hours in jail. The brew masters paternally wished me pleasant dreams.

An hour later a guard woke me with word that I was bailed out.

"No," I mumbled, "let me sleep." He shook me and said I was released.

"You can't release me," I said, waking up, "unless I sign release papers, and I will not sign."

At this point he guilt-tripped me: "Do you want those sweet Negro ladies who went through all this trouble to bail you out to leave empty handed?" I looked at Reavis, who told me, "You have to go." I shook hands with my client, promised the other two I would send them gifts, and signed myself out. Only then did I learn that it was not "sweet Negro ladies" but my staff waiting for me, pressured by Bronstein to post cash bail and even to tell the jailor how to lie to me. I was very annoyed but, recognizing the pressure on them, my anger soon eased.

Once out of jail I stopped at the nearest pay phone to call Amsterdam and tell him of the recent events and how I believed this was a potential test case to establish my rights—and also the rights of other unlicensed out-of-state lawyers—to represent civil rights workers in Southern courts. He pumped me for information and noted regretfully that since I had been arrested in Marengo County instead of Greene County only a few miles away, I was in the Mobile federal court's jurisdiction. This meant that instead of the preferable Birmingham court, my case would be heard by the notoriously hostile Judge Daniel Holcombe Thomas.

Amsterdam told me I'd better call Bronstein, which I did. The Boss bellowed at me for ten minutes and warned that one more act of insubordination and I was finished. I didn't respond. I was too tired. He hung up.

I arrived back in Selma a local hero: a jailed civil rights lawyer. The SNCC guys all came downstairs to kid the "excon." The national press had printed the story before I was released.[13] Letters of support and money later began to pour into our office. I was most touched by a note from Bill Kunstler's co-counsel Arthur Kinoy: "Your conduct and activity as a lawyer in the last months has been magnificent, and the highest tribute of all to your devotion . . . has been the recent attack on you."

I wished Bronstein could see it that way.

A week later *Jelinek v. Boggs* was filed in federal court, seeking a declaration that the state laws that had barred me were unconstitutional. It also sought to establish my right to practice in the Alabama courts and to restrain the prosecution against me. Further it stated that my clients could not obtain a fair trial in Southern courts without me and other lawyers in my situation—and that the whole incident was created to punish me for recent successes in court.

MEETING JUDGE THOMAS

Six days after my arrest Carmichael and his codefendants faced trial in Selma on incite-to-riot charges arising out of the sound truck incident. Again our attempts to move the trials to federal court failed, and I sought an injunction again based on the *Yick Wo v. Hopkins* precedent. Unluckily, this time I flew to Mobile, Alabama, to meet with Judge Daniel Thomas, who was also scheduled to adjudicate my test case.

Thomas was so antagonistic to the Civil Rights Movement that lawyers routinely sought to require a three-judge panel to hear civil rights–related cases assigned to him, hoping to create the potential for a two-to-one vote. Thomas was said to have provoked that provision of the Civil Rights Act of 1964 authorizing these three-judge federal district court panels, which became known as the "Thomas Amendment."[14]

In an effort to avoid having to rule on the injunction Judge Thomas had tried to persuade courageous black Mobile attorney Vernon Crawford not to "introduce" me to the court. Crawford refused to withdraw his sponsorship and Thomas was forced to admit me. It was clear, however, that there was little chance that an injunction would be granted. I notified Carmichael that he must be prepared to return to Alabama to stand trial in Selma the next day.

In the Mobile courtroom I was told to wait until my case was called. I cooled my heels for five hours as Judge Thomas ignored me and did not call the injunction motion. I rose a few times but was ordered to be seated and silent. At the end of the day the judge told me: "I'll give you an answer in the morning. Be in my chambers before court opens!" I pointed out that the trial was at 2 PM the next day, but he walked off the bench without responding.

I was very upset. I called the Selma office to say I would not be back that night. I didn't even have a razor or toothbrush, which was not as important as it felt. I slept poorly in a low-priced Mobile hotel.

The next morning I sat in the anteroom to the judge's chambers. I stood up when Thomas walked in, but he walked right past me and into his office. When he emerged twenty minutes later, I softly asked him for his decision. He ignored me and headed for the inner door to the courtroom. At that my nerves, temper, and patience all burst at once. I jumped into his path, blocked the door to prevent him from leaving, and demanded: "You promised me a decision this morning! The trial is this afternoon!"

From above the billowing majesty of his black robes Judge Thomas glared at me contemptuously. "You are the worst enemy the Negro people have," he barked, "and you represent those who do violence to harmonious relations between Negroes and whites in the South! *I don't sign injunctions for Stokely Carmichael!*"

He then roughly grabbed my shoulder, shoved me onto a bench, and walked into his courtroom as all rose in respect to this symbol of fairness and equal justice.

I immediately called Carmichael and took a cab to the airport. He had been on a brief vacation, and I let him know I would meet him at the Montgomery airport. I arrived just in time but almost missed him; he looked like a Green Beret dressed in an army field jacket, olive drab fatigue pants, and boots. We jumped into my car, which had been left at the airport, and retraced in reverse the route of the Selma-to-Montgomery march. We drove past a large billboard still displaying a menacing Black Panther and the message, "Pull the Lever for the Black Panther and Go On Home." We passed through Lowndes County where Carmichael's major Alabama organizing had taken place and where Seminarian student Jonathan Daniels and Viola Liuzzo were shot to death.

We were both depressed. We knew that he and the others would be convicted in the Selma Recorders Court, sentenced, and locked in the jail. Carmichael was feeling dejected about shortening his vacation; he had met a woman, he said, but barely had any time to spend with her. And he really didn't feel like going back to jail.

I was worried that Carmichael and me in one car might be considered a good target for a sniper. Thanks to the RentaCar spy at her booth in the Montgomery airport, everyone knew we were now on the road. When I asked Carmichael if he was frightened, he admitted that he thought about a sharpshooter's bullet but then patted his jacket pocket. I never learned or asked if he was armed.

As we crossed the bridge into Selma a police car was immediately on our tail. Then we saw the national press. *Why was I surprised?* Of course they would be here to witness the latest trial of the notorious black power advocate. I parked a few blocks away from the court. As the reporters ran toward us I was sagging, dreading them and their questions. Carmichael, however, came alive with a big grin spreading over his face.

Bounding out of the car, he took one look at my listlessness and punched me, hard, in the shoulder. I was stunned, wondering what I had done wrong. Then he exploded into raucous laughter, making jokes about the mayor and the judge. I found myself punching him back. When the press arrived we were like two adolescents, joking and shoving each other.

When reporters asked Carmichael what he thought his chances were in court he said, "Ask my lawyer." I laughed as I produced three bail petitions for convictions that had not yet taken place. Carmichael then made a serious statement just short enough to fit uncut into the evening news. After that we walked to the court to join the other defendants.

As I was barred from many state courts by now, including Selma, my clients that day were forced to present their own evidence while I prepped them—mostly to ensure that they did not give too much away in advance of an injunction hearing in federal court where I would *not* be barred.

To no one's surprise Judge E. P. Russell convicted all three with sentences of up to sixty days. Soon they were back in jail and just as soon I had them bailed out. I filed an action in federal court for a permanent injunction to stop further prosecution. I then filed to place Judge Thomas in a three-judge court group.

SET UP BY JUDGE FRANK JOHNSON

On November 26, 1966, three days after Carmichael's Selma trial and a few days after my own test case was filed, Conley frantically telephoned me. "We are in trouble," he said. "Judge Johnson has checked with the US Supreme Court and you are not admitted to practice there." I had no idea what Conley was talking about, but I knew whatever it was, if it involved Johnson accusing me of something, I was in trouble—serious trouble.

I immediately drove to Conley's offices in Montgomery where he told me that Johnson had called him at home that morning, directing him to appear at his chambers. Once there the judge had shown Conley a letter from the clerk of the US Supreme Court stating that my name did not appear on the list of lawyers admitted to practice before the high court. I sat still wondering what all this had to do with me. It was true that I'd never bothered with the formality of being admitted to practice before the US Supreme Court, but it was not clear why that would make any difference to Judge Johnson.

Conley continued, ". . . and Johnson then said you misrepresented yourself by remaining silent while I stated you were admitted, and . . ."

I burst in at this point. "Of course you told him that you never mentioned the US Supreme Court when you introduced me."

I looked Conley in the eye, but he looked away as he said, "I'm not quite sure what happened in there since there was no court reporter to take it down, but I have a vague recollection that I mentioned it and that you had once told me so."

I sputtered and swore, but Conley would not back down. He would not oppose the powerful Johnson and was already preparing his position.

Had I immediately called Amsterdam he would undoubtedly have told me, "No problem, even if a mistake was made, I'll straighten it out." But I lacked the calmness that leads to good judgment. *Not you, too, Johnson!* I thought. *Not you, too, against me! I can't take anymore!* As if to dramatize the point an ulcer from my New York days shot acid into my gullet.

I called Bronstein and accepted his suggestion that I see Johnson and straighten it out myself. An act of proposed contrition.

It was Friday. I called and made an appointment to see him the coming Monday. After a sleepless weekend during which I told no one of my predicament, I drove to Montgomery for my appointment. I tried to convince myself that by sheer logic he would realize that his memory must be faulty.

As I drove to court I went over how I would explain all this. Being admitted to practice before the US Supreme Court is no honor, it only required that I be licensed to practice in a state court for three years (and I had twice that), obtain written endorsement from two lawyers already so admitted (I could easily obtain two dozen), and pay a small fee. Since being admitted to the US Supreme Court is just a formality, I simply hadn't seen any benefit in applying to the court until I was ready to argue a case there. Besides, the much more material fact was that I had already been admitted to the sister federal court in Birmingham. I also wanted to ask the judge why he thought I would lie about something so easily checked.

When I finally found myself in Judge Johnson's chambers, the confident arguments I had framed in the car seemed to melt into mush. After mumbling through my presentation I finished with a defensive flourish. "I'm not a liar," I heard myself whining.

Johnson remained unmoved. His only comment was "What does Mr. Conley say?"

Of course the judge knew the answer.

"He backs you up."

Johnson stared down through his half-moon glasses at me as the acid in my stomach produced a new wave of pain.

By now I was practically groveling. "I'll withdraw from your court if you wish."

He dismissed me with an "I'll let you know."

As I awaited his judgment I declined both physically and emotionally. I picked fights with my staff and my girlfriend, and I found myself waking up at night screaming about a client who was being executed because I was not allowed to speak in court.

When she saw my hands shaking, a civil rights worker and member of the Medical Committee for Human Rights "ordered" me to rest in the Miami sun with Rogow. I agreed and called my old Mississippi ACLU pal, who was living in Florida with the white woman he left with from Jackson. He welcomed me to visit.

When I arrived Bruce could see I was withering and sent me to his doctor, who recommended my retirement from civil rights work. I started to cry. I told him that life was terrible, that we lost day after day, and even when we won it only set us up for bigger losses. But I could not leave, I told him. I had to be there for legal and moral support for those on the front lines.

The doctor handed me a heavy dose of tranquilizers.

The Florida sun was glorious and soon I was feeling a little better as well as considerably high from the medication. My office called me in Miami with an alert that Conley had revoked his recommendation of me to Johnson "in view of the misunderstanding with respects to [Jelinek's] admission to practice before the United States Supreme Court."[15] And that Johnson wanted me to withdraw from his court immediately.

Conley's convenient amnesia left me in a situation where it was my word against that of the judge. It was still difficult for me to imagine a man of Johnson's integrity "framing" me. Maybe he honestly thought that he had heard Conley pad my credentials without any disavowal from me.

On the other hand Johnson claimed to have believed I lied when he saw no mention of the US Supreme Court in my qualifications listed in my test case lawsuit. Was this explanation plausible? There was, after all, no reason for him to have read a pending lawsuit that was filed in a different court—and in a case he was not to judge. Moreover once the question of my admission rose, why did he take the dramatic step of writing to the clerk of the US Supreme Court for information easily obtained by asking me or my lawyers? And if this was really a serious infraction, why was I not formally reprimanded instead of simply allowed to resign from his court?

I felt that I had no chance to prevail in this argument. I surrendered and sent him a telegram which announced my intention to "withdraw my application for membership." Unfortunately there was an allegation in my "test case" lawsuit that I was "admitted" into Johnson's court. This would now become an issue at the trial.

What had happened?

In hindsight it's clear that whatever Johnson thought he heard, he had seized the opportunity to create havoc for me. I represented everything he despised: a lawyer who enthusiastically represented those willing to ignore his court and attempt to obtain their constitutional rights in the streets. Johnson had sacrificed everything: his reputation, his family, and risked his very survival to desegregate the South. He was not about to allow SNCC, much less their lawyer, to bypass his efforts to bring about racial justice in Alabama.

I had become collateral damage.

14

No Blacks on Southern Juries

I first met Paul and Pat Bokulich during my first week in Selma in June 1966. A religious white Catholic couple in their twenties, they had come from Detroit to Alabama in 1965 to join Dr. King's SCLC, working for voting rights. Afterward they elected to live in nearby Greene County, where they set themselves up in the black community adjacent to an acre of borrowed land that they tilled with a borrowed mule.

Paid a traditionally low SCLC stipend, the Bokulichs were among the poorest folk in the county. Their shack was one of the worst in town, and their diet as bad as that of the poorest sharecropper. They bathed by heating water on a wood stove then took turns pouring the hot water over each other while standing up in a large basin. Their black neighbors could not fathom why any sensible person, especially a white one, would choose to live in such squalor, but they loved the Bokulichs all the more for it. It was said, with only some exaggeration, that if they departed the poverty rate would decline markedly in Greene County.

The day I met the Bokulichs I was told how Paul had led an "almost successful" campaign to unseat William Lee, the incumbent sheriff of Greene County, a month before I arrived in Alabama. After a high-spirited account of the campaign Pat turned somber; she wanted to be sure I would represent Paul if anything happened to him in retaliation for the campaign.

THE ARREST

Paul snorted, dismissing his wife's fears, but she turned out to be prescient. That very night he was arrested and jailed, accused of robbing a poor black sharecropper neighbor of a few coins—his life savings.

Immediately after the arrest Pat called and told me what had happened, carefully emphasizing that the old black man had obviously been coerced into framing her husband.

"Don't worry," I assured Pat cavalierly, "I'll have him out on bail by morning at the latest."

But the next day, to my amazement, the judge refused to set any bail. Paul was to stay in jail—the US Constitution and even Alabama law notwithstanding.

I had never encountered such recalcitrance in my time in the South. Mississippi courts always granted bail, albeit often at outrageously high amounts. On the other hand I had never before represented a civil rights client who had tried to oust an incumbent Southern sheriff and failed. I could appeal the denial of bail in many courts, but by the time I eventually would have succeeded Paul would have spent over a month behind bars in a jail run by Sheriff Lee.

Nothing in law school or on Wall Street provided me with a strategy to short-circuit this process. But here in the South I had heard of an approach that would allow a lawyer to jump through the whole court system in one day. The strategy required instigating a series of quick losses (or rebuffs) until you leapt out of the state courts into the federal system. So I planned to file writs of habeas corpus (Free the Body) at every tier of the Alabama and federal courts to be heard at two-hour intervals.

Expecting to lose all the way to the federal appeals court in New Orleans, which had a favorable bench, I began in Greene County where the judge had turned down bail in the first place. As expected he glanced at my papers and said he would contact me when he had time for a habeas corpus hearing. Thanking him, I then filed papers in the next court charging that I had been denied an appropriate hearing in the prior court. There the clerk filed my papers but also without scheduling a hearing. Thanking the clerk, I immediately headed for the Supreme Court of the State of Alabama in Montgomery.

THE BENEFICENCE OF THE ALABAMA SUPREME COURT

To my surprise I was taken seriously here. I was escorted into an opulent, round, oak-paneled chamber where the justices sat wearing their black robes. They seemed almost friendly in their approach to me. When I was chided for not using the extra-large, three-holed, redlined legal paper that was required in their court, I apologized for my ignorance but noted that a writ of habeas corpus is so powerful a legal instrument that it would be valid even if I had written it on a napkin.

One justice, who barely hid a smile over my cavalier approach to Alabama court rules, tolerantly noted that it was no doubt my lack of Alabama training that had caused the error and that it would be better if I enlisted the aid of Alabama counsel in the future.

Then I was asked an unexpectedly candid question: "Aren't you just attempting to bypass the state courts to reach the federal system?" I gave a less-than-candid answer that I was convinced I could obtain justice in the state system—the federal courts were just for insurance purposes. I could tell my answer had been well received and after some factual questions, to which I believed they already knew the answers, I was ushered out of the chamber so they could begin their private deliberations.

When I was recalled the presiding justice told me he had spoken with the Greene County judge who was now prepared to grant a bail hearing the next morning. That judge must have been as shocked as I was!

"Is that what you want?" I was asked, "Or do you want a civil rights martyr and a slap at the Southern court system?"

"No martyrdom!" I was clear. "Remember, I'm from New York City," which received raucous laughter. Of course I accepted the morning bail hearing.

I left the court wondering what had just happened. That I had just been permitted to speak informally, privately, and personally with the entire bench of a state Supreme Court was, and remains, unprecedented in my experience and that of my peers. I was uncomfortable that I had no proof of the next day's scheduled bail hearing—nothing on paper and no phone calls made in my presence—but I had been in the South long enough to believe that, although you couldn't count on justice from Southern courts, the word of a Southerner was usually as good as a document. I had no doubt that the bail hearing would begin the next morning.

I called Pat with the good news and then headed for Greene County to see my client in jail. Although I was flushed with excitement Paul was placid, convinced that God was on our side and my success was merely proof. The result was *His* will.

I then told Paul my plan. Ordinarily a bail hearing deals only with the likelihood of the accused returning for the trial with the bail set accordingly. However, since the judge had now been called out by his superiors, this might give me leverage to demand that Paul be freed without bail because I would make evident to the judge that he was actually innocent. I would subpoena the "victim" to confirm under oath that the date of the alleged theft is the same as detailed in the charging papers, and then I would prove that Paul had an iron-clad alibi: he had been present in Atlanta at a national press conference the day of the alleged theft.

The risk, however, was that after Paul's alibi was announced the witness would be forced to say, "I was mistaken. It was probably the day before or after."

THE BAIL HEARING

The next morning I started questioning the unfortunate black accuser in a tense, densely packed courtroom. He had the very problem I feared: he could not give a firm answer as to the date. But after making me agree not to "hurt" the old man, Paul had told me how to pin him down. The date listed in the charging documents was the first Wednesday of the month: the day the "Candy Man" came around, selling boxes of candy to a few farmers who, in turn, sold the candy to the community for a few pennies profit.

"Was it the day of the Candy Man?" I asked.

"Yes," his eyes lit up. "That's the day. The Candy Man had just left my home when Mr. Paul arrived."

"Are you sure it was that day?"

"Yes."

"Not the day before?"

"No."

"Or after?"

"No."

"Right after the Candy Man came?"

"Yes."

"How many minutes after?"

"I reckon just a few."

I was satisfied. Now it was a free ride. I looked the old man in the eye and spoke softly to him. "Paul's your friend. He's risked his life to help you and your people. Are you going to send him to prison on a lie? *Did Paul really steal from you?*"

Although in any normal court I would have been held in contempt just for asking the question, the judge didn't stop me. I knew that Paul was furious and desperately whispering to me to cease this line of questioning, but I didn't acknowledge him.

There was an absence of sound in the courtroom as the witness looked at me, at Paul alongside me, and at Paul's pregnant wife behind

Don Jelinek plowing on "Bokulich" land (Donald A. Jelinek papers [M2225]. Department of Special Collections and University Archives, Stanford University Libraries, Stanford, California).

him. Then he looked to the other side of the courtroom where the sheriff stood surrounded by armed deputies, his arms crossed menacingly. Abruptly breaking the silence I shouted, *"Did he?"*

The poor man's mouth opened. Then he passed out. I rushed to the stand to grab him, but the deputies got there first. They took him to a locked room as I protested to the judge to no avail.

After a recess the poor fellow returned to the witness stand, flatly contradicted his prior testimony, and corrected the date. He again positively identified Paul as the thief. Bail was set low and Paul was soon a free man, at least temporarily. His case was to be presented to a grand jury in three months.

THE BOKULICH INJUNCTION: ALL-WHITE GRAND JURIES

By the time I actively began preparing Paul's defense I had become good friends with him and his wife. I was a regular visitor at their home and often stayed over, showering in a large bucket with Paul pouring hot water over me. I also helped plow their borrowed acreage with the borrowed mule.

One night back in Selma I encountered a friend of the Bokulichs, who asked, "Will Paul be indicted by the grand jury?"

"Yes, he will," I replied.

"What will happen to Paul at the trial?"

"Well, we can prove he was in Atlanta when the phony theft occurred," I paused, "but that probably won't matter. An all-white jury will convict him. Then we'll appeal," I assured her. "We'll go to federal court and argue that the verdict was unjust because blacks were not permitted to serve either on the grand jury or the trial jury. It probably will work."

"If not, then what?" she asked.

"If not," I shrugged, "Paul will face the choice of prison or fleeing the South and . . ."

". . . knowing him, he'll choose prison . . ." she interjected.

". . . where he'll probably be killed," I said, completing her thought.

"Can't you do anything?" she asked.

"I'm doing all I can," I said, a little too defensively. I was tired of feeling I was responsible for a racist, corrupt court system and the injustices it imposed.

"All I can do is present the evidence and then appeal over the lack of blacks on the juries. You can't stop a grand jury," I said and then paused, fresh thoughts racing through my head. "At least no one ever has. But . . . why not?" I was talking to myself now: "Why wait until after he's convicted to file an appeal? Why not stop the illegal all-white grand jury from issuing an indictment in the first place?"

It would be unique. *But was it possible?*

The starting point was easy. Though flagrantly ignored in most Southern courtrooms it had been unconstitutional to systematically exclude black citizens from juries since 1880.

In that year the US Supreme Court reversed the murder conviction of Taylor Strauder, a "colored man" who had been sentenced to hang. He was tried before a jury which, under West Virginia state law, excluded members of his race from serving on juries. On appeal the high court rhetorically asked: "How can it be maintained that compelling a colored man to submit to a trial for his life by a jury drawn from a panel from which the State has expressly excluded every man of his race, because of color alone . . . is not a denial to him of equal legal protection?"

The court answered itself, writing that the Fourteenth Amendment, adopted eight years earlier, was "one of a series of constitutional provisions having a common purpose; namely, securing to a race recently emancipated, a race that through many generations had been held in slavery, all the civil rights that the superior race enjoy."[1] (It is noteworthy that the 1880 US Supreme Court—which saved a black man from hanging—used the language of its day to describe whites as the "superior race.")

In more recent years civil rights lawyers had found racial exclusion on juries to be an effective point to raise on appeal in federal court after conviction and many verdicts had been successfully overturned. Although the federal courts loathed intervening in the state judiciary process and risk the accusation that they had violated states' rights, the power to do so clearly existed in federal law in order to "prevent irreparable injury which is clear and imminent."[2]

A challenge to all-white juries had been brought in Greene County in 1964, although it had ended with little more than a stern admonition (which was ignored) plus a slap on the wrist. Nonetheless it was in the record. As a result I would be asking the federal courts to stop an all-white grand jury from handing down an unjust indictment and enforce its own earlier order.

I drove to Birmingham to see US District Judge H. H. Grooms, who had issued the 1964 order. He was cordial, even stimulated by my approach, but he was a cautious man and not one to "break" new legal ground. After he reluctantly refused to intervene I flew to New Orleans to appear before the US Court of Appeals.

After hearing my argument the appellate court issued a one-week injunction to allow time for me to go back and try again to convince Grooms. The fact that my argument had been taken seriously at the federal appellate court—which is just below the US Supreme Court—stiffened Grooms' spine and this time he signed an unprecedented injunction against the convening of an all-white grand jury. As a result the Greene County grand jury system grounded to a halt. No one could be indicted by a grand jury in Groom's district, including Paul Bokulich.

It was a victory to enshrine, so I rewarded myself by visiting the Birmingham Humane Society to adopt a dog, which I promptly named Bokulich. When Paul and Pat complained that it was sacrilegious to name an animal after a human, I explained the dog was not named for them but for the landmark injunction that now and forever would bear the Bokulich name.

THE BOKULICH HEARING

Later the federal court convened in Birmingham to hear evidence that the Greene County Grand Jury had systematically excluded blacks from its deliberations since Reconstruction: that Groom's 1964 federal court order had not resulted in any change.

The Greene County jury system, like most Southern institutions, was an example of de facto segregation. On paper no citizen was excluded from jury service as a result of his race. Instead Alabama law required juries to be made up of legal residents who were "generally reputed to be honest and intelligent and . . . esteemed in the community for their integrity, good character and sound judgment."[3] In practice, however, the "good character" determination was made only by whites and few, if any, blacks had ever been found to possess sufficient "integrity" and "honesty" to be eligible for jury duty.

In court I described the machinery used to keep the system in place. The governor always appointed white jury commissioners; each jury commissioner in turn chose a clerk whose job was to prepare a "well-bound book" in which were listed the names of every potentially eligible juror in the county. In Greene County the number of blacks that were "generally reputed to be honest" was virtually zero.

At the hearing and in response to my questions the clerk of the county's jury commission admitted that she did not try to obtain the names of any potentially eligible black jurors to add to her list. She didn't know that she was required to do so, nor did she know how it could be done even if she were to attempt to comply. Although she said that sometimes she used the telephone directory to compile the list (in a county where the overwhelming majority of black residents did not possess a telephone), she admitted that she did not use the tax assessor's list (where the names of black farmers would appear) and almost never used the voter registration list, which by now contained the names of many black residents.

While she knew a few Negroes living in town, she said she did not know any rural blacks in the county except those who had been "in trouble." She knew no Negro ministers and had sought no names from black churches or organizations. Having no list of blacks to work from or any means of judging their reputations, the jury commission typically just used the previous year's list. The result was that by 1966—two years after Groom's order—the list of "eligible" jurors contained only 19 percent blacks in a county that had almost two black residents for every white resident.

SEEKING THOSE GENERALLY REPUTED

Kathy Veit, a twenty-four-year-old volunteer in our ACLU office, was a self-described "preacher's kid" who graduated from Western Washington State University in 1966—after which time she came South. Working out of the ACLU office in Selma, she had conducted a five-month census of every black male in Greene County to demonstrate the extent to which the county's jury selection process had overlooked qualified blacks. We already knew the county was planning to explain the low number of blacks on the grand jury selection lists by demonstrating that few "qualified" blacks were available.

The attorney for the state maintained that the ratio was slow in changing because "younger and better-educated Negroes" were migrating to the North. Veit testified that more than sixteen hundred eligible blacks in Greene County had been overlooked by the jury commissioner—the data she presented demolished the state's defense to our charges.

SUBPOENAING GOVERNOR WALLACE

Ascending the ladder of culpability, we decided to examine the manner in which county jury commissioners were chosen. We summoned Governor George Wallace to appear in court so we could question him as to which blacks he had interviewed or consulted to make his choices. After obtaining a subpoena a quintessential old-time Southern US Marshal advised the court that it was served on the governor. The next day, however, Wallace's lawyer appeared in court to "quash" the subpoena because it had been served on an aide. The marshal explained that he had first offered it to the governor who directed him to hand it to his aide.

When the court ruled this was not proper service the same US Marshal was dispatched again to serve the governor. Again Wallace's lawyer appeared to object to the new subpoena because the proper "witness fee" had not been offered to the governor. I exploded and demanded the marshal take the stand; he admitted that he had been serving subpoenas for years and knew all about the fees.

I demanded he be held in contempt and then began yelling at the judges when they refused. One judge snidely whispered, "You're lucky the old fox [Wallace] isn't on the stand, making a fool of you."

Chief Judge John Cooper Godbold of the New Orleans Court of Appeals ordered me to calm down. Veit pulled on my sleeve trying to get me to sit and quiet down, but I was out of control and accused the judges of "rigging the hearing to protect the governor."

At this point I was warned, "One more word. . . ."

Veit pulled me down again and urgently whispered, "Don, we're going to win the case. Don't blow it." I stood, chalk faced, biting my lip.

Godbold saw my struggle and called a recess, suggesting that I use it to calm down. In the bathroom I punched a tile wall as a stand-in for Governor George Wallace and the judges that were protecting him. Finally I composed myself with the aid of a Valium, which I carried for such occasions. Returning to the court I conceded that without Wallace I could not prove that part of our case which "failed for want of proof."

The court ruled unanimously, however, that the Greene County Jury Commissioner had followed "a course of conduct which [had resulted] in discrimination in the selection of jurors on racial grounds." Although the court attempted to soften the blow by stating that the result *could be* "just innocent failure," it strictly enjoined any further discrimination and ordered the county to prepare a new list that would be in conformity with the laws of Alabama and the US Constitution.[4]

Writing for the US Supreme Court, Justice William Douglas held that "there comes a time when an organ or agency of state law has proved itself to have such a racist mission that it should not survive a constitutional challenge. . . . In the Kingdom of Heaven, an all-white . . . [jury] commission could be expected to do equal justice to all races. . . . But, [not] where there exists a pattern of discrimination. . . ."

Local white officials had lost their "right" to an all-white grand jury. Two years later the Bokulich injunction was made permanent, and Paul was never indicted, charged, tried, or convicted.

Fired and Banished

T he tumultuous year of 1966 was in its waning days. In just a matter of months I had participated in a near-physical confrontation with one federal judge in Mobile and was "removed" from a federal court in Montgomery by another. I was forbidden to practice law in any state court in Alabama and was facing possible criminal prosecution for having done so.

Life was bad. It was about to get worse.

The week after the confrontation with Judge Johnson over the issue of my status before the US Supreme Court and my subsequent removal from his court, I found myself in the offices of my local associate counsel Chuck Conley, desperately pleading for his cooperation in a state court hearing which was literally a matter of life and death.

TWO DEATH CASES

A twenty-year-old black laborer named Leroy Taylor, a pulpwood worker with a seventh grade education, had no criminal record except two misdemeanor offenses for public drunkenness. In May 1963 he told his uncle that he had held a seven-year-old black girl under water until she drowned; the uncle brought Taylor to the police. Speedy Southern-style justice then commenced: crime, confession, indictment, arraignment, examination by three mental illness experts, trial, conviction, and death sentence—*all in forty-one days!* After a member of Taylor's family approached me to try to save his life, I looked into the grisly details of the case. I concluded that although there was no question that Taylor had killed the girl, it was equally clear to me that an all-white legal system had precipitously condemned an obviously crazy man to death.

There had only been three days remaining before Taylor's scheduled execution date when I first approached Conley. I attempted to persuade him that although this was not, strictly speaking, the sort of civil rights case that we normally handled, it was a classic example of race-fueled injustice in which we should be involved. Since I was barred from the state courts Conley would have to sign papers to stop the execution. Then we would be able to fight for reversal, citing the fact that there had been no blacks on the jury that had convicted Taylor.

After Conley signed the petition, I called the sentencing judge.

"When is all this to end?" the judge growled. "What more do you want?"

What I wanted, I answered, was a stay of execution and a new hearing. After outrageously bluffing that I could get the US Supreme Court to intervene in the remaining hours of Taylor's life, the judge reluctantly agreed to stop the execution but only if the papers bearing Conley's signature were delivered to him at his home that very evening.

Only one person on my staff had been available that dark and stormy night to make the three-hour drive to the judge's residence: a woman with faulty night vision. In response to her fears of driving that evening I imperiously reminded her that we were here in the South to die, if necessary, and if the price was too high for her she should pack up now. She delivered the papers and returned with a stay of execution; a hearing was set for a month later.

Most of my staff did not speak to me for over a week.

But now on the eve of that hearing Conley refused to attend. Feeling that he himself had narrowly escaped censure from Judge Johnson, Conley announced that he no longer wanted any part of me. He would not show up for the death penalty case hearing the very next day. Although he called the sentencing judge to ask for a postponement in order for me to obtain new local counsel, the judge refused. Since I was barred from practicing in the courtroom on my own it would mean that there would be no attorney present at the hearing.

"You have to go!" I insisted, "and that's all there is to it. Just walk through the door with me and then leave. If you're not there I'll be challenged and our client will die."

I thought Conley had reluctantly agreed.

I was wrong.

The next morning I met Conley at his office but he refused to go, no amount of begging and threatening could move him. Instead he sent a telegram to the judge withdrawing "because of physical exhaustion" and "the pressure of work pending."

After an hour of heated but futile argument I was forced to telephone the judge. After apologizing in cryptic terms for Conley's absence, I begged the judge not to send a man to his death because of these "logistical problems." The judge informed me that he had gotten out of a sick bed to come to court and would not postpone the hearing.

With no lawyer present at the hearing the condemned man himself was called upon to address the court. When he testified that he didn't know the contents of his own petition, the judge dismissed his legal papers as "groundless and baseless and not made in good faith." The execution was rescheduled for a month later; a newspaper headline read: "Attorneys Miss Death Hearing."[1]

I began a search for another Alabama lawyer—no small problem given my increasingly toxic reputation in the state. Searching desperately through my files I discovered a letter I had received from Erskine Smith, a white lawyer and chairman of the Alabama State Advisory Committee, US Civil Rights Commission. He had written to thank me for testifying at one of his hearings. While I assumed it probably would be futile for me to ask a white Birmingham-based lawyer for help, there was no choice. To my amazement and relief he accepted.

Unfortunately Conley's withdrawal and the dismissal of our petition meant that our likeliest vehicle for an appeal had been thrown out. With less than a month to go I scrambled for another plausible way to show that Taylor's civil rights had been compromised by his hasty conviction and sentencing. I came up with nothing.

I reread for the tenth time the record of the trial judge's appointment of the three local doctors, all experts "in mental and nervous disorders," who had found him totally lucid. This time though I read it aloud to my secretary Carol Lottman, who casually remarked, "Who would imagine they even had three shrinks in a small Alabama county?"

Who indeed? I looked up suddenly as did she.

She was exactly right. The three doctors who offered testimony were neither psychiatrists nor psychologists; they were merely MDs whose familiarity with mental disorders extended no further than a required medical school course in "mental and nervous disorders." Their examinations of Taylor had taken no more than fifteen minutes each. An insane man was being railroaded to the electric chair without a proper evaluation.

Within days I arranged for one of the finest psychiatrist-neurologists in the nation to fly to Kilby Prison in Montgomery. After an extensive examination the doctor found Taylor to have suffered an "acute psychotic episode at the time of the acts charged against him [and that] he lacked understanding of the nature and quality of said acts." Further, he was prepared to testify that Taylor was incompetent to stand trial.

I prepared the paperwork for a series of appeals up to and including the federal court and then turned the case over to Erskine Smith with little more than a note from me: "I am sure by now you are neglecting the work that supports your wife and children for a case no one else wanted to bother with, for which you probably will receive gratitude only from this grateful writer."

Erskine Smith was successful and Taylor's life was spared.

A short time later I read about the imminent execution of another black man. Edward Boykin Jr. had robbed a drugstore at gunpoint and then fired a shot into the floor, which ricocheted into a little girl's leg. In Alabama the death penalty could be imposed even for unarmed robbery. Although Boykin pled guilty his confession did not win him any leniency and he was sentenced to die. I wanted to file a stay of execution for him but I could not file any papers under my name.

As the days passed and Boykin's scheduled execution date drew closer, I waited for word that some local lawyer or civil rights law group would act. When no one came forward I called around the civil rights legal community to ask if anyone was going to represent him. The answer was "no one has asked us."

On the eve of the execution I decided to involve myself even though I was uninvited. I went to Kilby Prison where I was well known as Taylor's lawyer and gave the impression that Boykin had asked to see me. When he walked in I sat him down and whispered, "I'm a civil rights lawyer and I can save your life. Sign here." Boykin smiled and signed. Only then did we talk and get acquainted.

With another black man unfairly sentenced to die, I again went searching for another local lawyer. Acting on a recommendation from Erskine Smith, I located one more fine Alabama lawyer: E. Graham Gibbons, a white attorney from Mobile. Together we worked on the legal papers to stop the execution.

Gibbons eventually won a landmark victory in the US Supreme Court. Henceforth "Boykin" would become a lawyer's household name for the proposition that the record must indicate that an accused had intelligently and knowingly pleaded guilty with full knowledge of the consequences.[2]

I was aware that I had been attempting to walk a very narrow legal tightrope, but I was successfully negotiating it . . . or so I thought.

FIRED BY THE ACLU

On January 2, 1967, I was summoned to Mississippi for a conference with Al Bronstein and Henry Schwarzschild, which I had assumed was a peace meeting intended to clear the air.

Arriving in Jackson and driving down North Farish Street, I felt a burst of nostalgia and comradeship; war weary and shell-shocked, I was glad to be back. Bounding up the steps to the office, I hugged Julie, Bronstein's secretary and wife-to-be, and gave her a present I had brought with me. Curiously, although she hugged me back, she immediately left the room in tears.

Bronstein and Schwarzschild were waiting for me in the main office. I felt my first twinge of alarm when I was asked to close the door behind me. My apprehension was heightened when Bronstein began a flattering evaluation of my six-month stint as head of the Alabama office. As every lawyer knows, when the "judge" begins by praising you it usually ends badly.

It didn't take long for Bronstein to get to the point. "I have no choice but to remove you from your post." I was shocked. In his view, he went on to say, I had become a "gangrenous arm" that was jeopardizing the Movement's entire Southern legal operation.

The specifics followed. I had become a "wild man," my conduct becoming increasingly irrational, unprofessional and excessive. I had blurred the distinction between ACLU and the radical Black Power advocates, even allowing SNCC leaders and workers to use ACLU living quarters, office, and resources—and supporting their positions in the press. I was insubordinate, he continued, most recently when I fought his order to accept bail after my arrest during the Reavis trial.

Further, I had managed to alienate almost everyone of importance in Alabama, including Amelia and Bruce Boynton, the middleclass black leadership in Selma; Chuck Conley; Judge Johnson; Judge Thomas; and the entire Alabama Bar Association. In addition there were questions surrounding my missed court appearance at the Leroy Taylor death case hearing. Though Bronstein allowed that he didn't know enough about what happened in Judge Johnson's chambers to evaluate my behavior in that instance, "but whatever happened, you must realize that your credibility is now suspect."

I had roiled the waters so much, he concluded, that there was no way I could win my test case and that ACLU had decided to withdraw it. As for the legal charges against me he had negotiated a settlement: the charges would be dropped if I left Alabama.

At that moment I hit rock bottom. While I was well aware that Bronstein never regarded me as a "good soldier," and although I admittedly experienced setbacks in my first six months in Alabama, I had also been confident that the victories were more than sufficient to balance the defeats. Through all my difficulties I had no doubt that I was doing the job I had been chosen to do.

FAINT-HEARTED

I should have known better. There always had been less to the ACLU than met the eye. For over half a century it had been the champion of civil liberties and prided itself, appropriately, for the defense of its ideological enemies on the right: American Nazis, the Klan, and John Birchers, all who received a top-flight defense. However the ACLU had been fainthearted when the attacks were on organizations to its left: American Communist Party (CP) members, draft resisters, other left-wing radicals, and even civil rights workers in the beginning.

In truth its stance was understandable, if ignoble. When ACLU affirmed the right of American Nazi George Lincoln Rockwell to speak at New York's Union Square—where he called for the shipping of Jews to the ovens and "Niggers" to Africa—it could brag that it defended the civil expression of all views "including those we detest." But the liberal ACLU feared many would not believe it "detested" Communist views.

To avoid guilt-by-association and the chance that it would be declared "subversive"—as had the NLG—the ACLU constantly strived to show its loyalty, to prove it wasn't un-American, and even to develop and maintain close relationships with the FBI. That meant trying to advance its struggle while not excessively "rocking the boat." Better, it reasoned, to spend its time and money defending civil liberties rather than itself.

In 1940 the ACLU had expelled founding member Elizabeth Gurley Flynn for her membership in the American CP, and went on to exclude all then-current CP members from its ranks. In the 1950s—responding to increased Cold War pressures—the ACLU secretly fed lists of its staff to the FBI to search for "Reds" and alerted them of ACLU members who campaigned to abolish the House Un-American Activities

Committee. One ACLU state officer even proposed a civil liberties award for J. Edgar Hoover.

The ACLU strived to define its commitment to civil liberties by those it did *not* defend. Communists were not defended, blacklisting during the "Red Scare" years was largely ignored, and it found no civil liberties issues in the death sentences against Julius and Ethel Rosenberg, convicted on charges of atomic bomb espionage. The organization had even balked at mounting a defense of early civil rights workers until pressured by Alabama attorney Charles Morgan, who was celebrated for his noble protest of the Birmingham bombing of four school children.

Bronstein and Schwarzschild had already warned me that William Kunstler and his partner Arthur Kinoy were probably Communists—or "might as well be!" They were members of the NLG and as such they were not to be trusted. Kinoy was also a member of the Emergency Civil Liberties Committee, an organization explicitly formed to handle civil liberties cases rejected by the ACLU.

Even though I realized that it was probably hopeless, I attempted to answer the charges against me. But other than the Leroy Taylor accusation, I felt guilty as charged. I spoke hesitatingly at first, unprepared, feeling my way.

I began with the test case. What would be the consequence of dropping it? If I dropped the case, who else would get arrested and take up the fight? And if nobody was willing to do it, wouldn't the effect be to solidify the tactic to entirely block out-of-state civil rights lawyers? And what about all the people who risked their lives and livelihood to follow my lead in the agriculture cases? How could I buy my freedom by abandoning them and sacrificing all we had fought for in Alabama?

Then, as the initial shock began to wear off, I took a more belligerent tact: "You can fire me," I said, "but you have no power to drop the test case. You're only the lawyers, I'm the client—and I fire *you*, here and now! I'll hire Kunstler and Kinoy to replace you." I grabbed Bronstein's phone and dialed Kunstler in New York. Kunstler, who was never in, picked up the phone at his desk and quickly agreed to represent me. I promised to call him that night to explain what he was representing me about.

Schwarzschild intervened to break the test case stalemate. "We're worried about the effect that losing it could have on us all. Even Tony Amsterdam," he added ominously, "fears that you will lose the test case." That rattled me. I had never heard this from Tony, but I kept up my offensive.

"Okay," I demanded, "call a meeting in New York, your lawyers and mine."

Schwarzschild quickly agreed. Bronstein had stopped speaking, not accustomed to face-to-face insubordination. I stormed out of the room. Then I walked back in.

"How long do I have?"

"Till February," they responded in a chorus. *One month!* I walked out again and spied Julie at her desk with tears in her eyes. I didn't stop to speak. I went out to North Farish Street for my last time as an ACLU lawyer.

I began to digest what had happened during the flight back to Alabama. I remembered my initial fantasy of coming to Selma: how I would negotiate an understanding with the local power structure and resolve all the problems with charm and force of will. Now I was being ousted because I had hardly been able to effectively communicate with anyone on either side. Was I indeed, as Bronstein put it, a "bull in a china shop" knocking over everything and everyone in my path?

It was a moot point now. I had to launch a systematic retreat and wrap everything up before the money was cut off. I also had to prepare for my future, which might include time in a Southern prison.

Arriving at my Selma office I announced, "I've been fired!"

Civil rights workers from the two floors poured into my office and listened to the details. Firebrands from SNCC vowed to attack at once. They would establish picket lines outside the ACLU Alabama, Mississippi, Louisiana, and New York offices; launch a boycott of ACLU legal help; file lawsuits; and more. I asked them not to; they, as they so rarely did, accepted my advice in service of the "greater good." I knew that SNCC might have the power and moral force to reinstate me, but I lacked the fight to cooperate.

Three days later I took my girlfriend Jean with me to the New York City meeting—in part for emotional support but even more because we both knew that it was soon to be over for us as a couple. Though we had successfully lived together amidst the swirling currents of black militancy, she was convinced (and I agreed) that with me gone she would be harassed if she were to stay in Selma. She decided to try to relocate to Detroit where she had family and where I had friends to help her get a good job. We did not even consider trying to pursue an interracial relationship in the North.

Realizing that my life as I had known it was over, I sat with a "barf bag" on my lap for almost the entire flight north. Walking off the plane,

I promptly lost my lunch in the men's room and was sick for the rest of the day. I wanted to call off that night's meeting, but Jean guessed I was suffering more from nerves than a stomach bug and urged me to get the meeting over with.

Kunstler represented me. Bronstein and Schwarzschild represented the ACLU. Amsterdam was the impartial intellect. Amsterdam started off, setting forth the pros and cons of the decision I had to make.

There were, he said, valid reasons to fight on. I had a chance of winning the test case, and if so my ability to function in Southern courtrooms would be restored and my legal problems would go away. He also acknowledged my strong commitment to continue my efforts for the sharecroppers.

But, he continued, there were also powerful reasons to drop the case: mostly the expected testimony (*He lied to me!*) by Judge Johnson, who only a few weeks earlier had made the cover of *Time* magazine as *the* heroic pro-civil rights judge in the South.[3] Tony argued that the real impact of a loss in court would be on the ACLU and its ability to function in the South. Even though my name was on the test case, he said, it really was an ACLU case and not mine. He conceded that sound judgment on the question could go either way, but since I was unable to continue my work he believed that Bronstein and Schwarzschild should make the lawsuit decision.

Everyone had said what they were expected to say and would now wait for me to decide.

Jean and I spent the night as houseguests at Kunstler's home.

Privately I had earlier asked Amsterdam to assess the extent of my legal jeopardy. *What would happen if I stayed and lost the case? Would I still be allowed to practice law in New York? What about California where I eventually planned to relocate?*

"At the very worst," Tony said solemnly, "you face prison in Alabama, the loss of your license in New York, and problems with the California Bar. Or not," he hastened to add.

I asked Kunstler also, but he had no firm opinion. It was going to be up to me, he said, to make my "personal decision."

The next morning I made a telephone appointment and then called a psychiatrist I had known in New York. I asked him for advice, or at least to help me confront my indecision. But he snapped at me: to even think of staying and fighting, risking prison and disbarment was a "masochistic urge" on my part.

I was almost paralyzed with irresolution. Should I stay, fight, and risk imprisonment and the loss of my livelihood, or should I take the deal Bronstein had negotiated and leave Alabama and my potential legal jeopardy behind?

I felt like a sellout for even considering leaving without a fight. As Jean hugged me tears of regret combined with a sense of terror. I feared the thought of prison: picking cotton and facing beatings, rape, and perhaps even death.

So notwithstanding all those who risked their lives and livelihoods to stand with me, and despite the importance of the test case, I backed out. My troubles had begun by overzealousness but in the end I was defeated by lack of nerve.

I agreed to drop the test case, stipulated that I was leaving the employ of the ACLU and would leave Alabama "at this time." I further pledged that I would not practice law "illegally" in the state courts of Alabama. In exchange all charges against me were to be dropped. I insisted, however, on my right to return to Alabama and demanded a "qualifier" letter that nothing in the agreement prevented me from practicing law in the federal courts of Alabama.

I also received a written statement from Judge Johnson stating that in his opinion "Attorney Jelinek was never a member of the Middle District of Alabama and was never disbarred. . . . In the event that the Bar Association of California or any other state was to inquire [of him] concerning this matter, he would be happy to explain the same."

His action enabled me to apply to practice before the US Supreme Court and answer "No" to the question of whether I had ever been disbarred or suspended. I quickly applied. With Amsterdam and Kunstler as my sponsors, I took the oath and paid my fee. I was welcomed to practice before the high court by Chief Justice Earl Warren, credited for the unanimous decision in *Brown v. Board of Education*.

As I prepared to leave Alabama I still had to face my clients. They were very gracious, assuring me that I should take measures to protect myself. My SNCC friends bitterly blamed it all on Bronstein, but Shirley Mesher damned me for selling out.

The civil rights newspaper the *Southern Courier* agreed with her. My good friend Michael Lottman, who was also the paper's editor and whose wife worked for me, wrote a blistering editorial under the headline, "LCDC Sells Out."

The Lawyers Constitutional Defense Committee (LCDC) [of the ACLU] has deserted the civil rights movement in Alabama. One of the reasons for LCDC's existence, supposedly, is to give legal representation to Negroes and civil rights workers. But by dropping its federalcourt suit in Mobile this week, LCDC guaranteed that for a long time to come, movement people will come to state courts friendless and alone.

From the time he arrived in Selma last summer, LCDC staff counsel Donald A. Jelinek performed in state courts like a bull in a china shop. He didn't want to be friends with opposing lawyers and biased judges—he just wanted to help his clients, and often he did. Jelinek's attitude seemed to be consistent with LCDC's determination not to compromise away people's rights in order to stay on the good side of local officials.

Like other LCDC attorneys, Jelinek was not licensed to practice here. His presence in court, then, could only be seen as a challenge to Alabama's power to deny movement people their right to counsel.

Finally, Alabama took up the challenge, Jelinek was arrested for practicing without a license, and LCDC had a chance to make its point. . . .

Since Jelinek and LCDC deliberately muddied the waters for civil rights lawyers, they had an obligation to finish what they started. Instead, they chose to give up. And so a case that might have been one of the movement's greatest victories ended in a sordid deal that was worse than defeat.[4]

How reading the editorial pained me—and still does half a century later. Eventually the *New York Times* also piled on with an article headline "Yankee Lawyer Go Home," suggesting that I ran out to save my skin.[5]

The final word belonged to District Attorney Boggs, who had had me arrested during the Reavis case. My FBI file quoted his answer to the question of why he had dropped the charges against me: ". . . the main thing we wanted to do was to get rid of him," he admitted, "and we did."[6]

No court decision ever did restore the rights of outside attorneys to practice in Southern courtrooms, and the ACLU never did return to Alabama.

California

My road to California was not paved with gold. In fact it more resembled the trek of a pathetic hunched-over cowboy who had been told to "get out of town by sundown!"—and did.

I arrived in San Francisco without a job, money, or California law license and with painful reflections ahead. Fortunately two long-time friends and expatriate New Yorkers invited me to share their home. A month's rest in their eclectic culture calmed both me and my ulcer. Beginning to sleep peacefully and awakening without fatigue, I mostly spent my days strolling through a Japanese Tea Garden, visiting exotic locales, and watching buffalo roam in Golden Gate Park.

I also began reading, first for recreation and then in a search of some understanding of what had gone wrong. My reading included a return to my mentor, the fifteenth-century Italian civil servant and teacher of princes: Niccolò Machiavelli. Whenever I have made serious mistakes in my adult life, it was in part because I had not remembered what I had learned in *The Prince*.

> *One ought to be both feared and loved, but as it is difficult for the two to go together, it is much safer to be feared than loved, if one of the two has to be wanting.*[7]

I had not been short of love, but what had protected me was the Southerners' fear of messing with me as a civil rights lawyer. When I lost that I became vulnerable to the hate I had stirred up among my enemies as well as among some of my allies.

> *[One] who wants to act virtuously in every way necessarily comes to grief among so many who are not virtuous.*

I should have been tougher, formed stronger alliances, and paid more attention to protecting myself.

> *People are impressed by appearances and results.*

I never developed a significant constituency that would support me when I was in trouble. I should have better publicized my accomplishments and become a "name." Then I would not have been so vulnerable.

> *A prince ought to take care never to make an alliance with one more powerful than himself.*

At least not with *my* personality. Not that I had a choice, but with ACLU as my boss and chief ally it was inevitable that I would be ousted once I became too independent and militant.

As I started thinking what I could have done differently, Machiavelli seemed to shout at me: *Don't deny your roots! You are a middle-class lawyer; capitalize on it!*

I wanted a second chance. As my frustration, anguish, and guilt began to fade, warm memories of my life in the South grew more vivid.

If I could get another chance this time I would create my own base from which to operate. In addition to SNCC I would try to break into the moderate Atlanta civil rights power structure. I would continue to rely on Dr. King for advice and prestige, but I would make no controlling alliances. I would raise my own money and build my own organization. If there was to be a "next time" there would be no one to fire me.

What I needed was money, an organization, a respectable image, a program, and a way to avoid being jailed as soon as I set foot back in Alabama. *That's all*? I laughed to myself.

I started with money.

A year earlier, appearing before a NLG convention, I had made my usual remarks about the USDA's misuse of federal crop subsidy funds and its link to racism, which was well received. Afterward I was described as a progressive Marxist demonstrating that control of the South lay in taking over the means of agricultural production. Those were, in fact, my views but I never thought of them as Marxist.

Sometime later I was invited to address a meeting in Berkeley, California, alongside Victor Rabinowitz, a prominent Manhattan lawyer who was then serving as president of the NLG. A full-bearded sage and veteran of many political battles, he took special pride in representing Cuba and Fidel Castro. Rabinowitz was also an influential voice in a family foundation that aided budding progressive political organizations.

I decided to approach him for help. Without ACLU to support me I could not afford the luxury of being poor. Rabinowitz happily offered me $5,000.

The timing was perfect: the federal court hearing to stop Stokely Carmichael's incite-to-riot trial was fast approaching, and I had already been admitted to the federal court in which it would be held. And somehow SNCC had coerced ACLU to both finance my travel back to Selma to handle the case and to keep the money flowing until it was over.

On Easter Sunday 1967, one month after my departure, I was back in Selma. My many friends there didn't seem surprised to see me.

16

Unsung Heroes of Selma
The Fathers of St. Edmund

A friendly Justice Department attorney telephoned in mid-1967 to warn that Stokely Carmichael and I had been marked for assassination. It could be that night, he said, but the attack was more likely set for the next morning. Perhaps as we walked up the steps of a Selma courthouse to seek an injunction to block the prosecution of the "incite to riot" charges against Carmichael and others.

Having heard of many such threats, I asked, "What is the reliability of the information?"

"Very," the attorney answered me. "We have someone on the inside."

That was convincing enough for me to inquire, "What about federal protection?"

Although he answered bureaucratically, it essentially boiled down to *we can't, and the FBI won't!* Sarcastically I inquired, "Doesn't the FBI work for you?"

He ignored the question and went on to ask if the hearing could be called off for a few days. Tempers were running high, he said, and not helped by the "multiple subpoenas you served on many Selma officials."

"We cannot back down," I said. "If we did any future threat could prevent our ability to function in the South."

Despite my gutsy words I took the threat seriously enough to accept an invitation to spend that night in the rectory of the Society of St. Edmund in Selma. (There are few secrets in a small town.) The Edmundite priests were already well known in the civil rights community in Alabama and recognized as the unsung heroes of the 1965 Selma March. At

Don Jelinek with Stokely Carmichael and Thomas Lorenzo Taylor,
November 20, 1966 (Donald A. Jelinek papers [M2225]. Department of
Special Collections and University Archives, Stanford
University Libraries, Stanford, California).

the time the priests presided over the only integrated Catholic Church
in Selma, and perhaps even in the entire rural Deep South. As such they
were accustomed to threats of violence. Of all the places I could go this
was the safest by far. Carmichael was also invited but declined.

The night passed uneventfully and I met Carmichael in the morning
at the SNCC office. I had urged him to wear a suit to make a good impression on the three-judge federal panel. Instead he showed up wearing
a colorful dashiki and a cap. I knew that among the other contentious
issues on the docket that day, I would have to fight for his religious right
to wear that cap in court.

Carmichael was obviously pleased with his show of sartorial bravado.
I tried to summon up some bravado of my own as we walked up the
steps of the courthouse. Although I felt a blazing bull's eye on the back
of my head, nothing happened. I took a deep breath as we entered the

courtroom and announced: "Ready in the case of Stokely Carmichael versus the city of Selma."

I began by telling the court that the charges against Carmichael and the others were official harassment of legitimate electioneering taking place in the final hours of a political campaign, and that this harassment violated our clients' rights under the US Constitution as well as the new Voting Rights Act.

I then started calling local officials as witnesses, men not accustomed to a court not controlled by local authorities. In addition to winning my goal in this trial was to hold the Selma officials up to ridicule, especially in the eyes of those who had been terrorized by them for generations.

First to testify was a policeman who swore he hadn't used his shotgun to smash a sound truck that had been used to campaign in the streets of Selma before the election. He then sat speechless as Kathy Veit unveiled a poster size photo of him in *flagrante delicto,* using his shotgun to do just that.

He remained frozen in the witness chair as I asked him to explain the photograph.

The gambit was successful. Unsure of what other photos we had, city and county officials grew so fearful of potential federal perjury charges that virtually the entire true story came out of their mouths.

Eventually the mayor of Selma took the stand. He explained in an incoherent manner how Carmichael's one-man picket line had incited a riot that never occurred. Despite the lack of a riot, incited or otherwise, in its later decision the court gratuitously added a solemn postscript: "Freedom of Speech does not give license to incitement of a riot."[1]

When the hearing ended I walked out of the courthouse, threats of assassination forgotten, and joined Carmichael in delivering a SNCC-style Black Power harangue before the television cameras.

The decision was to come *four years later*—almost a record for delay. The court waited until SNCC had largely left the South to rule that Carmichael and the others would never stand trial on these trumped-up charges—the temporary injunction was made permanent. As requested the judges also prohibited future use of Alabama's antiriot act, which criminalized acts "calculated to . . . outrage the sense of decency and morals or . . . violate or transgress the customs, patterns of life and habits of the people of Alabama."[2]

I can only guess that it took some politicking from the other two judges to convince Judge Daniel Thomas—who had previously vowed never to grant an injunction for Carmichael—to participate in a unanimous ruling in favor of the Black Power leader. This may have been achieved in part by the unexplained removal of Carmichael as the lead plaintiff and the case name changed to *Taylor et al v. City of Selma*.[3]

That evening I returned to the rectory to retrieve my belongings, but Father John Crowley told me there was no rush for me to leave; the other priests gave a gracious "amen." My presence, Crowley said, meant that the three greatest hates of the Klan—Blacks, Catholics and Jews— would now all be present in their house.

So I kept my comfortable room in the rectory, became accustomed to black children calling me "Father," and cherished my evening meals and discussions of religion and civil rights with the priests. I lived full-time in the rectory for over a year.

THE SOCIETY OF ST. EDMUND

The Society of St. Edmund was founded in France following the French Revolution, but the priests were forced to flee after the French government enacted the 1901 Laws of Association, which authorized the state to expel any religious community and seize its properties.

In the 1930s, after Pope Pius XI urged religious orders to work among the "colored," Archbishop Thomas J. Toolen of Birmingham invited the Society to come to Selma, Alabama, for that purpose. Edmundite Father Nicole visited Selma and assessed the potential and problems associated with the offer.

In 1936 he wrote a letter in which he expressed his impression of the plight of "*les noirs*" of Alabama:

> I have just returned from my trip in Alabama. . . . It is a ministry which is very unrewarding humanly speaking, difficult because of the degradation of the Blacks and because of a social segregation in which they find themselves, a segregation which those who work amongst them will have to share without hope of finding in the near future amongst the blacks themselves an alleviation from this segregation . . . I have the impression that a mission amongst them is as difficult as a mission in China or Africa—there, at least, one does not have to suffer the isolation of caste.

Nonetheless on January 22, 1937, the Society of St. Edmund agreed to "establish a colored mission among the colored population in Selma [who are] among the most abandoned population in the country." Two Fathers were assigned to the new mission.

To Archbishop Toolen, "saving the Negroes" had referred mainly to their souls, but as soon as the two Fathers looked around and saw the separate but very unequal schools, the lack of medical facilities and general total neglect, they became very pragmatic. They called for other Edmundites to come down and invited the Sisters of St. Joseph from Rochester, New York, to join them. Together they built a church, school, and hospital for blacks in Selma and others nearby.

Merely by their presence within the black community the priests became the enemies of the white community. Fearing for their own safety, a knock on the door of their home would be answered by one priest holding the leash of a German shepherd and the other with a loaded shotgun. A good relationship with the Irish chief of police lessened the tension but didn't spare a priest from arrest when he unthinkingly accepted a haircut from a black barber. He was plucked out of the barber chair and jailed for violation of the segregation laws.

Although the Archbishop intervened and obtained the priest's release, he took the occasion to warn of the dangers Catholic clerics faced in this state. He related the story of an Alabama priest who performed a marriage ceremony between a Catholic and a Protestant; the latter's father shot and killed the priest—and was acquitted!

Aware that the Archbishop could banish them as easily as he had invited them, they attempted to conform. But three years later, in 1959, when cofounder Father Casey died, the Edmundites defied the segregation laws by holding an integrated wake. The beloved priest was carried to his grave by fellow white priests and local black parishioners.

In 1960 Father Maurice Ouellette was assigned as pastor of the Edmundite Church in Selma. Two years later he met black SNCC worker Bernard Lafayette, who was quietly attempting to establish a base in Selma. Fifteen years later Father Ouellette told me the story of their meeting:

> I met Bernard outside the church one morning. I invited him inside and we talked for many hours, and then for many days. He taught me that we could spend all our time supplying Band-Aids, but if we didn't get to fundamental rights, we really weren't helping. He asked for a location for voter registration training; I gave him use of our facilities.
>
> I was called before the City Council, accused of organizing and making things happen, and asked to leave the city. "You're really

behind all this," I was told, "and if you don't leave someone is going to shoot you and there will be nothing we can do about it." Afterward I was called before the Grand Jury, called a Communist, and told that I was using the church to prepare people to fight violently.

Around the fall of 1964 Dr. King was brought in [to Selma]. SCLC led the activity and met usually at [the black Baptist] Brown Chapel. Our church was the meeting place [separately] for SNCC and the US government.[4]

Thirty-eight-year-old Edmundite Mission Director John Crowley arrived in Selma a half year before the 1965 Selma march. Two nights after arriving in town he watched Sheriff Jim Clark arrest a woman outside his church, sparking protests from black teenagers who were attending a church dance.

"Before you knew what was happening," Crowley told me, "Clark sent out an emergency call and soon the whole church block was surrounded by his posse. The sheriff asked me to close down the dance and started to chase the kids. I told him, 'They are only children.' Clark responded, 'No, they're not, and they're smoking.' Fortunately calmer heads prevailed and Clark backed off. That was my initiation to Selma."[5]

The first major protest of Dr. King's Selma voting rights campaign took place in January 1965 with sixty-seven violent arrests followed by hundreds more arrested. A few weeks later Dr. King was behind bars, arrested with fellow demonstrators. Crowley visited him in the Selma jail. The two ministers met for the first time, sized each other up, and made plans to work together.

At this point Father Crowley began to take steps leading to open and formal support of the Civil Rights Movement. He arranged for King to visit the Edmundite hospital and attend a testimonial luncheon where he received a plaque for his contribution to the rights of Selma blacks.

Aware that the whole nation was watching Selma, Crowley was disturbed that there was no local Catholic voice speaking out. The Archbishop was silent and all the other Alabama Catholic churches were segregated. So Crowley purchased a full-page advertisement in the Selma press to make a statement that was calm and dispassionate, every fiery word excised in anticipation of an eventual showdown with the Archbishop—who was not shown a copy in advance.

On February 7, 1965, the article "The Path to Peace in Selma" proclaimed that the Edmundites' support of the black struggle was consistent with and grew out of Christian principles:

Should we who are Christians ever forget that we are indeed brothers and sisters in Christ? This is not mere sentimentality. Christ clearly points out to us [that] on the last day . . . He will turn to those on His left and say I was hungry and you gave Me not to eat. I was thirsty and you gave Me not to drink. I was in jail and you visited Me not. And they will say to Him: "Lord, when did we see you hungry, thirsty, in jail? If it had been You, surely we would have helped you." And He will answer them saying, "When you refused it to one of the least of my brethren here, you refused it to Me."[6]

Later, after Ouellette returned and the first march was imminent, word came to him from the Archbishop forbidding clergy to participate in any demonstrations. Ouellette never disobeyed him:

I never took part in a single demonstration. It was very difficult for me. I was encouraging my parish to participate but I couldn't be there. I didn't want to be a coward. Once as I was starting to march, people told me not to. They said, "We don't want to lose you, don't jeopardize your presence here."

Although the march was scheduled for Sunday, March 7, 1965, few believed it would take place at that time. Dr. King was in Atlanta, and Crowley was in the air on his way to see Cardinal Richard O'Boyle, one of the most powerful and liberal Catholics in the United States. But the march *did* take place on what became known as "Bloody Sunday," and marchers were brutalized by Jim Clark's posse.

In response Catholic priests and nuns from all over the country, joined by their counterparts of other religions, poured into the Edmundite Church. Selma became the "staging area for an assault on the entire structure of ecclesiastical opposition and resistance to involvement of Catholic clergy." None paused to ask permission of Archbishop Toolen.

The Edmundite church and hospital were made available to those who marched. The clergy slept on mattresses on the floor of the Edmundite Hospital. Few of the Catholics present had ever experienced an instance where their vows of obedience to church authority had come into direct conflict with the demands of their social conscience. By the time they left Selma "religious disobedience" took its place alongside the philosophy of civil disobedience. Some would go on to become famous as members of the "Catholic Left" during the late 1960s and early 1970s.

Three months after the march Archbishop Toolen banished Father Ouellette from Alabama. No explanation was given. Toolen merely said, "I don't have to give any reason, I just want him to leave."

However Father Ouellette told me that he was told the reason in private:

> The Bishop received a lot of flak over me. State troopers were always following me with cameras recording wherever I went, but more significantly he felt I was destroying his life's work to establish a true separate but equal life for the Negro. Toolen told me I was going to get killed if I stayed and he didn't want a dead priest in the Diocese.

Father Ouellette expressed his belief that the church had forever changed. "The Second Vatican in 1962 had opened the door for social change for the church, but Selma was different—it was concrete." The rebellion of the priests and nuns who came to Selma to march in defiance of an archbishop led to clergy speaking up for what they believed. There would be no more waiting for words from above. There would be no more respectful silence.

When I had begun living with the Edmundites I brought with me a negative perception of Catholics. As a boy in the Bronx I had been beaten up by young Irish hoods on my way to Bar Mitzvah instruction. The Rabbi told me that the Catholic priest probably egged them on. My year in the Selma rectory changed all of that. The priests were always open and welcoming to me. By the end of my stay we had become close friends, and my relationship with them was one of the most rewarding experiences of my three years in the South.

Just as the radical community organizer Saul Alinsky advised political leaders to spend contemplative time in jail, I would say that a rectory can serve the same purpose—though jail is usually easier to arrange. I left the church after a year with great regrets and wonderful memories. But I still visited and dined with the Edmundites while I remained in the South.

17

The Unimaginable Poor

After being fired I returned to Selma and I called for a large gathering of activists: black farmers, civil rights workers from previous campaigns, and what was left of my staff. H. "Rap" Brown stood in for Stokely Carmichael, who was out of state.

I started the meeting with an organizational vision I had developed while in San Francisco: a plan for a new march on Washington by representatives of the nation's impoverished rural citizens: blacks, whites Chicanos, Indians . . . everyone.

In that connection I had met with Chicano leader Cesar Chavez, to whom I had been introduced in California. Considered the "Martin Luther King Jr." of the Mexican American farm workers, he had founded the United Farm Workers, which aimed—and succeeded—at improving working conditions for agricultural workers through nonviolent strikes and boycotts. Chavez liked the plan and had sent a high-level aide to Selma as his representative; I introduced him to the group.

All were positive about the idea and pledged their support while wondering, as did I, how this small group could organize and finance such a momentous concept.

Next I relayed that the Carmichael injunction hearing had been postponed for a few months, meaning that the ACLU would pay the bills while we began to develop the march. A small cheer went up.

The last item on the agenda was the impact of my ouster from the ACLU. Jac Wasserman of the NSF offered the opinion that I should seek support from moderate organizations and that he could arrange such a meeting in Atlanta. Maybe they would even consent to serve on the board of directors of a new organization to replace the ACLU, Jac added.

This, I realized, would be no easy task, my reputation having preceded me to Atlanta. A meeting was put together, but many of those in attendance openly loathed SNCC—and my firing by the ACLU, in part for allegedly subsidizing SNCC, had been major gossip for over a month. I appeared at the meeting wearing a well-pressed suit, well-shined shoes, and a new tie, representing a serious attempt to counter my "wild man" image. I already had friends among a few of the groups, including the social action arm of the Quakers: the American Friends Service Committee.

I began the meeting by discussing the link between federal agricultural policies and rural poverty. I knew it would not be news to this sophisticated gathering how important it was to end discrimination in the USDA. I stressed that the work we were proposing would be single-minded in its focus on bringing changes in Washington to improve the lives of the rural poor.

This message apparently resonated and the meeting went much more smoothly than I had expected. Many of those present signed up for the board of directors. The board was eventually rounded out with representatives from Dr. King's SCLC and Carmichael's SNCC.

To my disappointment, however, the newly formed advisory board promptly advised me that the name I had proposed—Organization of the Rural Poor—sounded too much like an old-time Communist front organization and would drive away potential supporters and donors. I had to compromise on a more innocuous-sounding name: the Southern Rural Research Project (SRRP, pronounced "surp"). For our logo we chose a figure of a black farmer with a hoe laboring under a bright yellow sun.

A modest mission statement was later drafted:

> The Southern Rural Research Project is not fighting for the right to vote, the right to go to the 'white' school, restaurant, or motel, nor for the right of civil rights workers to demonstrate. SRRP is fighting only for people to have the basic essentials of life.

I felt a quiet satisfaction as I walked out the door following the Atlanta meeting. Although I had not been totally comfortable with the politics of some in the room (nor they with mine), they comprised an impressive amalgam. From now on my work would aim to further this broad inclusiveness. I could afford no new enemies and vowed that there would be no further animosities, if I could help it. Bronstein would even be invited to speak at future SRRP conferences. I feared my idealism

Southern Rural Research Project (SRRP) logo (Donald A. Jelinek papers [M2225]. Department of Special Collections and University Archives, Stanford University Libraries, Stanford, California).

was slipping away as I took the first steps toward respectability, yet I preferred to think that I was only shedding arrogance and unfettered self-confidence.

I became director of SRRP with Kathy Veit as associate director. It was my great fortune that Veit had stayed on after securing data for the Bokulich case about ignored-but-qualified potential jurors. We decided to launch our own "Mississippi Summer," a mini version of the massive voter registration campaign that brought a thousand student volunteers down South in 1964. This was still an era when all one had to do to get young recruits was to drop the word at a few campuses and place a free ad in the underground press. Veit and I recognized that this would be a relatively inexpensive method of turning SRRP into a functioning organization and an advantageous way of securing permanent staff.

THE SURVEY

As we settled into our new operation in Selma, Veit and I decided to formulate a comprehensive survey to collect detailed information that would describe the intersection between local farmers and the agriculture programs that purported to serve them. The results of this survey would function as hard data for SRRP to present to potential funders. It could also be used as a vehicle for launching what I then thought would be key lawsuits to achieve agriculture policy reform.

In order to draft the survey questions I invited civil rights veterans who could offer insight into what should be asked of sharecroppers and their families. We began with specific details of the farmers' relationship to the land they farmed: *Did they sharecrop the land or rent it? What were the conditions under which they worked? Did they use a tractor or a mule? How many hours did they typically work? What was their typical harvest?*

Then came questions about their relationship with the federal government: *How much did they know about agriculture programs designed to help them? Had they met government officials designated to relay information to them? Had they received government aid to which they were entitled? Had they ever been able to vote in an ASCS election?*

We seemed to have covered everything we needed but Paul Bokulich, the only one among us who actually lived alongside poor farmers, urged us to dig deeper. He pointed out that since the USDA also operated food programs for the needy, we should ask questions as to whether food needs were being met: *Do you get free food? If so, what food do you get and how much of it? Are you able to afford food stamps? What do you and your family eat?*

Another civil rights veteran suggested we ask about health care: *Access to doctors and dentists? Prenatal care?*

"Well," a member of the drafting group added, "if we're going this far, why not ask about living conditions?" *How many people sleep in one room? Is there heat in the winter? Running water? Are there holes in the floor? Is there a dirt floor? Are there rats in the home?*

After composing several drafts and some dry-runs, we finalized our questions and turned them over to professionals at the Division of Behavioral Science Research at Tuskegee Institute, a historically black university in Alabama. There the survey was honed down to a twenty-threepage questionnaire which a properly trained interviewer could complete in twenty minutes.

By the time we launched the survey in late June 1967 more than a dozen volunteers had trickled in. I had also recruited clients and friends from Mississippi. As we spread out across the region we met other people, including students from Tuskegee, who offered to help conduct the survey. All told, on a good day we had as many as thirty volunteers in the field.

They fanned out into the countryside with a weekly stipend of five dollars. Unfortunately they did not look as innocent as Veit had when surveying black farmers for the Bokulich case and Southern whites reacted. Volunteers were threatened and ordered to leave plantations at pistol point, scores of questionnaires were confiscated by police, one student was arrested for trespassing, and another had his room shot into.

THE SURVEY RESULTS

Still, when it was completed, our effort became one of the largest door-to-door surveys of rural blacks in Southern history: accounting for 1,800 heads of households in eight counties, and representing more than 10,000 persons.[1]

Although the experts at Tuskegee determined that the SRRP data was "sound," I found the results almost too extreme to be credible.[2] I feared that the volunteers had exaggerated the results to "help" black families by making their situation appear worse than it was. No one could possibly eat that little, I thought, or live that unhealthily and survive. So Veit and I began to crosscheck a sample to witness the conditions for ourselves.

We confirmed that the results were accurate—and devastating. The survey determined that the typical black rural Alabama family consisted of as many as four adults and twelve children living in an unpainted three-room, wood-frame shack. Cooking and very limited heat was typically provided by a small wood-burning potbellied stove. Most of the windows were equipped only with loose-fitting wood shutters which did little to protect against dampness during the rainy season or severe cold during the winter. Some dwellings had no floors. Over 70 percent were infested with rats, fleas, or lice.[3]

The families surveyed suffered from massive food deprivation. Most used up their limited income before the onset of winter and then were typically forced to skip meals. Federal programs like free Surplus Commodities had once provided a limited supplement to the few vegetables grown in the family garden, but when the free food distribution in a county was replaced by food stamps many of the poorest families could not afford to purchase them.

Without government food aid half of the black farm families ate no vegetables, rarely ate beef, and did not consume fresh milk. Mothers' breast milk was often scanty or lacking due to poor health and a low-protein diet, and as a result many infants received no milk at all.

Two-thirds of rural black babies of those surveyed were born at home. Almost 13 percent of mothers who had been pregnant within the previous five years received no prenatal care and one-fifth of the babies received no medical attention whatsoever during their first year of life. Fifteen percent of the babies viewed had distended stomachs; in some cases their abdomens were so bloated that toddlers were not able to balance themselves while walking. Over one-third of the children suffered from open sores and oozing, pus-filled scabs. Doctors who observed similar deprivation in Mississippi told me that the lack of essential food and medical care, coupled with unhealthy living conditions, doomed the sharecropper families, especially the children:

> We do not want to quibble over words [the doctors reported] but "malnutrition" is not quite what we found. The boys and girls we saw were hungry—weak, in pain, sick; their lives are being shortened; they are, in fact, visibly and predictably losing their health, their energy, their spirits. *They are suffering from hunger and disease and directly or indirectly they are dying from them—which is exactly what 'starvation' means.*[4]

ROMANTICIZING THE POOR

The survey results revealed conditions that were infinitely worse than imagined. Civil rights activists had been working in the rural South for almost a decade, and as a practice we ate with the sharecroppers and stayed over with them whenever we could. So how were we not aware that the food was that pitiable and the home conditions so appalling?

We had chosen to view the courageous sharecroppers as noble warriors—uncorrupted by the decadence of bourgeois society. We saw them as dignified and virtuous persons who overcame their deprivation to join in the fight for their salvation. In other words, we "romanticiz[ed] the poor."[5] We worked for their right to vote, the integration of their children's schools, but we—or at least I—had mostly not paid attention to what they ate nor to their living conditions and health.

Our vision had been distorted. We began to realize that the poorest of the poor did not register, did not vote, did not attend meetings, and hid in the bushes when the marches went by. It took all of their effort simply to survive. We had rarely met those who came to be known as the "invisible poor."

With this survey information SRRP now had a firm organizational goal: to spread word of the results and to take action on this grim state of affairs which was killing those we were fighting for—both in flesh and in spirit. When I called Dr. King and read him a thumbnail summary of the survey results, he was appalled. He asked for a copy immediately.

18

The Fight for Food

By the end of the summer of 1967 and with the survey completed, SRRP was a functional organization with a focused mission: to provide food for hungry and malnourished rural minority families. Even so, the FBI designated SRRP as one of "those organizations that appear to be of a potential [sic] dangerous nature. . . ."[1]

Kathy Veit and I next turned our attention to raising money. We wrote letters, attended meetings and conferences, and groveled at the feet of foundations. Perhaps our limited fundraising success was caused in part by the FBI, which had ordered an investigation into SRRP's "sources of funds."[2] As the results of the survey were tabulated I spent more and more time wondering what, if anything, could be done with these bleak findings—especially in view of our lack of funds.

I took a few days off to think, relax, and visit Paul Bokulich and work his one-acre plot. The mule, as usual, showed his contempt for me by either refusing to move, or, when he did, shifting to one side so the plow would dig across the furrow I had just turned over. In his spare time the mule would try to kick my dog that was encouraging more mule power by snapping at its heels.

By nightfall I was exhausted and dripping with sweat as I stood in a washbasin while Paul poured hot water over me. After dinner I settled down to read an article written by a lawyer who had been one of my very best volunteers. Howard Thorkelson, then twenty-seven, was in the ACLU office in Selma when Stokely Carmichael was arrested on incite-to-riot charges and had worked with me for thirty-six straight hours to prepare a most important brief for an ASCS case. He went on to become the director of the Pennsylvania Legal Services and served as director of the Pennsylvania Department of Labor's Bureau of Disability Determination.

In his article "Food Stamps and Hunger in America," Thorkelson flatly declared that the prime cause of hunger in the South and elsewhere was the improper application of the USDA food programs. He placed the responsibility squarely on the shoulders of the US Secretary of Agriculture who, he established, could end "mass hunger and slow starvation" in rural America by declaring a "national disaster," which would permit the flow of emergency relief.[3]

I threw the magazine into the air and yelled to my exhausted host, "I must talk to Howard, now!" Paul stared at me. "The nearest phone is miles away," he pleaded, "and by the time we get there it will be almost midnight." I knew how tired he was but I insisted, "I must talk to Howard tonight!"

Reluctantly Paul drove me to the phone. As soon as Thorkelson accepted the charges for my collect call, I began yelling: "Howard, your article is great! We're going to do it, you and me! We're going to Washington, DC, and we're going to do it BIG: a full-frontal attack with no holds barred—we will walk through the front door, not tiptoe through the back door! With enough people clamoring for food, we can bring this famine into national focus!" Though he could barely comprehend what I was saying, he signed on.

This was how SRRP could use the results of our survey! I fantasized about "abducting" USDA Secretary Orville Freeman to the rurals and forcing him to live in "black" homes and eat "black" food.

Not that Secretary Freeman was unacquainted with the issue of rural hunger. Senator Robert Kennedy had already trained a megawatt spotlight on the issue earlier in the year when he traveled to the Mississippi Delta. His investigation of starvation in April 1967 revealed suffering and pain beyond his belief. Kennedy famously viewed a child sitting on the floor and saw that his "tummy was sticking way out just like he was pregnant," according to a news report. "Bobby looked down at the child . . . picked him up [and started] rubbing the child's stomach." He promised to go "back to Washington to do something about this."[4]

Two months later a team of doctors led by Robert Coles, a child psychiatrist, Harvard professor, and Pulitzer Prize winner, followed in the Senator's tracks to Mississippi. The group reported on the conditions they found: "Not only are these children receiving no food from the government, they are also getting no medical attention whatsoever. . . . They are living under such primitive conditions that we found it hard to believe we were examining American children in the twentieth century."[5]

In response to all this pressure and publicity Secretary Freeman shrugged and said that he did "not want to upset the entire [food] program by either giving free food to these negroes in the delta or by lowering the amount of money they have to pay for food stamps. . . ." Freeman added he was awaiting a comprehensive food program from Congress.[6]

But despite the prominence and influence of those who had visited Mississippi, none of the national figures who had returned from fact finding in the South were able to "do something" in Washington to address rural hunger.

A Kennedy food bill was effectively stalled in Congress. In July 1967—while SRRP was conducting its survey—an emergency food and medical bill finally passed in the Congress but was derailed by the Texas chairman of the House Agriculture Committee. In November 1967 Congress finally approved the bill, but its execution was stalled. Frustrated by the legislative logjam, Dr. Coles agreed to help SRRP and recruited three of his group of doctors to come with us to Washington. Since a Congressional approach was going nowhere, maybe the SRRP actions could shake things up.

I was elated! We would go to the nation's capital to mount a major assault aimed at eliminating starvation from rural America. Would Dr. King go along with such a plan? I went to Atlanta to sit in on his weekly staff meeting held in the same café where I had first spoken with him and his staff. It would be the last time I would see him alive.

Invited to present my case, I explained that I planned to file a class action lawsuit for desperately needed food based upon the SRRP survey with claimants from across the Deep South, Appalachia, and the West, including American Indians and Chicanos recruited by Cesar Chavez. While I worked on the legal front with poverty lawyers throughout the United States, I hoped Dr. King and SCLC would undertake a political offensive, attracting media attention with demonstrations, marches, and speeches.

I suggested to Dr. King that he might make another "I Have a Dream" speech. "You know," I babbled enthusiastically, "you could even refer to Jesus and the bread and fish multiplying!" I only stopped talking when I noticed that everyone had burst into astonished laughter at the spectacle of a Jewish lawyer attempting to instruct them on the New Testament. Chastened and red faced, I summed up quickly: "We don't even need

Congress," I concluded. "President Johnson can do it with an executive order—and maybe, just maybe, he'll do it to get us to leave."

Everyone waited for Dr. King's reaction. After a long moment he smiled. "Tell me more," he said quietly. I elaborated for another half hour before I was asked about money. "Oh, we'll raise money easy enough," I responded breezily. Again Dr. King laughed, though he was gracious enough not to remind me of the $100 I had recently borrowed from SCLC to purchase mimeograph paper. Dr. King told me to talk it over with SCLC director Andy Young. "Let's have a report tomorrow."

I met Young that night for dinner at his home only to find that he had spoken with Dr. King and they had expanded the idea. The SCLC, Andy said, has a nationwide constituency which also has an acute need for "welfare, medical care, jobs, and housing. All of this must be addressed, too."

"No!" I almost yelled, "This must be a single-issue campaign: *'Feed the starving!'* Adding other issues will destroy the focus."

He looked at me and I imagined his thoughts: *SCLC has been doing this stuff for ten years and here is this newcomer telling us how to protest.* He may have also heard the charge that once I get a strong idea, I'm immovable. He excused himself to make a phone call, after which we debated most of the night with neither convincing the other.

"If we ask for the world, we lose," I summed up.

"It must be all," Andy said, eyes drooping.

"Then I'll have to go it alone!" I reluctantly told him, amazed at my own presumptuousness.

"As you should," he concluded. "It's a fine idea."

Dr. King and SCLC did not join SRRP in this project because they chose a broader impact by including other issues. SCLC instead went its own way and began the groundwork for what became the "Poor People's Campaign." Nevertheless we remained dedicated to the same goals and worked together on other matters.

Whatever would eventually happen on the "political" front, I had to turn to the pressing business of gathering individual plaintiffs to add to SNCC, which had already signed onto the suit. Throughout that fall and winter Veit and other SRRP staffers scoured the region. They talked to representative households from six counties, including one family whose baby had recently perished from the effects of malnutrition. They located families living in counties providing only minimal "surplus commodities" in lieu of food stamps or were eligible for food stamps beyond their means. They also found families in counties that did not allow *any* federal food programs. It took the better part of a month to explain the suit to our potential farmer plaintiffs—and the dangers of participating in it—and for us to document the details of their lives.

Because the plural of "person" in Southern black patois is "peoples," we designated as lead plaintiff a farmer named "Arlett Peoples," so that our lawsuit would be officially titled *Peoples v. USDA*.

Meanwhile the legal skeleton of the lawsuit was taking shape based on nothing less than the constitutional guarantee of life. With the raw data provided from the survey we were prepared to document living conditions in the "starvation belt" of the South. We eventually came up with that rare legal document that made even its drafters weep.

The suit was in three parts: the first dealt with the federal surplus commodities program, the second with food stamps, and the third with those localities that had no federal food programs at all. The federal surplus commodities (free food) program was an agricultural price stabilization effort. Its primary purpose was to keep agricultural commodity prices high by purchasing and then giving away those crops for which market prices had fallen below the cost of production. The fact that there was food that could be distributed to needy people without cost was only an incidental benefit, according to USDA officials.

The free food for the most part consisted of cornmeal, cheese, grits, flour, rice, and beans. The lawsuit charged that even in the counties where this free food was distributed, our clients were slowly starving to death on these inadequate, mostly starchy products.

Eight plaintiffs were in this category and had average household income of $110 per month. The typical household had nine members who ate only one meal a day, mostly consisting of starches supplemented by some garden vegetables.

People living in counties that allowed access to food stamps were in better shape in theory because they could purchase food of their choice for a reduced amount of money. Unlike the surplus commodity program, the federal food stamp program was explicitly designed to "raise the levels of nutrition among low-income households." Unfortunately the majority of rural black Alabamians could not afford the minimum purchase price of the stamps. Many of those who elected to purchase the stamps often did so with money that would otherwise have gone for basic health care and medication.

The households of sixteen plaintiffs from these food stamp counties had a typical income of $138 per month. Many in this group existed solely on credit provided by their landlord and almost never touched a dollar bill or handled a coin.

One representative household consisted of a mother, eight children, and seven grandchildren living on $188 per month with expenses for clothing and school supplies for the children and her debt to the plantation owner for rent, food, and farming supplies. This cost them $165.05 monthly, leaving them a little less than $23 to purchase food for thirty days.

The daily life of one pathetically poor woman was described in depth in the legal papers. She lived with her six children in a wooden frame shack on an income of $150 per month. She could not raise the $60 required in her county to buy the equivalent of $100 worth of food stamps. Her six-week-old son Chester had died from the effects of severe malnutrition.

Her family ate only one meal a day, although some of the children received free lunches at school. The meal typically consisted of seasonally available garden greens, cornbread, rice, and occasionally pork parts.

Theoretically food stamps would enable that amount to stretch further but only if they could pay the minimum required. We would prove that a policy that looked very generous on paper was in reality abetting slow starvation.

But as bad as conditions were in the counties that participated in the federal food programs, they were far worse in the counties that did not allow any federal food assistance. The households of three families in those counties averaged nine persons. One had no cash income, one had $50 per year, and the third existed solely on Social Security.

These were the "walking dead," as our doctors were prepared to testify.

After outlining the severe nutritional deficits afflicting the nation's rural poor, we demanded that the USDA declare a state of emergency to force federal food programs into the counties that were blocking them and to radically reform the programs that were already in operation. We called for the cost of food stamps to be drastically reduced or even provided at no cost to the hardest hit of the rural poor. We argued further that the government should ensure that the free food brought into rural areas truly promote a diet that conforms to USDA's own nutritional standards. In short our suit insisted that the USDA follow its mandate and ensure that no family would ever again face famine in a land of plenty.

To my surprise and dismay most of the nation's civil rights groups opposed the SRRP suit. Some considered our tactics too belligerent, some were clearly uncomfortable with SNCC's support of the effort, and we assumed all knew about the SCLC choosing not to participate.

Even members of the SRRP advisory board, reflecting the sentiment of their organizations, held back funds. "Bobby Kennedy thinks you're wrong and believes you would hurt *his* bill for food," I was told. "Everyone thinks you're wrong! How can you be so sure you're right?"

Although I responded with carefully thought-out explanations, privately I brooded. At root I believed that Kennedy's failure in the Congress was convincing proof that celebrity, political influence, congressional laws, and doctors' reports would not be enough—that the system, especially with the power of Southern segregationists, would not yield until the victims came to the gates of power.

To get them there, however, would take money: The cost for the three buses needed to transport one hundred and thirty farmers and families eight hundred and fifty miles to DC was $3,600. Without contributions from the civil rights community this figure might as well have been a million dollars. Fortunately, Winifred Green, part of the SRRP board, member of the Quaker staff, and a friend, broke the ice. She told me and others that while she wasn't sure we would succeed, she wanted us to be able to try. With her help we raised the money to pay for the buses one day before it was due.

The die was now cast. For better or worse the buses would leave for the nation's capital in late March 1968 to demand food from the US Congress.

With the publicity surrounding the trip—and the lawsuit—came threats to the bus company and to our clients. I wondered what more could happen—then my beloved dog Bokulich died from poisoning. A neighbor later told me he saw a car drive by and someone threw him a ball of hamburger meat, which he ate. It was laced with strychnine.

Accompanying me as I drove to a meeting later that night, Bokulich was making strange whimpering noises but I ignored him and yelled at him to stop carrying on. About a half hour into the meeting he walked through an open door, came to me, peed on the floor, and collapsed spread eagle.

I drove to a nearby phone but was too hysterical to dial; others phoned a white Selma veterinarian. Although it was very late he got out of bed and met us at his clinic where he pumped my dog's stomach and then gave him a sedative to quiet him. I held him as he fell asleep, never to awaken. The veterinarian—no friend of mine or of civil rights—muttered, "I will kill the dog murderers when I learn their identity."

I fell into a deep depression and couldn't work for the next three days. All civil rights workers knew we could be killed at any time—but at least we had made that choice. My dog was innocent and helpless. I couldn't bear his death, a cowardly killing of me in effigy.

Then one evening the phone in the church rang. It was the familiar voice of Dr. King offering his condolences. He told me that he and Coretta were praying for Bokulich, who they considered a martyr to the cause. I barely managed to thank him through my tears, but his call lifted me from my paralyzing depression.

Four days before the arrival of the buses I flew to DC and began to work with Estelle Fine, a thirty-two-year-old PhD candidate and a reporter for *The Southern Courier*. She prepared for the arrival of the farmers and their families. The group ranged in age from six weeks to seventy-five, including one mother with fourteen children. Fine miraculously accomplished obtaining places for all to stay and food to eat. One local church provided shelter, another parish provided cots, a nearby college offered blankets, a supermarket reduced its food prices for the visitors, and others provided towels and soap. Most of the black Alabamians had never before taken a real shower, and some admitted they were afraid at first.

Churchwomen cooked and local school children of many races pooled their spending money to purchase candy for the children, which they wrapped in pretty boxes with fancy bows of silk ribbon. A steady stream of private individuals brought in used clothing and children's shoes. The first night a girls' glee club serenaded the Alabamians. The farm families submitted to medical examinations administered by doctors who were prepared to testify about the health conditions they found.[7]

As we later entered the courthouse black jurors from another case were so moved by the news coverage that they "chipped in" for the families to tour the Capitol. The FBI also took notice and was advised by an informant that SRRP was bringing "suit against the United States Department of Agriculture in an attempt to obtain free food stamps of negligible cost, for surplus food for the poverty stricken," and that we "planned to sit in the courtroom as witnesses [but] without demonstrating, picketing, or visiting the USDA."[8]

The hearing took place in the courtroom of US District Judge George L. Hart Jr. on March 25, 1968. He promptly rebuked me for "traipsing" the plaintiffs to DC "for what I suspect to be purely political purposes rather than to seek quick justice." He added, "I believe you have done this as a publicity stunt and I can tell you that it leaves a bad taste in the court's mouth."

I politely replied, "I don't believe we can get justice anywhere but here in the Capital of the United States." I didn't add that the justice sought could *not* be obtained in his court either but only by the political pressures brought about by the appearance of the farmers in his courtroom. I also stated that among other reasons to bring the sharecroppers all the way to Washington was that while here they could get medical help denied them in Alabama.

"If that is true," the judge interrupted, "then that's about as heavy an indictment of the medical profession as I have ever heard. Don't doctors in Alabama take the Hippocratic Oath?"

"Yes," I replied, "but it's a segregated Hippocratic Oath."

Then Judge Hart announced (to my great disappointment) that he would not permit any live testimony at this hearing, pointing out that it was in his discretion—because this was an injunction proceeding—to allow only testimony by written affidavit. Angry at me for bringing all these farmers to the hearing—and possibly fearing that I intended to put all of them on the stand along with the doctors—he excluded testimony from the clients, the doctors who had toured the South, as well as the doctors who had examined the farmers a few days earlier. But he said he would allow an "offer of proof," a summary from me (for purposes of an appeal, if necessary) of what I contended the live testimony *would* have shown, if permitted.

Taking the podium I spoke for almost an hour presenting the results of the SRRP survey highlighting the disturbing findings concerning lack of food as well as the doctors' reports. I told in detail of the woman with the dead baby and the courage the plaintiffs had displayed to come here despite widespread threats. I then discussed the USDA's food programs, stating that even with food stamps priced as low as fifty cents, many couldn't afford them and therefore receive no food assistance at all.

"You are saying," Judge Hart scoffed in disbelief, "that if you have no money, it still costs fifty cents for the stamps?" The judge looked over to the table of the USDA lawyers for rebuttal, but they just lowered their heads. He mumbled, "You mean it's true?"

I felt Judge Hart's attitude was starting to shift as I continued, although he still declined when I asked him if he would like to hear from the farmers or the doctors. After many hours the judge announced his decision. Based upon what he had heard in his courtroom, he agreed that "the food programs are inadequate," that "many of Alabama's poor people are facing starvation," that "there is not sufficient food available to them," and that an improperly balanced diet can cause irreparable injury to the persons involved.

Nonetheless, he concluded, the primary objective of the original statute was the removal of agricultural surpluses. Any benefit derived by the poor and undernourished were at best an incidental objective, and therefore the farmers had no legal standing to sue.[9] The appellate court would later reverse this line of reasoning, holding that the poor "are aggrieved" and are entitled to their day in court.

"The remedy is with the Congress," Judge Hart concluded, "and the sooner the better."

After we left the courtroom I met with the farm families who were thrilled by the judge's compassionate tone and comments. To them it was clear that we had "won." Talking within clear earshot of the press I tried to set the judge's action in a narrative context. The Johnson administration, I said, had promised that poor people would get food stamps for free, but Agriculture Secretary Orville Freeman wouldn't do it because he is a puppet of Congressman Jamie Whitten of Mississippi who controls USDA money.

And why didn't Whitten want to make life a little easier for poor people? Because, I said, with the onset of automated cotton picking, he wanted the newly restive and suddenly troublesome black rural population out of the South. If he couldn't get them out any other way, I charged, he was willing to starve them out.

Their official duties over, it was now tourist time for the families. Bottles of whole milk were brought for the youngsters, but not accustomed to such rich fare they could not stomach it. They did eat bologna sandwiches, however, and then got on the buses to see the Capitol, President Kennedy's grave, and the Lincoln Memorial. Some copied Lincoln's Second Inaugural Address from the engraving on the monument.

The next day they got back on the chartered buses for the long ride home as the *New York Times* ran a major story about a judge who had rejected a demand to order free food for families that "were starving." The *Times* lead editorial that day also called for prompt Congressional action.[10] This coverage set the tone for the nation's press and even some foreign press.

The next month I received word that Bobby Kennedy had congratulated our efforts. Dr. King did so directly in a telephone conversation. It was the last time I would speak to him before he was assassinated.

Predictably enough Southern media were quick to deem our effort a failure. The *Montgomery Advertiser* gloated:

Probably the most surprised person in [the] courtroom Monday was Donald Jelinek, lately of Selma. What Jelinek was trying to do was to get the judge to force the Agriculture Department to give away Food Stamps, rather than requiring some recipient participation. The way the program operates, it encourages some initiative. From the hamhanded manner that Jelinek went about it, he doesn't want it that way.

Jelinek obviously doesn't know what to do and hasn't helped by taking his ducks to the wrong market.[11]

But it was soon abundantly clear that Washington, DC, was the *right* market for inspiring a national sense of shame and guilt around the issue of rural hunger. Within three days of the mass-media spotlight attracted by the court hearing, the USDA declared "starvation emergency" areas in Elmore County and two other counties that barred federal food aid.[12] It also announced that its new policy would be to bypass local governments and, if necessary, provide the food programs on its own. It also agreed to begin fortifying its surplus commodities distributions with vitamins, one of the recommendations of our panel of doctors. A USDA official conceded that the *Peoples* case "made it easier for us to move into Elmore County."

Nick Kotz, a reporter for the *Des Moines Register,* wrote a story within a month after the hearing. "Not until April 1968 [when the farmers departed DC] did interdepartmental haggling [over the Congressional food bill] finally ebb enough so that someone could begin dispensing what was supposed to be 'emergency' aid to the sick and hungry poor."[13]

By mid-1968 the USDA was providing food in forty-two counties that had previously refused to distribute federal food relief to the poor. In time all of the nation's rural counties would have some form of food assistance. The surplus commodities program was improved, the price of food stamps was sharply lowered, and the food crisis, while still severe, was brought closer to manageable proportions.

Food stamp offices were suddenly responsive to SRRP's suggestions. Miscalculations were cleared up with a simple phone call, and charges of abusive treatment were quickly addressed. The FBI noted that SRRP had "come into prominence. . . ."[14]

PROJECT HELP

In mid-1968 we were approached by the producers of a TV documentary being prepared for broadcast on CBS called *Hunger in America*. The

Don Jelinek at food distribution center in Alabama (Donald A. Jelinek papers [M2225]. Department of Special Collections and University Archives, Stanford University Libraries, Stanford, California).

filmmakers asked us to find hungry families in Alabama for them to film and interview. We agreed to act as their guides. Those who consented were interviewed and filmed as they lived and ate.

The finished show was broadcast on May 21, 1968, and, in the words of the network, "moved the nation to tears." The producers told us that the viewers seemed most touched by a fourteen-year-old who said he "was ashamed" when he could not pay the twenty-five-cent cost of a school lunch and had to sit and watch the other children as they ate.

Since our name was listed in the credits at the end of the film, money began to pour in (by our standards). We received $3,000 in contributions in amounts as small as $1.25. I wanted to use the money to keep SRRP functioning, but my staff overruled me, insisting that the money be donated to feed the hungry. So we introduced a plan to purchase and distribute food in the counties where the documentary had been filmed. We called it "Project HELP." As word of the effort spread people began sending food on their own: 500 cans and boxes of food arrived plus an entire railroad car from Duluth, Minnesota, which carried 42,000 cartons of desserts.

Since our survey had revealed that 25 percent of the respondents ate no fresh meat at all, we decided to purchase hamburger meat in bulk: two-and-a-half tons. Sunday, July 14, 1968, was spent inside our rented Hertz freezer truck making 10,000 half-pound meat patties.

To help demonstrate the inadequacy of the USDA's surplus commodities program, we had decided to bring our food to the USDA's food distribution site on the same date, time, and place that the fed's free food was to be given out. When USDA officials advised that they would deny us access to their site, I alerted the media, promising them that "if the gates are closed, we'll crash the fence with the Hertz truck!" When the hour of the promised confrontation approached the USDA docilely opened the gates in front of the television cameras and even provided a long table for our distribution effort.

As we gave out hamburger meat for each household we conducted an impromptu survey and learned that most sharecroppers couldn't even remember when they last, if ever, had seen beef. I spoke to the recipients: "This fresh meat is *not* being given to you by the government. It's being given to you because the government won't feed you. Because people all over the country heard that the government won't give you enough food."

Moved by the power of the event, I looked squarely at the TV cameras and spoke words I had uttered privately many a time: "The US Department of Agriculture and the Secretary of Agriculture are the murderers of every black baby who starves to death in the South." So much for my painstakingly and carefully constructed moderate reputation.

For their part the recipients were far more interested in the meat than my rhetoric. Those who picked up the food were offered food tips: "The meat can be cooked in a frying pan or broiled in an oven. It can be made tastier by adding garden green peppers, onions, and 'running' tomatoes." Each household was also given the name of a Northerner who had written to us after the television program wanting to help.

This scene was repeated the next week in another county which had been filmed. Again officials from the USDA allowed that it was "perfectly alright" for us to use their facilities to give people food. Federal agriculture officials also announced that they planned to extend food programs in 165 "reluctant" counties throughout the nation within three months—*thus feeding tens of thousands!*

The success of the fight for food in the tempestuous summer of 1968 remains one of the proudest moments of my life.

19

Goodbye to SNCC ...
and the South

On June 11, 1967, the phone rang while Kathy Veit and I were in the home of a professor at Tuskegee Institute. He picked it up and then handed it to me. I heard the nearly hysterical voice of Lowndes County SNCC leader Johnny Jackson. "Don, we're trapped in Dan Houser's home in Prattville!" He yelled into the phone, gunshots audible in the background. "A whole army's outside shooting at us. We're all going to be killed. . . ."

Then the phone went dead. Turning on the radio we heard an announcer state that martial law had been declared in the small town of Prattville, Alabama, fifteen miles northwest of Montgomery, after Stokely Carmichael had caused a riot there. Then Johnny Jackson called again. "No calls can come into the house," he explained breathlessly, "but I am able to call out—at least for now." He then repeated that armed men were surrounding the house. *Please do something!*"

I called Atlanta SNCC and was told that they had also been contacted and that "carloads of armed blacks are leaving from five different points, but," a staffer added, "it will take them many hours to get there." I was only an hour away. I said I would leave immediately.

"You will be the first to arrive," I was warned, and then given instructions and a message to deliver to the commanding officer of the surrounding forces if I got through. "Good luck."

Apologizing to my host, I explained that I must leave immediately for Prattville. Despite my request that Veit stay back, she defiantly walked out of the house and planted herself in the car. I was secretly delighted. It would help to ease my raging anxiety to have someone to talk to, though I didn't tell her the details of the message I was to deliver.

Judge Frank Johnson, in a later written opinion, would compile and file a chronology describing the events that unfolded in the hours before I had received Johnny Jackson's call. He accepted as credible the testimony of a sixteen-year-old black teenager and the notes of a newspaper reporter, both of which he relied upon as evidence of what had happened that day.

According to Johnson, Carmichael had arrived in Prattville at 3 PM to speak to the Autauga County Improvement Association meeting in a local churchyard. The rally was in response to the killing of a black man, who was shot in the back while in police custody by Prattville police officer Kenneth Hill.[1] Although Carmichael's rhetoric was angry, the gathering was peaceful until the police arrived.

"We advocate that all black people get some guns and learn to use them," Carmichael was quoted as saying. "The only way to get Kenneth Hill off the police force is to organize Black Power in this area and use your guns."

Seeing troopers driving by, he raised his fist in the air and shouted, "Black Power!" When the driver turned the car around and returned, the crowd took up the call chanting, "Black Power! Black Power!" The first trooper who emerged from the car was Kenneth Hill.

"Listen, you," he said, pointing his finger at Carmichael, "You don't go 'round shouting and going on, hear?"

"Would you like to speak to me?" Carmichael mocked the police officer. "I'm Mr. Carmichael."

"I don't give a damn who you are!" Hill said. "You've got no business shouting like that."

Ignoring the officer, Carmichael turned back to the crowd. "You know the only time black people are allowed to meet without interference is to pray and to dance. Whenever black people get together for any other reasons, the hunkies get scared and come out to beat and kill us."[2]

"Shut up, *boy*!" said the increasingly red-faced Hill. "I'm the law around here."

Facing the fuming officer, a fiery Carmichael challenged Hill. "Take off that tin badge and drop your gun! I'll show you something, hunkie!"

"You're threatening me?" Hill growled.

"Do you want to arrest me?

"No, we don't want to arrest you. Our job is to protect the people."

"These hunkies want to send us to Vietnam to fight the Viet Cong," Carmichael said, turning again toward the crowd. "But our war is right here in the United States of America!"

By then more policemen had arrived on the scene while Carmichael continued addressing the crowd.

"From now on it's going to be an eye for an eye, a tooth for a tooth, and a hunkie for every black man killed!"

That proved to be too much for Hill, who placed Carmichael under arrest and pushed him into the back of a police cruiser. When a local woman protested Carmichael replied jauntily, "Well, that's right, Baby!"

Another police officer responded by striking him through the open window of the police car. Then, noticing a reporter from the *Southern Courier* taking photographs and a newswoman from a radio station recording the incident, he roughed them up as well. "No publicity!" he yelled. Their cameras and microphones were confiscated.

Carmichael was then taken to the same jail where the black man had recently been shot in the back.

Approximately seventy-five people followed local leader Dan Houser to his nearby home to discuss strategy. Many were inside the house, some posted outside when the first shots rang out. Those outside dove for cover as bullets struck the house.

"Prattville, Alabama, literally became an armed camp," concluded Judge Johnson, describing the scene. "Numerous members of the Alabama State Troopers arrived; all available deputies and special deputies for Autauga County were called into active duty, and [later] a contingent of the Alabama National Guard [was] sent to the Prattville area."[3]

I had stopped for gas about a half hour from Prattville when I heard a radio news flash: "Stokely Carmichael is dead. He was killed in Prattville!" I ran to the men's room to vomit and then spoke to a tearful Veit: "I think I'm going to die tonight."

We continued our drive, passed a Prattville city limits sign used by passing motorists for target practice, and then saw the road ahead blocked by a wooden barricade manned by two National Guardsmen. They looked as young and innocent as I must have appeared during my own days in the guard. When I stopped the car one pointed his rifle at us while the other flashed his searchlight into the car. Identification was demanded.

"I'm Stokely Carmichael's lawyer!" I bellowed at them. "I want to speak to your commander immediately! This involves *his family*!"

They were momentarily confused by my authoritative tone. Keeping my arms visible, I slowly opened the car door. The guardsmen said nothing as I exited, but as I stepped on the ground my knee buckled and I fell. One of the young men readied his rifle, apparently fearing my fall was an aggressive maneuver. I immediately assured them that I had fallen over a rock. I rose very slowly hoping they would not guess that fear had buckled my knee.

Again I demanded to see their commander. One of the guardsmen went to look for him while the other kept me under guard and under the beam of his large flashlight. After ten minutes an officer in military garb approached and ordered me to leave. I told him that I knew his troops were firing at unarmed blacks, including children, and that I wanted my friends out of that house safely. He scoffed and said, "It is *your* friends who are doing all the shooting and. . . ."

"If so," I broke in, "I'll be happy to drive to the house and bring them out, unarmed and unharmed."

"You'll be shot," he answered.

"You know that's not true," I rejoined. "I'm their lawyer and friend. They won't shoot at me, even if—as you apparently believe—they are crazy enough to take on a whole army."

That was enough debate for the officer, who now reverted to his official status. "That's the end of this conversation. Now leave or you will be arrested!"

I had been dreading this moment, which I had hoped would not be necessary. "I have a message for you," I said. "It's from Atlanta." This stopped him, and he waited to hear what I had to say.

"I've been told to tell you," I stated without emotion, "that if Stokely Carmichael or the others were or are killed, there are people in Atlanta who will kill you and your wife at your home [and I gave the address], and your children at their school [and I gave the name of the school and its address]." I added softly, "That is the message." I worried what the commander would do now.

He flinched, paled, and then said that Carmichael was alive. The news flash was wrong, he assured me, and no harm will come to those in the house. This time when I was again ordered to leave, I obeyed. Veit and I drove back to Selma.

I later learned that at about the very time I was speaking to the commander, the sheriff received two phone calls making similar threats against him and his family. One of the callers even gave his name and phone number in case the sheriff wanted to verify that this was not an anonymous crank call.

Soon thereafter the National Guard ordered all shooting to cease. Later that night over a loudspeaker the sheriff promised safety to the group if they left the house. Ten to twelve blacks were arrested, and all but Houser were taken to the county jail. He was brought to the city jail where he was severely beaten.

In his account of the Prattville events Judge Johnson noted that "a large group of hostile white people" were allowed to congregate night and morning near the jail, that two police cars were fired upon, and that two policemen and a "dog boy" (a bloodhound handler) were wounded by shotgun pellets fired by "unknown individuals."[4]

On the basis of these facts Johnson concluded that "the fault lies on *both* sides," alleging that blacks "did harass . . . police officers and other citizens. . . . This court unequivocally and emphatically condemns any advocacy of violence or the use of violence at any time," Johnson would write, "and particularly in connection with activities that are ostensibly designed to secure full rights of citizenship to members of the minority race."[5]

Only then would Judge Johnson express disapproval of "the excessive use of force or power . . . on the part of police officials. . . . Even though the use of the term 'black power' offends the sensibilities of many citizens, both white and Negro," he wrote, "it cannot justify the action of the police."

When Veit and I returned to Selma we were relieved to hear that Carmichael was in fact alive and that the last of the group were safely out of the Prattville house. Nonetheless I had a fitful night worrying what I would do when Carmichael was arraigned in a state court from which my presence was barred and to which I had agreed never to return. I knew what a negative impact an incident in a state courtroom could have on my plans for SRRP.

A day later I drove from Selma to the Prattville city jail and hugged a very alive Carmichael who was only now finding out about the news of his "death." When he later appeared in the courtroom to answer the charges of disorderly conduct, I was seated at the defense table as he pled "not guilty." As he was taken back to his cell he threw me a broad wink.

Following my appearance in the Prattville courtroom, the Alabama Bar Association called Bronstein to ascertain if I was reneging on my agreement. When Bronstein checked with me, I assured him that this was a one-time matter and that it would not happen again. And it didn't. Never again did I step foot in an Alabama state courtroom.

Perhaps inevitably, word came from Atlanta that many on the SRRP board were upset by my action. In response I repeated the message that I had given to Bronstein, assuring them that I was well aware that SRRP's viability depended on my keeping a low profile—and that included my avoiding being any more directly linked with SNCC than I already was.

H. "RAP" BROWN

There was one problem with my genuine intention to keep my distance from SNCC, however, and that problem's name was H. "Rap" Brown, Carmichael's successor as chairman of SNCC as well as a SRRP board member.

Rap Brown had issued a fiery statement to the press after Prattville: "We will no longer sit back and let black people be killed by murderers who hide behind sheets or behind the badge of the law. . . . It is clear that the law cannot and will not protect black people. . . . It appears that Alabama has been chosen as the starting battleground for America's race war."[6]

Prior to the time that the twenty-four-year-old Brown stepped up as chair of SNCC in 1967, he and I had become real friends. Bombastic, lovable, and good-humored, the lanky young man drifted in and out of Selma, his role in SNCC vague and his tasks undefined. When he was arrested for breaking into the SNCC house over a lover's quarrel, I had to wake up a judge to arrange for bail. ("Not *him* again," the judge groused.)

Much of our time together was spent arranging contests for our dogs. His was named Sapphire (an in-joke from the *Amos and Andy* radio comedy show). We would compete: Could Sapphire jump, fetch, return, and race as fast as my dog? Then he and I would wrestle, drink booze, and tell exaggerated stories. Mostly when Rap was in town he would make evident how he earned his nickname from his days as a student in Bogalusa, LA, where he was always "rapping."

While I liked Brown and welcomed him to live in the ACLU house when he was in town, I had trouble taking him seriously as SNCC's new leader mostly because it was difficult to imagine an old friend as a new national (and controversial) celebrity. It had been easier with Carmichael, who was already a well-established leader before I met him. When I was later asked how well I knew Brown, I would answer, "Very well," but then I would typically add, "but I don't think I know the Rap Brown that's famous."

Now a new and deadly serious Brown was coming into his own, soon to overshadow Carmichael bearing the torch of Black Power to militants across the nation. He had emerged, almost unnoticed, in Newark, New Jersey, on July 20, 1967, at the National Conference on Black Power. There he was only one firebrand among many. But then he drove to Cambridge, Maryland, where he told a black audience, "If America don't come around, we're going to burn America down, brother." When a black section of that town was later set aflame, he was charged with inciting the riot.

Then began a series of speeches and arrests. Eventually Brown was charged with fourteen separate counts in forteen separate parts of the country. Setting aside the intellectual appeal of Carmichael, Brown used the raw rhetoric of the nation's urban ghettos. His signature line was "Violence is as American as cherry pie!" and his autobiography was entitled *Die Nigger Die!*

He struck a raw American nerve. Ghetto dwellers listened to him as he talked of the evolution of the black struggle from the early days of civil rights, to the nonviolence of Dr. King, and culminating in the Black Power advocated by Carmichael. Brown was now prepared to carry the Black Power banner in ever more violent battles. Impatient urban black residents proved a receptive audience.

As Brown's controversial national profile continued to grow, I began to receive strong entreaties and then outright threats from Atlanta: "If Rap Brown's name remains on the SRRP board of directors, we will resign." As our donation stream, already a trickle, shrank still further, Rap himself advised, "Jerk, drop my name and take the bread!" But I would not remove his name, arguing that if we claimed to be an all-inclusive civil rights organization then we must act as such. His name remained on the SRRP letterhead, and in the end no one resigned.

But the effort to keep the big tent of the Civil Rights Movement intact and upright seemed an increasingly quixotic mission. The ideological and emotional gap between SNCC, the civil rights establishment, the US government, and the Democratic Party had grown into a chasm.

VIETNAM AND ISRAEL

In the wake of the "betrayal" at the 1964 Atlantic City convention, Carmichael had stated that SNCC needed to become independent of the US government and the Democratic Party. Nothing could declare that independence more unequivocally than opposition to President Johnson's escalation of the Vietnam War.

In early January 1966 twenty-two-year-old Navy veteran Samuel Younge Jr. was shot in the back of the head in Alabama by a white gas station attendant for attempting to use a whites-only restroom. Younge had been a "key figure" in student demonstrations at Tuskegee Institute.[7] Three days after his death SNCC issued a heated statement describing their organization as supporting "the men in this country who are unwilling to respond to a military draft [to] compel them to contribute their lives to United States aggression in Viet Nam in the name of the 'freedom' we find so false in this country."[8] The SNCC account compared the murder of Sammy Younge with "the murder of peasants in Vietnam, for both Younge and the Vietnamese sought, and are seeking, to secure the rights guaranteed them by law."[9]

The statement was fervently denounced as soon as it was issued. In the midst of the firestorm SNCC cofounder Julian Bond, who had just been elected to the Georgia House of Representatives, was denied his seat because he backed the SNCC position on the war. Although a unanimous US Supreme Court reinstated him, the impact of the anti–Vietnam War statement and opposition to the war in general continued to cause multiple problems for SNCC.[10]

Then SNCC upped the ante. On June 5, 1967, Israel became engaged in the Six-Day War against an overwhelming Arab force. For years prior to 1967 the Egyptian and Syrian armies had been rapidly and extensively building up thousands of tanks, artillery pieces, fighter planes, and military "advisors." In the months leading up to the war the Egyptian and Syrian media had been filled with boasts and threats that they would "drive the Jews into the sea."

A few days before the war began I discussed the Middle East with SNCC workers, expecting them to share my belief in Israel and my worry for its safety. After all, I noted, the Jewish nation was very much like SNCC: young, arrogant, uncompromising, and outnumbered.

It was a shock to me when they signaled their support for the Arabs. These SNCC activists demonstrated a sense of identity with the "black" Arabs—which increased when the Arab armies were defeated and utterly humiliated in less than a week.

During my next trip to SNCC in Atlanta I was shown a draft of an article to be published in the next issue of the SNCC newsletter. It asserted that "Zionist imperialists" were responsible for the permanent state of war between the Arab nations and Israel, and further that the US government's staunch support of "Zionism" was intended to advance its neocolonial ambitions in Africa. A cartoon accompanying the article showed a hand holding a lynch rope looped around the necks of a black man and an Arab; the hand bore a Star of David with a dollar sign inside the star.

That article, I predicted, would be devastating to SNCC and to the health of the civil rights community.

It would be hard to overestimate the importance of Jewish activists to the civil rights movement. Two of the three civil rights workers murdered in 1964 were Jewish, most of the one thousand volunteers in the 1964 Freedom Summer were Jewish, and most of SNCC's funding was being donated by Jews in the North. Jews, in fact, were the last major ethnic group who still refused to turn away from SNCC, sticking with it even through the drift into black separatist ideology. I knew and felt personally that the Jewish community would now feel stabbed in the back. When SNCC offended the Jewish people, it was effectively alienating their most loyal white constituency.

I asked if it was absolutely necessary to publish the article. After all, I argued, the Israel-Arab strife does not involve Southern civil rights. Neither, I was reminded, did SNCC's anti–Vietnam position "which you supported." My disagreement was of no consequence to the black militants.

My SNCC friends empathized with my personal discomfort and assured me the SNCC position was not anti-Semitic, but we all knew that such subtle distinctions would be lost in the headlines.

From the day the newsletter was released I never held a serious discussion outside of the South without being asked to justify SNCC's positions on Israel, Vietnam, and Black Power. As a white civil rights lawyer I was asked to justify black separatism. As a Jewish civil rights activist I was asked to justify SNCC's anti–Israel sentiments.

For me the SNCC position hit very close to home. I was labeled a traitor by my remaining New York friends. One lawyer colleague warned that I was "burning my bridges"—that I might never again be able to effectively practice law in New York, awash with Jewish clients, judges, and juries. I even received a letter addressed to "Judas, Selma, Alabama" which the post office somehow knew to deliver to me.

My parents, who now seemed noticeably less comfortable when I visited, reminded me that "the colored have always hated Jews."

But the anti-Israel position was not to be the final blow.

THE DEATH OF MARTIN LUTHER KING JR.

I was vacationing in New York on April 3, 1968, when Dr. King was backing black sanitation workers during strike in Memphis, Tennessee. That night he delivered a prophetic speech in a local church:

> Well, I don't know what will happen now. We've got some diffi-cult days ahead. But it really doesn't matter with me now because I've been to the mountaintop. And I don't mind. Like anybody, I would like to live a long life. Longevity has its place. But I'm not concerned about that now. I just want to do God's will. And He's allowed me to go up to the mountain, and I've looked over, and I've seen the Promised Land. I may not get there with you. But I want you to know tonight, that we, as a people, will get to the Promised Land. And so I'm happy tonight. I'm not worried about anything. I'm not fearing any man. Mine eyes have seen the glory of the com-ing of the Lord.[11]

The next day, as he stood on the balcony of a Memphis motel, he was slain by a sniper's bullet.

While blacks rioted throughout the country and machine guns were set up at the White House, I slumped before a television set and cried for the loss of Dr. King. I grieved for the nation and for myself. I telephoned a close mutual friend in Atlanta for consolation; instead I held a silent receiver for half an hour as she and I wept together.

A week later I called Carmichael to tell him that I could not go on any longer and that my time in the South was nearing an end. He confided that he would probably be leaving as well—to Africa. (There he would change his name to Kwame Ture—for President Kwame Nkrumah of Ghana and Sékou Touré, the first President of Guinea. He would remain in Africa for most of the last thirty years of his life.) I told him how much he had meant to me; he thanked me for risking my life to save him in Prattville and for always standing by him and SNCC.

I also had a final talk with Rap Brown. When we met in an Atlanta restaurant, he rose to embrace me and then introduced me to two FBI agents in a booth across the room.

"Meet my escorts," Brown told me. Everyone laughed. They seemed to appreciate it when Rap advised them that he and I would be having a long talk, so there would be time for them to order a large lunch. They thanked him for his consideration and did just that.

There was no real reason to meet as there was no business between us. It was a goodbye. He was soaring into new worlds that I could never enter, and it was unlikely we would ever meet again. We talked about dogs and the pros and cons of his fame.

And so it was that the journey that had begun with such bravado years earlier on the streets of Jackson and in the shacks and fields of Mississippi and Alabama was ending with the sight of the body of Martin Luther King Jr. laid to rest. Most of our battles were over and we had won our share. The South was shrugging off its long Jim Crow nightmare. Dr. King's SCLC barely functioned in Alabama, and SNCC had essentially decamped from the South.

Most significantly Dr. King was gone. I had had limited contact with him—phone calls, a few visits—and although he was only five years older than me I considered him my mentor. As long as he was laboring nearby I knew that I was in the right place, but now that was over.

THE JOURNEY

My journey had started out with fear, not just of death or serious bodily injury—although that dread was never far away—but also of failing others who relied on me. As a civil rights lawyer in the South in the 1960s I should not have expected many successes, but given the stakes that were involved it was easy to worry that one's efforts would fall short.

The experience was difficult. Conflicts were everywhere I turned: black versus white, North versus South, nonviolence versus militancy. I felt guilty for not becoming a full-time civil rights worker, for not being a sharecropper, and for being able to leave the Deep South whenever I was ready because I was not a poor, black Southerner who could not leave.

I was also concerned that I was losing my pride of being an American. I adored the Kennedys but now I wondered about the politics that kept them from intervening in Mississippi and Alabama. And there was the federal government I no longer revered—especially the USDA which helped impoverish black farmers and then denied them food.

Law Enforcement did not enforce the law, not just the Southern state highway patrol, county sheriffs, and local police, but the national police as well. I feared the FBI, the Justice Department would offer us no relief, and the local judiciary did not provide even the semblance of justice, nor did some Southern federal judges. Yet the law was the major tool for tackling white supremacy because we had so many people on trial and in jail. We lawyers could help, but it took civil rights workers and sharecroppers to stand up to Southern "justice"—civil rights lawyers could only lose with fervor.

I found myself once again saying goodbye to my many friends in the South, this time forever. I bid farewell to people who had fought to register to vote and bravely gone with me to various courts—many of whom had their courage rewarded by being shot at, evicted, or denied the credit they needed to eke out their meager life.

As I prepared to depart for a place where they would not follow, I told them I hoped that they understood and did not regret the battles we fought together. I told them I prayed that they would soon live in a time when they would have enough food to eat, decent homes to live in, adequate health care for themselves and their families, and decent jobs. I would never forget them.

Among the most moving farewells was one delivered on September 12, 1968, by the Edmundite Fathers. During a lavish dinner—it was jokingly called the "last supper"—they presented me with a scroll from the Book of Psalms. It read:

> He will free the poor man who calls to him and those who need help, he will have pity on the poor and feeble and save the lives of those in need; he will redeem their lives from exploitation and outrage, their lives will be precious in his sight. Prayers will be offered for him constantly blessings invoked on him all day long.

And then I departed the South.

LOST IN CALIFORNIA

Three years after I had come from New York to Mississippi as a three-week volunteer, I relocated to San Francisco to take the California Bar exam, begin a normal life, and earn some money. The FBI would add a postscript in a memorandum to my file: "Donald Jelinek, who was involved in civil rights activities in the Selma area, left Selma and Alabama in 1968 and has not been heard of since."[12]

Despite the ease of finding me—I had taken flights to and from California, had a telephone listed in my name, applied for the California Bar, and of course paid taxes—the FBI was figuratively right: *I was lost.*

Following my departure from the South I had no job, no license to practice law in California, was broke, and was heartsick. Every time I read a story about discrimination or poverty in the South I felt ashamed for having left. I continued to struggle with these feelings even after I obtained my license and began practicing law in California.

For more than three decades I never went back to the South nor had any dealings with those still living and working there. I avoided civil rights people, even those living nearby, lest they remind me of what I was trying to forget and cause my hurt to resume.

But I could not forget the love I had felt and received while living in the South.

In the evenings I would unburden myself to sharecroppers talking about joys of successes, despair at defeats and fear of what the next day would bring. They would congratulate, express regrets, and offer reassurances.

They would discuss what the future held for them, wonder out loud whether integrated schools were best for their children, and then display enormous faith that all would work out for them.

I would be asked about living in a church with priests, and I would regale them with tales about New York City and Wall Street. They would ask about my parents, and I would ask how their crop was coming and how their children were doing in the North. We would talk about the latest news in the farm communities, including births, marriages, and general gossip. Then I would play with the children until it was time to go to sleep.

My colleagues, the civil rights workers, became my adored extended family. We would exchange reports of workers in Alabama and other states and overall Movement chitchat. I would ask about their future life after civil rights, and we would discuss medical problems, girlfriends, boyfriends, and money problems.

By 1968 civil rights workers were almost all black, but I hardly noticed and nor did they, I thought. It was a camaraderie I had never experienced before with love beyond anticipation and of which I believed I would never find again.

Working alongside heroic sharecroppers and daring civil rights workers in Mississippi and Alabama I had encountered audacity and bravery beyond human expectation. Sharecroppers who risked their lives and livelihood by attempting to register to vote and by offering a bed and a meal to activists. Civil rights workers who organized black farmers in a place where the guns and the power were in the hands of an enemy who could kill, jail, or beat them with impunity.

Then in 2003 I met with a group calling itself the "Bay Area Veterans of the Civil Rights Movement." They too had had problems adjusting in the North and difficulty discussing their experiences in the South.

One woman told that she and another civil rights veteran had kids who grew up together but they did not discuss their time in the South. She consciously avoided getting too close to any civil rights workers.

A man told me that he had blanked out his experiences from his conscious mind for decades because thinking about the South hurt too much. Another woman told of horrible experiences in Georgia and how for many years she would wake in the middle of the night with sweats and nightmares. Others discussed joining cults to regain some sense of belonging.

Our experiences in the South, along with the act of leaving the sprawling, contentious, noisy, and joyful interracial community for which we had fought so hard and loved so much, continued to affect us in ways we could barely explain. Although we treasured our past it did not leave us unscathed.

We would discuss our highs, lows, and insights from that period. With this ultimate support group I no longer felt lost.

Perhaps someone should tell the FBI.

NOTES

PREFACE

1. Benjamin Muse, *The American Negro Revolution*, 141; Clayborne Carson, *In Struggle*, 322.

2. Matthew 5:39, "Whosoever shall smite thee on thy right cheek, turn to him the other also."

3. Cleveland Sellers and Robert L. Terrell, *The River of No Return*, 133.

4. Peniel Joseph, *Black Power Movement*, 2.

5. Sellers and Terrell, *The River of No Return*, 167.

6. Ibid.

7. Stokely Carmichael and Charles V. Hamilton, *Black Power*, 83.

I. GOING SOUTH

1. *JET,* "Nation Horrified by Murder of Kidnapped Chicago Youth," September 15, 1955, 6–9.

2. Mamie Till-Mobley and Christopher Benson, *Death of Innocence*, 101.

3. Ibid, 123.

4. Henry Hampton, Steve Fayer, and Sarah Flynn, *Voices of Freedom*, 6.

5. Till-Mobley and Benson, *Death of Innocence*, 212; W. B. Huie, "The Shocking Story of Approved Killing in Mississippi," *Look*, January 24, 1956, 46–50; *JET,* "Nation Horrified," 6–9.

6. For a full account of Emmett Till's murder, see Till-Mobley and Benson, *Death of Innocence*.

7. Rev. Jesse L. Jackson, foreword to *Death of Innocence*, xii.

8. *Browder v. Gale*, affirmed by the US Supreme Court; See www.crmvet.org for a collection of mostly firsthand accounts of these events provided by veterans of the Civil Rights Movement.

9. "Mississippi Summer Project," accessible at www.crmvet.org/tim/tim64b.htm #1964fs.

10. David Houze, *Twilight People*, 276.

2. LAWYERS FOR THE MOVEMENT

1. Ian McCrae, Raymond Berry, and John M. Prat, *Statement to Congressional Briefing*, National Council of Churches of Christ, June 22, 1965.

2. Sellers and Terrell, *The River of No Return*, 89.

3. *Brown v. Board of Education*, 347 US 483.

4. For its Deep South subsidiary the ACLU created the "Lawyers Constitutional Defense Committee of the ACLU," hereinafter referred to as ACLU, except when distinguishing it from the parent organization.

5. The reference to "Summer Soldiers" was derived from Thomas Paine, who had written in 1776: "These are the times that try men's souls. The summer soldier and the sunshine patriot will, in this crisis, shrink from the service of their country; but he that stands it now, deserves the love and thanks of man and woman."

4. MISSISSIPPI'S NEWEST CIVIL RIGHTS WORKER

1. Martin Luther King Jr., "I've Been to the Mountaintop," speech, April 3, 1968.
2. "The Sit-Ins of 1960," accessible at www.crmvet.org/info/sitins.pdf.
3. King, "I've Been to the Mountaintop."
4. "Freedom Rides of 1961," accessible at www.crmvet.org/riders/freedom_rides.pdf.
5. King, "I've Been to the Mountaintop."
6. "The Campaign Begins," accessible at www.crmvet.org/tim/timhis63.htm#1963 bhbegin.
7. "Civil Rights Movement History: Mississippi Freedom Summer Events," accessible at www.crmvet.org/tim/tim64b.htm.
8. Martin Luther King Jr., "I've Been to the Mountaintop," April 3, 1968.
9. "Selma and the March to Montgomery: A Discussion," accessible at www.crmvet .org/disc/selma.htm.

5. NOVICE COUNTY LEADER

1. Gunnar Myrdal, *An American Dilemma,* 947
2. Myrdal, *An American Dilemma,* 879–907, 927–956.
3. *Plessy v. Ferguson.*
4. By 1967 Thurgood Marshall would become the first black man to sit on the US Supreme Court.
5. *Brown v. Board of Education.*
6. Myrdal, *An American Dilemma,* 484.
7. *Benton County Freedom Train* vol. II, no. 10, September 1965.
8. FBI Memorandum, September 25, 1965, Donald Jelinek dossier. The author obtained parts of the FBI file dossier on him pursuant to the Freedom of Information Act. When those parts appeared insufficient, he filed a successful lawsuit to compel most of the information. Emphasis added by author.
9. Arguing that the arrest was racially inspired, the case was eventually transferred to the federal courts where it died in limbo.
10. Robert Bolt, *A Man for All Seasons,* 56.
11. Robert Williams, *Negroes with Guns,* 3; emphasis added by author.
12. Emilye J. Crosby, "This nonviolent stuff ain't no good. It'll get ya killed," 159.
13. Charles Evers and Andrew Szanton, *Have No Fear,* 36.

6. TIME TO LEAVE . . . AND RETURN

1. Removal Statute, 28 USC § 1441, et seq.
2. Clayborne Carson, *In Struggle,* 39.
3. *Moses v. Kennedy.*
4. Cox was the same judge who had dismissed federal indictments against those charged with the 1964 murder of three civil rights workers, claiming the slayings were not federal crimes. After Cox was reversed seven white Southerners were convicted for the murders. Cox also called blacks who appeared in his court "chimpanzees" and once yelled at me saying I was wasting his time calling more black witnesses because "THEY

will say anything a white man tells them to!" Ironically conservative Dwight Eisenhower appointed Southern federal judges of high integrity while liberal John Kennedy appointed many who were openly hostile to civil rights. "Senatorial courtesy" allowed US Senators to block nominees to federal judgeships associated with their states. This was a form of veto by which Democrats from Mississippi controlled the appointment of Mississippi federal judges. Republican Eisenhower had no Southern Republican senators to contend with.

5. *United States v. City of Jackson.*

6. David Kaiser, "Presumptions of Law and Fact," 254.

7. I would turn out to be wrong. Other related cases would occur, but this strategy would never again be quite appropriate.

7. FULL-TIME CIVIL RIGHTS LAWYER

1. The typical pay for SNCC workers was $40 per month.

2. The CIA was said to covertly funnel money to finance civil rights work and thereby enhance America's image overseas. This would have been illegal since it was, and still is, prohibited by law from conducting activities within the United States. Moreover it would have created a states' rights storm within the South. But the rumor also made for good conversation.

3. *Southern Courier,* "CR Lawyer Gets Slugged," June 17, 1967.

4. Stokely Carmichael with Ekwueme Michael Thelwell, *Ready for Revolution,* 89.

5. Milton Viorst, *Fire in the Streets,* 263.

6. Carmichael with Thelwell, *Ready for Revolution,* 92–94.

7. "MFDP Congressional Challenge, November 1964–September 1965," accessible at crmvet.org/tim/tim64c.htm#1964congress.

8. *Whitley v. Democratic Party of the State of Mississippi;* Carmichael with Thelwell, *Ready for Revolution,* 92–93.

9. A major part of the team was the brilliant Arthur Kinoy, Bill Kunstler's law partner, founder of the Center for Constitutional Rights and a professor at Rutgers University.

10. Donald Jelinek, *Attica Justice,* 82–83.

11. A year later I visited Washington, DC, to lobby for civil rights–related food relief. A Congressional aide, hedging support, volunteered that after Atlantic City his Congressman would not again trust the civil rights workers. "We offered them the world," he protested, "but they just couldn't compromise. They embarrassed us and let the gains we fought to get them slip through their fingers."

12. John Lewis and Michael Orso, *Walking with the Wind,* 291.

8. THE "RAPE" OF THE PLANTATION OWNER'S WIFE

1. Mack Charles Parker, a twenty-three-year-old black man, had been falsely charged with sexually assaulting a white woman and later taken from jail and slain.

2. Howard Smead, *Blood Justice,* 53.

3. Myrdal, *An American Dilemma,* xcviii.

4. Till-Mobley and Benson, *Death of Innocence,* 127.

5. This was true. Windom told me he had feared a lynching after the sentence.

6. Transcript of Judge Sebe Dale in the matter of *Alfred Windom, Petitioner, vs. State of Mississippi, Respondent,* on a petition for Writ of Eram Coram Nobis 5138 heard on June 9, 1966, at the courthouse in Lamar County, Purvis, Mississippi; emphasis added by author.

7. Ibid; emphasis added by author.

8. *Windom v. State of Mississippi; Windom v. Cook.*

9. A CRACK IN THE MOVEMENT

1. Dr. Poussaint wrote two provocative papers on the subject, each highly controversial within the Movement, in no small part for their titles; Alvin F. Poussaint and Joyce Ladner, "Black Power," 385–39; Alvin F. Poussaint, "The Stresses of the White Female Worker in the South," 401–7.

2. Poussaint and Ladner, "Black Power," 387.

3. Ibid, 388–89.

4. James Forman, *The Making of Black Revolutionaries* 412, 452.

5. Julian Bond, "Address to Freedom Summer Fiftieth Commemoration," Jackson, Mississippi, June 28, 2014.

6. Forman, *The Making of Black Revolutionaries,* 374.

10. WHITE LAWYER IN BLACK POWER SELMA

1. Bruce Hartford, *The Selma Voting Rights Struggle and March to Montgomery,* 10.

2. Charles Fager, *Selma, 1965,* 94.

3. Lewis and Orso, *Walking with the Wind,* 338.

4. Martin Luther King Jr., "Address at the Conclusion of the Selma to Montgomery March," March 25, 1965.

5. Barack Obama, "Remarks by the President Honoring the Recipients of the 2010 Medal of Freedom," February 11, 2011, whitehouse.gov/the-press-office/2011/02/15/remarks-president-honoring-recipients-2010-medal-freedom.

6. Carmichael with Thelwell, *Ready for Revolution,* 479.

7. Hasan Kwame Jeffries, *Bloody Lowndes,* 182.

8. Carmichael with Thelwell, *Ready for Revolution,* 448.

9. Ibid, 479.

10. Ibid, 466–70.

11. Jeffries, *Bloody Lowndes,* 82.

12. Sellers and Terrell, *The River of No Return,* 167

13. Susan Youngblood Ashmore, *Carry It On,* 153.

14. Carmichael and Hamilton, *Black Power,* 118–202.

15. Muse, *The American Negro Revolution,* 243–45.

16. Ibid 203–5; Joseph, *Black Power Movement,* 294.

17. Rob Warden, "Hoover Rated Carmichael as 'Black Messiah,'" *Chicago Daily News,* February 10, 1976.

18. Carmichael and Hamilton, *Black Power,* 47.

19. Ibid, 83.

20. Miriam Wasserman, "Farm Elections," 10–11.

21. FBI Memorandum, undated. The name of the informant was blacked out. One would have thought that the FBI would have noticed that SNCC had a well-staffed office on the floor above mine, but this was symptomatic of using raw data unchecked.

22. Carson, *In Struggle,* 201.

11. THE COTTON WARS

1. US Commission on Civil Rights, *Equal Opportunity in Farm Programs.*

2. Jeffries, *Bloody Lowndes,* 117.

3. Ibid, 128; Wasserman, *"Farm Elections,"* 10–11.

4. Ashmore, *Carry It On,* 203.

5. *Barlow v. Collins.*

6. Ashmore, *Carry It On,* 199.

7. Ibid, 230.

8. Forner, *Why the Vote Wasn't Enough for Selma*

9. Andrew Jackson Young was a pastor from Georgia, who later served as Mayor of Atlanta, a US Congressman and US Ambassador to the United Nations.

10. *William v. Freeman,* no decision, the defendants stipulated to the extension of the ASCS elections.

11. Exhibit "H" of *William v. Freeman; Miami Herald,* "Rights Groups Obtain Copy of Secret Report," August 8, 1966; emphasis added by author.

12. Excerpted from a speech by the author printed in Joanne Grant, *Black Protest,* 401.

13. *Birmingham News,* "ASCS to Let Rights Man Sit in at Sessions," August 9, 1966.

14. Jeffries, *Bloody Lowndes,* 118.

15. Testimony of Peter Agee, *William v. Freeman.*

16. P. Valentine, "Alabama Farm Election Postponed for a Month," *Washington Post,* August 11, 1966.

12. BLACK VERSUS BLACK IN THE 1966 ELECTIONS

1. Jill Konieczko, "Alabama Primary Facts and Figures: Compiled by the US News & World Report Library Staff," February 1, 2008, usnews.com/news/campaign-2008/articles/2008/02/01/alabama-primary-facts-and-figures.

2. John F. Kennedy, "Inaugural Address," January 20, 1961.

3. Ashmore, *Carry It On,* 221.

4. *Boynton v. Virginia.*

5. *Taylor v. City of Selma Alabama.*

6. Ari Berman, "Fifty Years After Bloody Sunday in Selma, Everything and Nothing Has Changed," *The Nation,* February 25, 2015.

7. Carmichael and Hamilton, *Black Power,* 103–7.

8. Its name and symbol was offered a year later to what became the California Black Panther Party headed by Huey Newton and Bobby Seale. This West Coast offshoot gained national prominence when members attended a session of the California legislature armed with unloaded rifles, pressing their demand for the rights of blacks to be armed.

9. Ashmore, *Carry It On,* 157.

10. Sellers and Terrell, *The River of No Return,* 154.

11. Carmichael and Hamilton, *Black Power,* 118–20.

13. THE DARK SIDE OF TWO FEDERAL JUDGES

1. *New Times Magazine,* "Here Comes the Judge: Frank Johnson, an American Hero for the FBI," December 9, 1977.

2. Museum of Living History, "Frank M. Johnson Jr. Biography." achievement.org/achiever/frank-m-johnson/#biography.

3. *Forman v. City of Montgomery.*

4. Carmichael with Thelwell, *Ready for Revolution,* 450.

5. Carmichael with Thelwell, *Ready for Revolution,* 451.

6. *Cottonreader v. Johnson,* 252 F. Supp. 492 (M.D. Ala. 1966). Emphasis added by author.

7. Sellers and Terrell, *The River of No Return*, 47.

8. *Yick Wo v. Hopkins.*

9. *Forman v. City of Montgomery.*

10. *Gideon v. Wainwright.*

11. *Selma Times Journal,* "Grand Jury has Advice on Court," September 18, 1966.

12. *Southern Courier,* "Three's a Crowd at Linden Jail," November 19, 1966.

13. *New York Times,* "Northern Lawyer for Rights Group Jailed in Alabama," November 17, 1966.

14. Fager, *Selma, 1965,* 42; Brian K. Landsberg, *Free at Last to Vote,* 118.

15. Letter from Charles S. Conley to the Honorable Frank M. Johnson Jr., 5 December 1966; Author's possession.

14. NO BLACKS ON SOUTHERN JURIES

1. *Strauder v. West Virginia.*

2. *Dombrowski v Pfister.*

3. Alabama Code § 8603.

4. *Carter v. Jury Commission of Greene County,* following the evidence presented in *Bokulich v. Jury Commission of Greene County.*

15. FIRED AND BANISHED

1. Robin Reisig, "Attorneys Miss Death Hearing," *Southern Courier,* December 17–18, 1966.

2. *Boykin v. State of Alabama.*

3. *Time Magazine,* "The Law and Dissent: Judge Frank M. Johnson," May 12, 1967.

4. *Southern Courier,* "LCDC Sells Out," March 4, 1967.

5. Richard Hammer, "Yankee Lawyer Go Home," *New York Times,* March 12, 1967.

6. FBI Memorandum, Donald A. Jelinek FBI File, undated.

7. Niccolò Machiavelli, *The Prince,* 66.

16. UNSUNG HEROES OF SELMA

1. *Taylor v. City of Selma.*

2. Ibid; Alabama Code Ann. tit. 14, § 407(1).

3. *Taylor v. City of Selma.*

4. Father Maurice Ouellette, interview by author, 1975.

5. Ibid, 1967–1968.

6. John Crowley, "The Path to Peace in Selma," February 7, 1965.

17. THE UNIMAGINABLE POOR

1. Southern Rural Research Project, *SRRP Proposal,* 4.

2. Howze, *Frequency and Percent Distributions.*

3. Southern Rural Research Project, *Survey of Living Conditions of the Southern Blacks in Alabama.*

4. Robert Coles, et al., *Children in Mississippi* (emphasis added by author). See also *Hunger and Malnutrition in America. Hearings before the Subcommittee on Employment, Manpower, and Poverty of the Committee on Labor and Public Welfare, United States Senate, July 11 and 12, 1967* (Washington, DC: US Government Printing Office, 1967), 47.

5. Saul Alinsky, *Rules for Radicals,* 111.

18. THE FIGHT FOR FOOD

1. Donald Jelinek Dossier, FBI Memorandum, April 4, 1968.

2. Donald Jelinek Dossier, FBI Memorandum, April 2, 1968.

3. Howard Thorkelson, "Food Stamps and Hunger in America," *Dissent,* July 1967, 479–84; Food Stamp Act of 1964.

4. Nick Kotz, *Let Them Eat Promises,* 3–4; Arthur M. Schlesinger Jr., *Robert Kennedy and His Times,* 794.

5. Coles, et al., *Children in Mississippi.* See also *Hunger and Malnutrition in America. Hearings before the Subcommittee on Employment, Manpower, and Poverty of the Committee on Labor and Public Welfare, United States Senate, July 11 and 12, 1967* (Washington, DC: US Government Printing Office, 1967), 46.

6. Joseph Califano, interview by Jean Stein, September 21, 1968.

7. Bernadette Carey, "Food Stamp Program is Protested," *Washington Post,* March 25, 1968.

8. Donald Jelinek Dossier, FBI Memorandum, March 28, 1968.

9. *Peoples v. USDA.*

10. *New York Times,* "Starvation in Mississippi," March 26, 1968.

11. *Montgomery Advertiser,* "Poverty Aid Should Begin at Home," March 26, 1968.

12. J. M. McFadden, "Ala. County Declared a 'Starvation' Area," *Washington Post,* March 30, 1968.

13. Kotz, *Let Them Eat Promises,* 3–4.

14. Donald Jelinek Dossier, FBI Memorandum, March 4, 1968.

19. GOODBYE TO SNCC . . . AND THE SOUTH

1. *Houser v. Hill.*

2. The word is a racial slur against white people, sometimes spelled "honkie" or "honkey" and in this case "hunkie."

3. *Houser v. Hill.*

4. Ibid.

5. Ibid; emphasis added by author.

6. Sellers and Terrell, *The River of No Return,* 191

7. Ibid, 149

8. "The Murder of Sammy Younge," accessible at crmvet.org/tim/timhis66.htm #1966younge.

9. "Statement by the Student Nonviolent Coordinating Committee on the War in Vietnam." Lucile Montgomery papers, 1963–1967; Historical Society Library Microforms Room, Micro 44, Reel 3, Segment 48. Wisconsin Historical Society. [accessible at http://content.wisconsinhistory.org/cdm/ref/collection/p15932coll2/id/35466]

10. *Bond v. Floyd.*

11. Martin Luther King Jr., "I've Been to the Mountaintop," April 3, 1968.; David J. Garrow, *Bearing the Cross,* 621.

12. Donald Jelinek Dossier, FBI Memorandum, undated.

BIBLIOGRAPHY

BOOKS

Alinsky, Saul. *Rules for Radicals*. New York: Vintage Books, 1971.

Ashmore, Susan Youngblood. *Carry It On: The War on Poverty and the Civil Rights Movement in Alabama, 1964–1972*. Athens: University of Georgia Press, 2008.

Bloom, Harold. *Alex Haley and Malcolm X's The Autobiography of Malcolm X*. New York: Chelsea House Publishers, 1996.

Bolt, Robert. *A Man for All Seasons*. New York: Random House, 1962.

Branch, Taylor. *At Canaan's Edge: America in the King Years*. New York: Simon and Schuster, 2007.

Brown, H. "Rap" (Jamil Al Amin). *Die Nigger Die!* New York: Dial Press, 1969.

Carmichael, Stokely, and Charles V. Hamilton. *Black Power: The Politics of Liberation in America*. New York: Random House, 1967.

Carmichael, Stokely, with Ekwueme Michael Thelwell. *Ready for Revolution: The Life and Struggles of Stokely Carmichael*. New York: Scribner, 2003.

Caro, Robert A. *The Years of Lyndon Johnson: A Passage of Power*. New York: Random House, 2012.

Carson, Clayborne. *In Struggle: SNCC and the Black Awakening of the 1960s*. Cambridge, MA: Harvard University Press, 1981.

Crosby, Emilye J. "'This nonviolent stuff ain't no good. It'll get ya killed.': Teaching about Self-Defense in the African-American Struggle." In *Teaching the American Civil Rights Movement: Freedom's Bittersweet Song*, edited by Julie Buckner Armstrong, et al., 159–73. New York and London: Routledge, 2002.

Dittmer, John. *Local People: The Struggle for Civil Rights in Mississippi*. Urbana: University of Illinois Press, 1994.

Evans, Sara M. *Personal Politics: The Roots of Women's Liberation in the Civil Rights Movement and the New Left*. New York: Knopf, 1979.

Evers, Charles, and Andrew Szanton. *Have No Fear: The Charles Evers Story*. New York: Wiley and Sons, 1997.

Fager, Charles. *Selma, 1965*. New York: Scribner, 1974.

Forman, James. *Sammy Younge, Jr.: The First Black College Student to Die in the Black Liberation Movement*. New York: Grove Press, 1968.

——. *The Making of Black Revolutionaries; a Personal Account*. New York: Macmillan, 1972.

Friedman, Leon. *Southern Justice*. New York: Pantheon Books, 1965.

Garrow, David J. *Protest at Selma: Martin Luther King Jr., and the Voting Rights Act of 1965*. New Haven: Yale University Press, 1978.

——. *The FBI and Martin Luther King, Jr.: From "Solo" to Memphis*. New York: W. W. Norton, 1981.

————. *Bearing the Cross: Martin Luther King Jr., and the Southern Christian Leadership Conference*. New York: W. Morrow, 1986.

Good, Paul. *The Trouble I've Seen: White Journalist/Black Movement*. Washington: Howard University Press, 1975.

Goodwin, Doris Kearns. *Lyndon Johnson and the American Dream*. New York: Harper & Row, 1976.

Grant, Joanne. *Black Protest: History, Documents, and Analyses, 1619 to the Present*. New York: Fawcett World Library, 1968.

Hampton, Henry, Steve Fayer, and Sarah Flynn. *Voices of Freedom: An Oral History of the Civil Rights Movement from the 1950s Through the 1980s*. New York: Bantam Books, 1990.

Hartford, Bruce. *The Selma Voting Rights Struggle and March to Montgomery*. San Francisco: Westwind Writers, 2014

Houze, David. *Twilight People: One Man's Journey to Find His Roots*. Berkeley: University of California Press, 2006

Jacobs, Paul, and Saul Landau. *The New Radicals: A Report with Documents*. New York: Vintage Books, 1966.

————.*To Serve the Devil*. New York: Random House, 1971.

Jeffries, Hasan Kwame. *Bloody Lowndes: Civil Rights and Black Power in Alabama's Black Belt*. New York University Press, 2009

Jelinek, Donald. *Attica Justice: The Cruel 30-year legacy of the Nation's Bloodiest Prison Rebellion, which changed the American Prison System*. Berkeley: Jelinek Publishers, 2011.

Joseph, Peniel E. *Black Power Movement: Rethinking the Civil Rights-Black Power Era*. New York: Routledge, 2006.

————. *Waiting 'til the Midnight Hour: A Narrative History of Black Power in America*. New York: McMillan, 2007.

————. *Stokely: A Life*. New York: Basic Civitas Books, 2014.

Kennedy, Robert F., Jr. *Judge Frank M. Johnson, Jr.: A Biography*. New York: Putnam, 1978.

King, Martin Luther, Jr. *Stride Toward Freedom*. New York: Harper, 1958.

Kotz, Nick. *Let Them Eat Promises: The Politics of Hunger in America*. Englewood Cliffs, NJ: Prentice-Hall, 1969.

Kunstler, William M. *Deep in My Heart,* New York: Morrow, 1966.

Lamont, Corliss. *The Trial of Elizabeth Gurley Flynn*. New York: Horizon Press, 1968.

Landsberg, Brian K. *Free at Last to Vote: The Alabama Origins of the 1965 Voting Rights Act*. Lawrence: University Press of Kansas, 2007.

Lester, Julius. *Look Out, Whitey! Black Power's Gon' Get Your Mama!* New York: Dial Press, 1968.

Lewis, Anthony. *Portrait of a Decade: The Second American Revolution*. New York: Random House, 1964.

————. *Gideon's Trumpet*. New York: Random House, 1964.

Lewis, John, and Michael Orso. *Walking with the Wind: A Memoir of the Movement*. New York: Simon & Schuster, 1998.

Loewen, James W., and Charles Sallis. *Mississippi: Conflict and Change*. New York: Pantheon Books, 1974.

Machiavelli, Niccolo. *The Prince*. London: Grant Richards, 1903.

Martinez, Elizabeth S. ("Betita"). *Letters from Mississippi.* New York: McGraw-Hill, 1965.

May, Gary. *The Informant: the FBI, the Ku Klux Klan, and the Murder of Viola Liuzzo.* New Haven: Yale University Press, 2005.

Muse, Benjamin. *The American Negro Revolution: From Nonviolence to Black Power, 1963–1967.* Bloomington: Indiana University Press, 1968.

Myrdal, Gunnar. *An American Dilemma: The Negro Problem and Modern Democracy.* New York: Harper & Row, 1969.

Oates, Stephen B. *Let the Trumpet Sound: The Life of Martin Luther King, Jr.* New York: Harper & Row, 1982.

Paine, Thomas. *Common Sense.* Charlottesville: University of Virginia Library, 1993.

———. *The American Crisis.* Charlottesville: University of Virginia Library, 1993.

Rabinowitz, Victor. *Unrepentant Leftist: A Lawyer's Memoir.* Urbana: University of Illinois Press, 1996.

Raines, Howell. *My Soul is Rested: Movement Days in the Deep South Remembered.* New York: Putnam, 1977.

Schlesinger, Arthur M., Jr. *The Age of Roosevelt.* Boston: Houghton Mifflin, 1957.

———. *Robert Kennedy and His Times.* Boston: Houghton Mifflin, 1978.

Sellers, Cleveland, and Robert L. Terrell. *The River of No Return: The Autobiography of a Black Militant and the Life and Death of SNCC.* New York: Morrow, 1973.

Smead, Howard. *Blood Justice: The Lynching of Mack Charles Parker.* New York: Oxford University Press, 1986.

Sojourner, Sue [Lorenzi], *Thunder of Freedom: Black Leadership and the Transformation of 1960s Mississippi.* Lexington: University Press of Kentucky, 2013.

Stampp, Kenneth M. *The Peculiar Institution.* New York: Knopf, 1956.

———. *The Causes of the Civil War.* Englewood Cliffs, NJ: Prentice-Hall, 1965.

———. *The Era of Reconstruction, 1865–1877.* New York: Knopf, 1965.

Till-Mobley, Mamie, and Christopher Benson. *Death of Innocence: The Story of the Hate Crime that Changed America.* Random House: New York, 2003.

Viorst, Milton. *Fire in the Streets: America in the 1960's.* Simon and Schuster: New York, 1979.

Webb, Sheyann, and Rachel West Nelson. *Selma, Lord, Selma: Girlhood Memories of the Civil Rights Days as told to Frank Sikora.* Tuscaloosa: University of Alabama Press, 1980.

Whisenhunt, Donald W. *Reading the Twentieth Century.* Lanham, MD: Rowman & Littlefield Publishers, 2009.

Whitfield, Stephen J. *A Death in the Delta: The Story of Emmett Till.* New York: Free Press: 1988.

Williams, Robert. *Negroes with Guns.* New York: Marzani & Munsell, 1962.

Woods, Donald. *Biko.* New York: Paddington Press, 1978.

JOURNAL ARTICLES

Kaiser, David. "Presumptions of Law and Fact." *Marquette Law Review* 38, no. 4 (November 1955): 253–61.

Lange, Fabian, Alan L. Olmstead, and Paul W. Rhode. "The Impact of the Boll Weevil, 1892–1932." *The Journal of Economic History* 69, no. 3, (September 2009): 685–718.

Poussaint, Alvin F. "The Stresses of the White Female Worker in the Civil Rights Movement in the South." *American Journal of Psychiatry* 123, no. 4 (October 1966): 401–7.

Poussaint, Alvin F., and Joyce Ladner. "Black Power': A Failure for Racial" Integration —within the Civil Rights Movement." *Arch Gen Psychiatry* 18, no. 4 (April 1968): 385–91.

Wasserman, Miriam. "Farm Elections: White Power in the Black Belt." *New South* (Winter 1967) 27–36.

REPORTS

Coles, Robert, Joseph Brenner, Alan Mermann, Milton J.E. Senn, and Cyril Walwyn. "June 1967, Children in Mississippi: A Report to the Field Foundation." In *Legislative History of the Select Committee on Nutrition and Human Needs,* by the US Congress Senate Select Committee on Nutrition and Human Needs, 9–13. Washington, DC: US Government Printing Office, 1976.

Douglas, M. Davison. *Bush v. Orleans Parish School Board and the Desegregation of New Orleans School.* University of Michigan Law School, Report for Special Project on Federal Trials and Great Debates in University, 2005.

Howze, Glen R. *Frequency and Percent Distributions of Items from Study of Rural Poverty of Selected Alabama Counties Conducted by the Southern Rural Research Project During the Summer of 1967.* Division of Behavioral Science Research, Tuskegee Institute, Alabama. March 18, 1968.

McCrae, Ian, Raymond Berry, and John M. Prat. *Statement to Congressional Briefing National Council of Churches of Christ,* June 22, 1965.

Southern Rural Research Project. *Survey of Living Conditions of the Southern Blacks in Alabama,* Summer 1967.

Southern Rural Research Project. *SRRP Proposal,* December 1969.

US Commission on Civil Rights. *Equal Opportunity in Farm Programs: An Appraisal of Services Rendered by Agencies of the United States Department of Agriculture.* Washington DC: US Government Printing Office, 1965.

———. *Twenty Years After Brown: Equality of Economic Opportunity: A Report of the United States Commission on Civil Rights, July 1975.* Washington, DC: Government Printing Office, 1975.

Yun, J. T., and Gary Orfield. *Resegregation in American Schools.* Civil Rights Project, Harvard University, 1999.

CASES

Barlow v. Collins, 397 US 159, 1970.
Bokulich v. Jury Commission of Greene County, 298 F. Supp. 181; 394 US 97,1970.
Bond v. Floyd, 385 US 116, 1966.
Boykin v. State of Alabama, 395 US 238, 1969.
Boynton v. Virginia, 364 US 454, 1960.
Browder v. Gale, 142 F. Supp. 707, 1956.
Brown v. Board of Education, 347 US 483, 1954.
Carter v. Jury Commission of Greene County, 396 US 320, 1970.
Dombrowski v. Pfister, 380 US 1116, 1965.
Forman v. City of Montgomery, 254 F. Supp. 17, 1965.
Gideon v. Wainwright, 372 US 335, 1963.
Henderson v. ASCS, 317 F. Supp. 430, 1970.
Houser v. Hill, 278 F. Supp. 920, 1968.
Moses v. Kennedy, 219 F. Supp. 762, 1963.

N.Y. Times v. Sullivan 376 US 254, 1964.

Peoples v. USDA 427 F.2d 561, 1970.

Plessy v. Ferguson, 163 US 537, 1896.

Strauder v. West Virginia, 100 US 303, 1880.

Taylor v. City of Selma, 327 F. Supp. 1191, 1971.

United States v. City of Jackson, 318 F.2d 1, 5 Cir., 1963.

Whitley, Johnson B. v. Governor of the State of Mississippi, 1967.

William v. Freeman, US District Court, District of Columbia, 2011.

Windom v. Cook, 423 F. Supp. 721, 5th Circuit, 1970.

Windom v. State of Mississippi, Action #5138 Cir. Ct. Lamar County, Mississippi, 1966.

Yick Wo v. Hopkins, 118 US 356, 1886.

STATUTES, CODES, AND LAWS

Ala. Code, 14, § 407(1).

Ala. Code, 1923, § 8603.

Food Stamp Act of 1964 PL 88–525, Section 4(b).

Removal of Civil Actions, US Code 28, 1940, § 1441, 1442, et seq.

INTERVIEWS

Father John Crowley, interview by author, 1967–1968.

Father Maurice Ouellette, interview by author, 1975.

Joseph Califano, interview by Jean Stein, Jean Stein Personal Papers, JFK Presidential Library, Boston, MA, September 21, 1968.

Robert Coles, interview by Jean Stein, August 2, 1968, Jean Stein Personal Papers, JFK Presidential Library, Boston, MA.

INDEX

ACLU House, 21, 76, 119, 123, 125, 242

Agee, Peter, 147–49

Agriculture Stabilization and Conservation Service (ASCS), 108, 133–36, 138, 141, 143, 145–49, 164, 172–73, 220, 224

American Civil Liberties Union (ACLU), 13, 15–19, 21, 29, 36, 65–68, 70–73, 75–77, 82, 83, 87–90, 92–93, 99, 104, 106–07, 110, 119, 123, 125, 132, 170, 173, 184, 193, 194, 200–06, 208, 217–18, 224, 242; Atlanta Project, 127, 129–30; Jelinek firing, 200, 203

Atlantic City "betrayal," 84–85, 122, 243

Benton County, 26, 28, 40–41, 43, 45–47, 49, 52–55, 57, 60, 63, 65, 72, 79, 108, 109; Freedom Train, 28, 47, 53

Black doll experiment, 51

Black Panthers, 84, 164–65, 181

Black Power, 47, 85, 99, 105, 119–25, 127, 130, 131, 134, 141, 152, 160–61, 166–67, 182, 200, 211–12, 238, 241, 243, 245; Movement, 85, 112–113

Bokulich, Paul, 186–92, 195, 220, 224–25; wife of, 186–88, 192

Bond, Julian, 244

Boykin, Edward, 199

Boynton, Amelia, 154–55, 200

Boynton, Bruce, 154, 171, 173, 200

Bronstein, Alvin J., 15–19, 23–25, 30–31, 33, 35–36, 45, 59, 63, 66–69, 71–75, 77, 79, 82–83, 99–100, 110, 125, 179–80, 183, 200–05, 218, 241–42

Brown, H. "Rap," 84, 123, 217, 242–43, 246

Brown, Jess, 89, 155

Brown v. Board of Education, 5, 16, 51, 137, 167, 205

Carmichael, Stokely, 84, 104, 111, 113, 117–19, 120–21, 123–24, 127, 129, 130, 142, 144, 147, 160–64, 180–82, 208–11, 217, 224, 237, 239–40; attack in Prattville, 237–39; as chairman of SNCC, 117; black power speech, 118; exclusion of whites, 113, 130–31, 245; incite-to-riot arrest and trial, 180, 208–09; in Lowndes County 118, 135, 162–64, 181; See also Meredith march

Chavez, Cesar, 217, 226

Christmas Eve Riots, 67–68, 72

Civil Rights Act of 1964, 14, 58, 82, 102, 126, 177, 180

Civil War, 3, 50, 53, 69, 72–73, 133–34

Clark, Jim (Sheriff), 39, 115, 119, 126, 151–52, 154–55, 161, 214–15

Clark, Kenneth & Mamie, and black doll experiment, 51

Congress of Racial Equality (CORE), 6–7, 38, 81

Conley, Charles, 171, 173–74, 177, 182–85, 196–98

Connor, Eugene, 38–39

Coopwood, Sam (Judge), 57, 64, 108

Corcoran, Howard (Judge), 144, 147, 149

Cotton, Dorothy, 139–43

Cotton elections, 108, 132–33, 135, 138, 141, 143, 149

Cotton money, 106–07, 112, 136

Crop subsidies, 132–33

Council of Federated Organizations (COFO), 6–8, 100, 134

Cronkite, Walter, 68–69, 71

Crowley, John, 212, 214–15

Dale, Judge Sebe, 90, 92–96,

Dallas County Voters League ("Voters League"), 152, 154–56

Democratic Party National Convention, 84, 122; *see also* Atlantic City "betrayal"

Edmundite Church, 213, 215; priests, 213–16
Elmore County, 234
Evers, Medgar, 14, 21

Farmers Home Administration, 145
Father Crowley, 212, 214
Fathers of Saint Edmund, 209, 212
Federal Bureau of Investigations (FBI), 11, 54, 68, 70, 121, 125, 140, 201, 206, 209, 224, 231, 234, 246–48, 250
Feiring, Phil, 6, 8–9
Food Stamps, 220–21, 225–29, 231–34
Forman, James, 105, 168–70, 172–74, 177
Free Voters Party, 151–56
Freedom House, 24–25, 28, 31, 58, 108
Freedom Rides, 5, 7, 16, 110, 118, 122, 155
Freedom Schools, 6–7
Freedom Summer, 6–8, 14, 16, 39, 79, 105, 117–18, 122, 134, 186, 245
Freeman, Orville (USDA Sec.), 138, 143, 225, 233
Futorian, Aviva, 25–28, 30–31, 35–36, 39–48, 50, 63–64, 66, 100, 111

"George," 37–40, 62
Gibbons, Graham E., 199
Godbold, John Cooper (Judge), 194
Greene County, 126, 179, 186–88, 192–95

Hamer, Fannie Lou, 80, 130
Hart, George L., 231–33
Higson, Mike, 77–79
Hildreth, Emmet F. (Judge), 175–78
Hill, Kenneth, 238
Holly Springs, MS, 21, 23–26, 28–29, 32, 35, 39, 44, 52, 57–58, 62, 64–66, 83, 91, 99, 102, 105, 107–08, 122
Hoover, J. Edgar (FBI Dir.), 70, 93, 121, 202
House, Stu, 158–60
Houser, Dan, 237, 239, 241

Hunger in America (film), 234

Israel, State of, 243–46

Jackson, Johnny, 237–38
Jackson, MS, 3, 8, 12–14, 17, 20–24, 26, 30, 35, 44, 63, 67–68, 71, 89, 92, 99, 102, 104, 109–12, 116, 122, 126, 184, 200, 247
"Jean," 130, 203–05
"Jim Crow," 3, 12–13, 75, 133, 247
Johnson, Frank M. (Judge), 166, 168–71, 182–84, 196–97, 200, 204–05, 238–39, 241
Johnson, Lyndon B. (President), 53, 80, 107, 154, 227, 244

Kennedy, John F. (President), 8, 14, 16, 71, 116, 151, 233
Kennedy, Robert, Jr. (Atty General), 70, 141, 168, 230, 233
King, Martin Luther, Jr. (Rev.), 6, 8, 29, 37, 53, 61, 84, 114, 138, 140, 150, 166, 217, 246–47; ASCS, 141,146; background of, 139; conflicts with SNCC, 117; death of, 246–47; final speech, 37–39; food suit, 226–27; Selma march, 116–17, 142, 168
Kinoy, Arthur, 180, 202
Ku Klux Klan, 38–39, 61, 116, 167
Kunstler, William, 70, 82–86, 169, 180, 202, 204–05

Lamar County, 87, 90, 96
Lawyers Committee for Civil Rights ("President's Committee"), 16–17, 75
Lawyers Constitutional Defense Committee (LCDC), 205–06
Lewis, John, 85, 115, 117–18
Liuzzo, Viola, 116, 162, 181
Lowndes County Freedom Organization (LCFO), 163–65

March on Washington, 7, 117, 217
Marshall, Thurgood, 51
Meredith, James, 25, 78, 116
Meredith march, 116, 118, 123

Mesher, Shirley, 125, 136–37, 152–53, 155, 205

Mississippi Freedom Democratic Party (MFDP), 79–85, 100, 130

"Mike," 13–15, 20

Mississippi Summer, 6–7, 39, 100, 104, 219

"Molly," 100–02, 105–12, 132

Moses, Robert ("Bob"), 38–39, 117

NAACP Legal Defense Fund, 16–18, 137

National Lawyers Guild, 16–17, 70, 83, 201–02, 208

National Sharecroppers Fund (NSF), 138, 147, 154, 217

New York Times Co. v. Sullivan, 29

Okolona, MS, 23–25, 27, 31, 33, 35, 40, 65–66, 83

Parker, Charles Mack, 88–90, 93–94

Parks, Rosa, 5, 139

Plessy v. Ferguson, 50–51

Poussaint, Alvin, 102–04, 106, 109–10,

Prattville, AL; Attack on SNCC, 237–39, 241–42

President's Committee, 16–17, 75

Rabinowitz, Victor, 208

Rankin, Harold, 45–46

Reavis, Richard (Dick), 149, 175–79, 200, 206

Reeb, James (Rev.), 116

Removal petitions, 69, 71, 169

Rogow, Bruce, 76–77, 89–93, 96, 110–12, 184

Root, Oscar, 43–44

Ross Barnett Reservoir beating, 78–79

Rules of Survival, 10–11, 41, 62

"Sally," 20–23, 35, 37

Schwarzschild, Henry, 65–66, 74, 76, 82–83, 110–12, 119–20, 128, 154, 200, 202–04

Seale, Bobby, 84

Selma march, 115, 117, 142, 154, 162, 168, 209

Six Day War, 244

Smith, Erskine, 198–99

Southern Christian Leadership Conference (SCLC), 6, 39, 115, 117, 123, 125–26, 136–43, 150–52, 154, 175–76, 186, 214, 218, 226–27, 230, 247

Southern Courier, 205, 231, 239

Southern Rural Research Project (SRRP), 218–21, 223–27, 229–32, 234–35, 241–43

Student Nonviolent Coordinating Committee (SNCC), 6, 23, 38, 72, 79–82, 85–87, 104–105, 111–13, 115–20, 122–27, 129–31, 134–35, 138, 142–43, 151–52, 154, 156–59, 161, 163–64, 166–71, 174, 179, 185, 200, 203, 205, 208, 210–11, 213–14, 218, 227, 230, 237, 242–47; civil rights workers, 123–24, 151–52, 179; exclusion of whites, 123–24, 127; Judge Frank Johnson, 168, 182, 238; Lowndes County, 126; anti-Zionism, 245; *See also* Atlantic City "betrayal"

"Summer Soldiers," 17, 19

Surplus Commodities, 221, 227–28, 234–35

Southwest Alabama Farmworkers Cooperative Association (SWAFCA), 137–38, 152

Taylor, Leroy, 196–99, 200, 202

Taylor, Thomas, 156, 158, 210

Thomas, Daniel H. (Judge), 180–82, 211

Thorkelson, Howard, 224–25

Till, Emmett, 3–5, 90

Toolen, Archbishop, 212–13, 215–16

United States Department of Agriculture (USDA), 108, 133, 135–36, 138, 143–49, 208, 218, 220, 225, 228–29, 231–36, 247

Veit, Kathy, 193, 211, 219, 224, 237

Vietnam War, 141–42, 239, 243–45

Voters League. *See* Dallas County Voters League

Voting Rights Act, 40–41, 52–53, 82, 86, 118, 138, 150, 154, 162, 168, 211

Wallace, George (Gov.), 14, 116, 152, 156, 194, 195
Windom, Alfred, 87–88, 90–94, 96, 99

X, Malcolm, xxi, 84

Yick Wo, 170–71, 180
Young, Andy, 142, 227
Younge, Samuel, Jr., 244